To

CHANGE

the

CHURCH

POPE FRANCIS *and the*
FUTURE *of* CATHOLICISM

ROSS DOUTHAT

SIMON & SCHUSTER

New York   London   Toronto   Sydney   New Delhi

Simon & Schuster
1230 Avenue of the Americas
New York, NY 10020

First Simon & Schuster hardcover edition March 2018

SIMON & SCHUSTER and colophon are
registered trademarks of Simon & Schuster, Inc.

For information about special discounts for bulk purchases,
please contact Simon & Schuster Special Sales at
1-866-506-1949 or business@simonandschuster.com.

The Simon & Schuster Speakers Bureau can bring authors to your live event.
For more information or to book an event contact the Simon & Schuster Speakers
Bureau at 1-866-248-3049 or visit our website at www.simonspeakers.com.

Interior design by Ruth Lee-Mui

Manufactured in the United States of America

10 9 8 7 6 5 4 3 2 1

Library of Congress Cataloging-in-Publication Data is available.

ISBN 978-1-5011-4692-3
ISBN 978-1-5011-4694-7 (ebook)

This one's for Gwendolyn, Eleanor, and Nicholas

For the Holy Spirit was promised to the successors of Peter not so that they might, by his revelation, make known some new doctrine, but that, by his assistance, they might religiously guard and faithfully expound the revelation or deposit of faith transmitted by the apostles.

—*Pastor Aeternus*, First Vatican Council, 1870

Therefore a man shall leave his father and mother and hold fast to his wife, and the two shall become one flesh. This mystery is profound, and I am saying that it refers to Christ and the church.

—Saint Paul, *Letter to the Ephesians*

"But that would be putting the clock back," gasped the governor. "Have you no idea of progress, of development?"

"I have seen them both in an egg," said Caspian. "We call it 'Going Bad' in Narnia . . ."

—C. S. Lewis, *The Voyage of the Dawn Treader*

Contents

A Personal Preface

This is a book about the most important religious story of our time: the fate of the world's largest religious institution under a pope who believes that Catholicism can change in ways that his predecessors rejected, and who faces resistance from Catholics who believe the changes he seeks risk breaking faith with Jesus Christ.

It is also a story that cannot be written about neutrally. The outsider to Catholicism is unlikely to fully grasp or appreciate the stakes, or to take the competing theologies as seriously as do the bishops, cardinals, and lay Catholics embroiled in the church's civil war. The insider, the believer, is likely to be pulled to one side or another, to see God's hand at work in either reform or resistance, to assume that the Holy Spirit has a favorite in the struggle. So it makes sense at the outset to briefly lay out my own background and biases, the experiences and assumptions that I bring to the telling of this fascinating and very much unfinished story.

I was not born a Roman Catholic, but neither did I join the Catholic Church as an adult. My family was Episcopalian in the beginning, and as a child I received a certain amount of religious formation—distinctively strange formation, in some cases—in various Protestant circles, Mainline and evangelical and Pentecostalist. Then I became a Catholic as a teenager, along with my family, in a shift that I welcomed but that was impelled more by my mother's spiritual journey than my own. So in the world of cradle Catholics and adult converts, groups that are often contrasted with one another and occasionally find themselves at odds, I belong to the little-known third category in between.

As a result I share something with each group, while lacking something each enjoys. Like other converts I did not recite Hail Marys as a child or experience the church as a deep ancestral inheritance, bound up with blood and class and ethnic patrimony. Instead I made an intellectualized religious choice, reading the books that converts tend to read and deciding the things that they decide, choosing Catholicism because its claims were more convincing than the Protestant churches of my youth.

But I did so while I was still half a kid, under strong maternal influence. Which meant that I also had elements of the cradle Catholic experience— a devoutly Catholic mother, confirmation classes with other teens rather than the adult-oriented conversion program, an after-school job manning the desk in my parish's priory, a hormonal adolescence and the attendant Catholic guilt. And it meant that like all cradle Catholics I have no way of knowing *for certain* if I would have chosen the church simply on my initiative, independently of family influence. My intellect says yes, but my self-awareness raises an eyebrow—because I have a strong interest in religious questions but relatively little natural piety, I can imagine myself lingering in the antechamber of a conversion, hesitating to pass inside.

When I went out into the world, to college and then into journalism, where my identity as a Catholic became important to my writing, this in-between feeling took on a new cast. In the secular world, my faith made me a curiosity and sometimes an extremist: I was *a real live Catholic*, not the lapsed or collapsed or Christmas-and-Easter sort that populate so many campuses and newsrooms, and what's more I had actually chosen to join the faith, deliberately signed on to all the strange dogmas and strict moral rules. And even if my friends and colleagues noticed that I didn't always live by them, I at least went to mass every Sunday and spoke up for something called "orthodoxy" in my writing, which was enough to make me seem like a zealot—the friendly sort, the kind you could have a beer and enjoy an argument with, but a guy with pretty strange ideas all the same.

But then if I went among my fellow true believers, both those who had converted and those cradle Catholics who were committed theologically as well as tribally, I was always conscious that my secular friends were wrong, that I wasn't much of a zealot after all, that I lacked something required for the part that I had been assigned in my professional life. My fellow serious Catholics seemed to have sincerity and certainty where I had irony and doubt. They went on retreats and knew whose feast day it was and had special devotions and prayed novenas; I was always forgetting basic prayers and Holy Days of Obligation. They seemed to approach the dogmas and rules as a gift, a source of freedom, a ladder up to God; I wrestled with them, doubted them, disobeyed them, constantly ran variations on Pascal's Wager in my head. They joined Opus Dei or attended Latin Masses; I was often at a 5 p.m. guitar mass, hating the aesthetics but preferring the schedule because it fit my spiritual sloth.

Sometimes I felt as though my conversion was incomplete, awaiting some further grace or transformation. At others I felt that I belonged to a category of Catholics that used to be common in Catholic novels and Catholic sociology, but had been abolished somewhere in the 1970s—the good bad Catholic or the bad good one, whose loyalty was stronger than his faith and whose faith was stronger than his practice, but who didn't want the church to change all the rules to make his practice easier because then what would really be the point?

This meant that, unlike many Catholics I knew who were loyal to the church as a community but doubtful of its doctrines, I did not want this tension to be smoothed away by understanding priests and broad-minded theologians; indeed, the conflict between what I professed and how badly I fell short was part of what made the profession seem plausible, because a religion that just confirmed me in my early-twenty-first-century way of life couldn't possibly be divinely revealed. No, I wanted the church to be *the church*, to vindicate its claim to be supernaturally founded by resisting the tides and the fashions of the age—

—but at the same time I didn't want that resistance to go too far, and actually forge the smaller, purer, Benedictine-monastery church that the most traditional and countercultural sometimes envisioned as Catholicism's future. Because I wasn't sure that such a church would have room for a Catholic as doubtful and slothful and erring as myself.

There is a tendency to see conservative Catholics, especially the sort who convert from more loosey-goosey faiths, as rigid people craving stability, traumatized by Protestantism's disorders or fearful of modernity's pace of change. No doubt I have some touch of this condition; I am, for instance, a child and grandchild of divorce, with views on the sexual revolution colored by watching multiple layers of my family peel apart. But in many ways my experience is almost the opposite. I am temperamentally quite comfortable with the ways of modern life, and like my transcendentalist New England ancestors I think I would do pretty well at weaving together a personalized form of faith. So I have always appreciated Catholicism because it doesn't fit my personality, because it unsettles and discomfits and destabilizes the also-rigid-in-their-way patterns of a secular existence, because without it I would be too self-confident in my ability to run my own life, too disinclined to pursue works of charity or mercy when there are works of ambition to pursue instead.

My temptation is not to imagine myself some perfect saint passing judgment on erring sinners and brazen heretics. Rather it's to romanticize my own failings, like a character in a Graham Greene novel, as some sort of existential wrestling match, rather than the rather ordinary and squalid sinfulness they are.

What all this means for my soul is known to God alone. But since there is a tendency to read all religious argument these days through the lens of psychoanalysis, I thought I should offer this brief confession preemptively, so that readers can judge for themselves how my spiritual struggles influence my analysis of Pope Francis's tumultuous reign.

My hope is that they influence this book for the better. Most accounts of recent Catholic history suffer from a kind of inevitabilism. When they're written from a secular or liberal perspective, there is a sense that, of course, eventually the church will simply have to make all the reforms that recent popes resisted, that those Catholics who believe some teachings simply cannot change are on the wrong side of religious history, that a kind of liberal Christianity is the destination to which Catholicism will sooner or later arrive. When they're written by conservative Catholics—and this was especially true during the heyday of John Paul II—there is a sense that wherever Rome has spoken, the argument is sound, the case is closed, and all the apparent tensions and contradictions within the global church will be resolved by the operation of the Holy Spirit, and smoothly, without the kind of chaos that has engulfed Catholicism in some of its ancient and medieval crises.

This book is not inevitabilist. It is conservative, in the sense that it assumes the church needs a settled core of doctrine, a clear unbroken link to the New Testament and the early church, for Catholicism's claims and structure and demands to make any sense at all. If the church is just a religious tribe with constantly evolving views, a spiritual party in which the party line changes with the views of the ecclesiastical nomenklatura, then for all the good works and lovely paintings and clever arguments the whole thing seems like a high-minded fraud, a trick upon the masses of believers, Philip Larkin's "moth-eaten musical brocade."

But at the same time, more than many conservative Catholics I think the recent history of the church should instill a certain amount of doubt about what exactly constitutes the Catholic core, where the bright lines lie and where they might be blurry, and what the church can do without touching doctrine and dogma to accommodate the modern world. And more than many, my doubts encourage me to envision scenarios—schisms and ruptures and striking transformations—that a certain kind of Catholic tends to rule out as impossible.

"To be deep in history is to cease to be a Protestant," wrote John Henry Newman, the nineteenth-century Anglican theologian turned Catholic convert and then cardinal, who will make further appearances in these pages. I believed this when I became Catholic, and I believe it still. But to go deep in *church* history, I have found, in trying to wrestle with this era of Catholic division and debate, is to find reasons to doubt all of the Francis era's competing visions for the church: the conservatives' because the church has changed in the past more than they are often ready to admit, the traditionalists' because the church has needed to change more than they seem ready to allow, and the liberals' because it is hard to see how the church can change in the ways that they envision without cutting itself off from its own history and abandoning its claim to carry a divine message, an unchanging truth.

So where does that leave us? With uncertainty, which is also where this book will end. But my uncertainty is confined to the outcome of these Catholic conflicts: About the stakes in the Francis era, their historic importance for the church and the wider religious world that Catholicism influences, I have no doubt whatsoever. Whatever comes, whatever changes in the church, we have the blessing and the curse of living in truly interesting religious times. This is a hinge moment in the history of Catholicism, a period of theological crisis that's larger than just the Francis pontificate but whose particular peak under this pope will be remembered, studied, and argued over for as long as the Catholic Church endures—and, if Catholics are right about their church, for as long as this world endures as well.

My hope is that most readers, religious and secular, Catholic and otherwise, will come away from this book convinced of the importance of its story, even if they are not always swayed by my interpretation of events. If I do not persuade, it is my own fault: As critics of my journalistic writings on Pope Francis have occasionally noted, my qualifications for telling it are those of a newspaper columnist and layman and self-educated student of church history, not a professional theologian or a clerical authority, which means that I will undoubtedly make blunders that a better education would have spared

me. Also, I am writing about an institution, the old and strange and complicated Vatican, in which even expert and well-sourced reporters struggle to
figure out exactly what is going on. I am not a Vatican insider; I have relied
on others' reportage and expertise, filtered through my own interpretation, to
tell this story. What is true is owed to others' work; the errors are all my own.

Finally, there are Catholic readers who will find this book's critical portrait of a sitting pope to be inappropriate, impious, disloyal. They may be
right; there I must rely on the mercy of God, which Francis has so eloquently
stressed, if I have strayed into presumption and failed in the religious duties
I assumed when I converted twenty years ago.

But the major duty I assumed wasn't to the pope; it was to the truth
the papacy exists to preach, to preserve, and to defend. I became a Catholic
because I thought that Catholicism had the most compelling claim to being
the true church founded by Jesus of Nazareth, whose radical message and
strange story offers the likeliest reason in all of recorded human history to
believe that God loves us, that *He so loved the world* that our sins will be
redeemed and our suffering will make sense in the end. I will die a Catholic;
there is no getting rid of me now. Here is a story about my church, my half-
chosen and half-inherited faith, a story that has added to my always ample
doubts, a story that needs to be told nonetheless because in the end, only the
truth can set us free.

To

CHANGE

the

CHURCH

One

THE PRISONER OF
THE VATICAN

At the center of earthly Catholicism, there is one man: the Bishop of Rome, the Supreme Pontiff, the Vicar of Christ, the Patriarch of the West, the Servant of the Servants of God, the 266th (give or take an antipope) successor of Saint Peter.

This has not changed in two thousand years. There was one bishop of Rome when the church was a persecuted minority in a pagan empire; one bishop of Rome when the church was barricaded into a Frankish redoubt to fend off an ascendant Islam; one bishop of Rome when the church lost half of Europe to Protestantism and gained a New World for its missionaries; one bishop of Rome when the *ancien régime* crumbled and the church's privileges began to fall away; one bishop of Rome when the twentieth century ushered in a surge of growth and persecution for Christian faith around the globe.

But all the other numbers that matter in Roman Catholicism have grown somewhat larger. When Simon Peter was crucified upside down in Nero's Rome, there were at most thousands of Christians in the Roman Empire, and only about 120 million human beings alive in the whole world. When Martin Luther nailed his theses to the Wittenberg door, there were only 50 or 60 million Christians in all of Europe. There were probably about 200 million Catholics worldwide when Pope Pius IX's Syllabus of Errors condemned modern liberalism in 1864; there were probably about 500 million a century later when the Second Vatican Council attempted a partial reconciliation with modernity.

And now—well, to start in the red-hatted inner circle, there are more than 200 cardinals, roughly 5,100 bishops, 400,000 priests, and about 700,000 sisters in the contemporary Catholic Church.[1] In the United States alone, the number of people employed by the church in some form—in schools and charities and relief organizations and the various diocesan bureaucracies— tops a million.[2] Worldwide, the church dwarfs other private sector and government employers, from McDonald's to the U.S. federal government to the People's Liberation Army.

That's just the church as a corporation; the church as a community of believers is vastly larger. In 2014, one sixth of the world's human beings were baptized Catholics. Those estimated numbers? More than a billion and a quarter, or 1,253,000,000.

Catholic means "here comes everybody," wrote James Joyce in *Finnegans Wake*. That was in the 1920s, when there were about 300 million Catholics, two thirds of them in Europe.

Now there are more Catholics in Latin America, more in Africa and Asia, than there were in all the Joycean world.

The papacy has never been an easy job. Thirty of the first thirty-one popes are supposed to have died as martyrs. Popes were strangled, poisoned, and possibly starved during the papacy's tenth-century crisis. Pius VI was exiled by French Revolutionary forces; his successor, Pius VII, was exiled by

Napoleon. Pius XII's Rome was occupied by Nazis. Five popes at least have seen their city sacked—by Vandals, Ostrogoths and Visigoths, Normans and a Holy Roman Emperor.

These are extreme cases, but even the pleasure-loving pontiffs of the Renaissance found the office more punishing than they expected. "Since God has given us the papacy, let us enjoy it," Giovanni di Lorenzo de' Medici is supposed to have said upon being elected as Leo X. But his eight years as pope included a poisoning attempt, constant warfare, and the first days of the Reformation; he died at forty-five.

Huns or Visigoths no longer menace today's popes, and their odds of being poisoned—conspiracy theories notwithstanding—are mercifully slim. But alongside the continued dangers of high office (the assassin's bullet that struck John Paul II, the Islamic State's dream of taking its jihad to Saint Peter's), there are new and distinctive pressures on the papacy. The speed of mass communications, the nature of modern media, means that popes are constantly under a spotlight, their every move watched by millions or billions of eyes. Papal corruption would be an international scandal rather than a distant rumor. Papal misgovernment leads to talk of crisis in every corner of the Catholic world. Papal illness or incapacity can no longer be hidden, and aging pontiffs face a choice between essentially dying in public, like John Paul II, or taking his successor's all-but-unprecedented step of resignation.

In an age of media exposure, the pope's role as a public teacher is no longer confined to official letters, documents, bulls. Not just every sermon but every off-the-cuff utterance can whirl around the world before the Vatican press office has finished getting out of bed (or returned from an afternoon espresso). And theological experts are left to debate whether the magisterium of the church, that lofty-sounding word for official Catholic teaching, includes in-flight chats with reporters or "private" phone calls from the pope to members of the faithful.

In past centuries the papacy's authority survived some of its worst occupants—from the sixteenth-century Borgias to the tenth-century villain John XII, who allegedly raped and murdered pilgrims—because their sins were out of sight and mostly out of mind for Catholics who didn't live in Rome or its environs. And across those same centuries, the papacy's claim to be a rock of unchanging teaching seemed more solid because casual papal utterances and speculations remained personal and private, with no iPhones to capture them, no Twitter to broadcast them to the world entire.

Now, though, the pope is a global celebrity, with all the scrutiny that entails. And the Vatican has mostly encouraged this shift toward papal stardom. From the nineteenth century onward, as the papacy lost its claim to secular power and was besieged by revolutionaries and totalitarians, a papal cult was fostered among faithful Catholics, which treated the living occupants of Peter's see in a style usually reserved for long-departed saints. In the twentieth and twenty-first centuries, as mass communication and airline travel expanded the papal presence further, actual papal canonizations became more commonplace. While the popes of the early church were almost all sainted, between the fall of Rome and the twentieth century, only thirty popes out of about two hundred were canonized. But two of the last five pontiffs have been declared saints, one has been beatified, and two have been declared Servants of God, the first step toward sainthood. And there will be a clamor (albeit from different camps among the Catholic faithful) for both the current pope and his still living predecessor to join those ranks once they've passed to their reward.

In fairness, recent popes probably have exceeded some of their medieval and modern predecessors in sanctity. But the trend still suggests an important transformation in how the papal office is presented and perceived, both among Catholics and in the wider world. The popes of the past struck monarchical poses and claimed sweeping political as well as spiritual powers. But with those claims came an implicit acknowledgment of their worldliness, which in turn invited lay Catholics to treat them as ordinary mortals—sometimes corrupt, sometimes foolish, sometimes in need of hectoring and correction, and always at risk of eternal damnation. When Dante Alighieri's *Divine Comedy* consigned several popes to the Inferno, or when medieval painters of the Last Judgment made sure to place a tiara-sporting pontiff in the flames of hell, they were making a theological point about the nature and limits of the papal office. No matter how much power God had entrusted to the papacy, the popes' personal sanctity was irrelevant to the church's central theological claims.

This is still the official teaching of the church. But it is not the implication that one would draw from the way that the papacy is—there is no other word for it—*marketed* today, the way that each pope is treated not just as the supreme governor of the church but as its singular embodiment, the Catholic answer to Gandhi or Mandela, the Beatles or the Stones.

With this marketing comes both outsize expectations and outsize vulnerability. Just as in American politics the president is handed both blame and credit for events that are far outside one man's control, so too the pope is treated like a minor deity, idolized by ultramontanists and cursed by anti-Catholics, and held responsible for good harvests and drowning floods alike.

Thus where the church seems to be growing or reviving it must be "the Francis effect" or a "John Paul II generation" bearing fruit. Where Catholicism is in crisis or decline everyone is quick to place the blame on failing leadership in Rome. When the Berlin Wall came down there was a rush to suggest that John Paul II had vanquished communism all-but-singlehandedly; when AIDS ravaged Africa there was a rush to claim that the Vatican's line on condoms had somehow cost millions of lives. When Francis joined the fight against global warming there was a lot of implausible talk about how the papal aura would transform the difficult politics of climate; when the sex abuse scandals came to light Benedict was regularly portrayed as a spider at the center of a global criminal conspiracy.

As with the American presidency, these expectations have encouraged an ongoing centralization: If you're going to be blamed for everything that goes wrong, after all, why wouldn't you seek more power, more control? As in American politics, neither the church's conservatives nor its liberals have offered consistent resistance to papal aggrandizement. Everyone wants a humbler papacy . . . right up until their man sits the papal throne.

And as in American politics, the centralization of power has not led to its effective use. Instead, in the years of Benedict XVI especially, the sheer incompetence of the Vatican, with its warring fiefdoms and Renaissance-court intrigues and speed-of-telegraph media operations, became the one issue on which the church's feuding theological factions tended to wholeheartedly agree.

But here a certain charity is in order, because of the central dilemma facing the modern papacy—which is that the Catholic Church has grown much larger and much weaker at more or less the same time.

There are many more Catholics than ever before, but the church's influence over secular politics has ebbed almost everywhere since the 1960s, and consumer capitalism rather than the church sets the cultural agenda and shapes the moral landscape for many of those baptized millions.

There are many more Catholics, but in the developed world they are increasingly secularized, while outside the West they're often just a generation or two removed from animism. With a few exceptions—the Philippines, Poland—the deeply inculturated, ethnically rooted Catholicism that was the norm for centuries has all but disappeared, and with it the church's easy, natural hold over its communicants.

There are many more Catholics, but they often inhabit not only different political and economic systems from one another but radically different moral and metaphysical landscapes. An African Catholic participates in a religious world in which magic and witchcraft still claim cultural authority, the validity of supernatural experience is taken for granted, and the miraculous is considered almost prosaic. An American Catholic, even the most fervent, lives and works and prays in a much more skeptical and disenchanted landscape. A Middle Eastern Catholic lives in a religious landscape out of the Thirty Years War, caught in the crossfire of Islam's bloody civil wars. Just a plane flight away, a European Catholic subsists in a religious landscape whose self-satisfied indifference can rival Gene Roddenberry's Star Trek.

There are many more Catholics . . . but on every continent and country they find themselves divided against one another, standing on different sides of a widening theological and moral gulf, arguably wider than the chasm that separated Catholicism from Orthodoxy and later from Lutheranism and Calvinism.

That gulf exists because of Christianity's complicated relationship with liberal modernity, which is both a rebellious daughter of the Christian faith and a rival—and essentially dominant—worldview. Every major Western religion, every faith tradition, has spent decades and centuries wrestling with how far to accommodate to liberalism, and when and where to resist. The lines have been drawn over scriptural interpretation and historical criticism, over Darwin's theory of evolution, over church-state separation and religious liberty, over race and eugenics and human equality, over liturgical customs and traditions, over the role of women and the nature of marriage, over clothing and music and entertainment, over the importance of missionary work, over theological concepts too numerous to name, and in our own time over the sexual revolution and all its works.

On all these issues, religious traditions that share a common theological patrimony have often ended up deeply divided. The specific controversies vary with the denomination, but there's an essential commonality to what separates liberal Episcopalians from conservative Anglicans, or the more liberal Evangelical Lutheran Church from the more conservative Missouri Synod Lutherans, or the liberal Alliance of Baptists from the conservative Southern Baptists, or the liberal Presbyterian Church (U.S.A.) from the Presbyterian Church of America and other Calvinist formations.

In each case disagreements over how far a faith can go accommodating itself to modernity are now the defining lines of division; those divisions have grown so deep and bitter that fellowship and communion are imperiled or broken; and liberal and conservative believers have either grown apart or gone their separate ways. And in many cases this sorting-out, this division, has been accelerated by the way globalization has brought the divergent metaphysical landscapes of America and Europe and Africa and Asia into tension with one another, hardening and accentuating the theological differences between, say, United Methodists or Episcopalians in the United States and their coreligionists in the developing world.

The case of the American Episcopalians, and the global Anglican communion to which they belong, is particularly striking, since the entire theory of Anglicanism from the Elizabethan age onward was that it was supposed to be capacious, tolerant, a house capable of containing all sorts of contradictions, with a wing whose theology was basically evangelical and a wing that considered itself Catholic in everything save submission to the pope. Yet this capaciousness failed to contain the divisions over the sexual revolution, which were heightened by the same-sex marriage debate. Instead of holding together, both the Episcopal Church in the United States and the Anglican Church in Canada simply split, with several conservative groups going their own way and seeking support from Anglican churches overseas, particularly in Africa. (The ironies of religious history have given us a world where South Carolinian Episcopalians descended from slaveholders prefer African archbishops to white liberals.) Anglicanism's central authority, the archbishops of Canterbury, have attempted to paper over these divisions—but those attempts have mostly confirmed that the worldwide Anglican communion as a communion no longer really exists.

Yet Roman Catholicism, which is more international than Anglicanism and seemingly less well suited to contain doctrinal contradictions, remains officially undivided. There have been small splinterings, yes: When the First Vatican Council defined papal infallibility in 1870, some liberal Catholics in Germany departed for what was styled the Old Catholic Church; when the Second Vatican Council made its peace with religious liberty and rewrote the church's liturgy, the Society of Saint Pius X went into a kind of quasi-schism on the traditionalist right. But there has been nothing sweeping and permanent, nothing to rival the Reformation or the break with Orthodoxy or the Great Schism of the Middle Ages, and, indeed, nothing that quite resembles the breakages in Anglicanism or the widening cracks in other Protestant bodies. Instead Catholicism has found a way to contain multitudes, to straddle various liberal-conservative and modernist-traditionalist divides, with a superficial similarity in formal commitments masking deep differences in fundamental belief.

These intra-Catholic differences, as in Anglicanism's schism, tend to burn hot with controversy when they touch on sexuality and gender and bioethics—when the issue is abortion or contraception or euthanasia, same-sex marriage or transgender claims, divorce and remarriage, the possibility of a married priesthood or the ordination of women as priests. But those issues, important as they are, are not the real roots of the debate. What lies beneath are often larger and more comprehensive disagreements: about the purpose of the church, the authority of the Bible, the nature of the sacraments, the definition of sin, the means of redemption, the true identity of Jesus, the very nature of God.

Chase the debate about same-sex marriage down far enough and it becomes an argument about the authority of Scripture generally, and whether the church's past teachings on any moral issue can be considered permanently reliable, or whether all things Catholic are subject to Holy Spirit-driven change. Pursue the debate about divorce and remarriage long enough and it becomes a discussion about whether Jesus's words in the New Testament are definitely *his* words, whether the gospels are reliable, whether Jesus could have made mistakes, and other questions that are foundational to Christology, theology, the church. Chase debates about abortion and euthanasia downward and you find yourself debating the essential questions of Christian ethics—are some acts intrinsically evil, or is everything a matter of relativized, situational perspective? And beyond that—is damnation a real danger? Does hell even exist? Is the devil just a metaphor?

The liberalizing tendency in Catholicism wants most immediately and intensely to adapt to the sexual revolution. But its adaptationist, evolutionist spirit is older than today's controversies, and its premises often point toward a more fundamental sort of change. They would make Catholic Christianity open to substantial reinterpretation in every generation, and transform many of its doctrines into the equivalent of a party's platform or a republic's constitution—which is to say, binding for the moment but constantly open to revision based on democratic debate.

This liberal spirit is not just confined to a few pockets within the Catholic ecosystem, or to people who are disconnected from the institutional church. It extends throughout the Catholic intelligentsia, the Catholic academy, the Catholic theologate, and up through the clerical ranks into the hierarchy. Thus the strange Janus face that contemporary Catholicism presents to the Western world. Viewed from afar it still often looks like the most antique of institutions, a last premodern bulwark in an otherwise postmodern world, a strange ark from the Middle Ages still somehow afloat in the twenty-first century's squalls. But then viewed from the inside, from a more intimate angle, it can seem more liberal, more modernized and diverse and permissive, than many of the evangelical churches that once damned Rome as an obdurate foe of human liberty and progress. Depending on where you look, that is: If you look in other areas, it can appear as conservative or traditional as its public image would suggest.

These tensions and contradictions are not a new problem for the church or the papacy that governs it. Prior to the 1960s and long before the sexual revolution, popes sought to suppress liberalizing tendencies, launching internal purges and imposing theological loyalty oaths, treating most accommodations to modernity as heresy in the making, and insisting on an all-but-changeless vision of the Catholic faith—*semper idem*, "always the same," in the motto of Cardinal Alfredo Ottaviani, the doctrinal watchdog of the church in the years just before Vatican II. Then in the 1960s and 1970s, during Vatican II and afterward, the popes shifted to a strategy of accommodation and adaptation, which embraced certain aspects of the modern liberal consensus and encouraged or accepted—for a while, at least—various grassroots experiments that sought to push the reconciliation with liberalism further.

What happened after that, under John Paul II and Benedict, is a story that will be told—and told, and told—from three separate perspectives in the next chapter. Suffice it to say that both men succeeded in holding the church together, even as many other religious bodies split, without in any way resolving the deep tensions between its factions. And how they might be resolved is a difficult question to answer.

The pope, given his powers and prominence, might seem like the man to answer it. But he doesn't just preside over Catholicism's contradictions, he's also imprisoned by them. A conservative pope can prod, he can exhort, he can reprimand or silence the occasional dissident theologian—but he cannot actually suppress theological liberalism without breaking the church apart, forcing a series of rebellions that would leave Catholic institutions broken and bankrupt, and countless baptized Catholics shepherdless.

Indeed, even that dire scenario is hard to imagine because the pope's authority is channeled through structures that make a purge nearly impossible to execute. The layers of Catholic bureaucracy are no less theologically divided than the wider church, and the effective liberalism of countless Catholic functionaries means that much of a conservative pope's theoretical power is just that—a power of the bully pulpit, a power over certain high-level appointments, but not a power that can remake the church without being balked, resisted, turned aside. In an anecdote often repeated by his conservative admirers, an ally lamented to Benedict XVI how little of the church reflected the pontiff's intentions and agenda. At which point the former Joseph Ratzinger supposedly gestured to his office door. "My power ends there," he said.

But it is not only a conservative pope who is frustrated by the system. A liberal pope, once a hypothetical but arguably no longer, has the same dilemmas and faces the same dangers, but with this added wrinkle: Many of the changes that liberal Catholics might want a pontiff on "their side" to institute threaten to dynamite the very theological authority required to implement them, because that authority depends for its legitimacy not just on the papacy's aura and antiquity, but on its claim to transmit the Catholic faith intact from generation to generation, rather than making sharp and controversial breaks.

Procedurally, papal powers can look near-absolute. If a pope decided tomorrow to canonize Hitler or declare Oprah the fourth person of the Trinity, there is no Catholic Supreme Court that could strike his ruling down. But substantively the pope is supposed to have *no* power to change Catholic doctrine in areas where it is long established and defined. He is bound to what Catholics call the "deposit of faith"—the teachings revealed in Scripture and defined by previous papacies and councils, which cannot be altered without making the pope's own claim to authority fray and come apart. These teachings can be "developed" toward greater detail and specificity, they can be clarified where ambiguous, they can be applied to new dilemmas and debates. But they cannot be reversed or contradicted or transcended.

This rule comes, quite obviously, with many gray areas, and a great deal of room for debate about where development ends and contradiction starts. But it still imposes some hard limits, and it has effectively restrained popes from incautious doctrinal experiments for most of the church's history. In the Reformation era there were lively debates about whether a pope could be a heretic, and the borderline examples are all cautionary tales. Nobody wants to end up like the unfortunate Pope Honorius I, anathematized after his death for a flirtation with the Monothelite heresy (he "did not attempt to sanctify this Apostolic Church with the teaching of Apostolic tradition," his successor witheringly declared, "but by profane treachery permitted its purity to be polluted"), or John XXII, whose heterodox speculations about the nature of the beatific vision provoked a successful theological rebellion.

The nineteenth-century definition of papal infallibility—the claim that a pope cannot err if he teaches authoritatively on faith and morals—has, if anything, tended to restrain papal experimentation even further, by reminding the pontiffs of the weight that a truly authoritative pronouncement has to bear, the requirements of consistency and continuity that it has to meet, and the limits that it would impose upon future pontiffs. ("I am only infallible if I speak infallibly, but I shall never do that," John XXIII is reported to have said.) Since it was defined, the only explicit exercise of infallibility came in 1950, when Pius XII promulgated the dogma of the Virgin Mary's bodily assumption into heaven—controversial with Protestants, but much less so within the church. At the Second Vatican Council, the popes were very careful to build overwhelming consensus for the most controversial reforms, the ones that lay in gray areas between *semper idem* and self-contradiction: The conciliar pronouncements that seemed most like developments in doctrine, on religious liberty and Judaism, passed with fewer than a hundred dissenting votes out of more than 2,300 cast. And in the years since, even when they were clearly reaffirming long-standing church teaching on controversial issues, Paul VI, John Paul, and Benedict were always careful to leave a certain ambiguity as to whether infallibility had really been invoked.

This caution reflects the core reality, obscured by papolatry and papaphobia alike, that popes have rarely been the great protagonists of Catholic dramas. For good or ill they tend to move last, after crises have percolated for decades or generations, after arguments have been thrashed away at for many years or lifespans. Circumscribed by tradition, hemmed in by bureaucracy, fearful that any too sudden move might undo their authority or shrink or break the church, they lack real power commensurate to their prominence— and never more so than in our own age of papal celebrity and Catholic civil war.

But what happens when a pope sets out to defy this reality, to slip through the bars and evade the constraints, to act in the way that a watching world—and above all a watching media—seems to want the man at the center of the earthly church to act? What happens when a pope decides that he can deal with the church's crisis, its deep divisions, in a swift reforming march, and reshape Catholicism according to his vision?

What happens when a pope decides to change the church?

Two

THREE STORIES
ABOUT VATICAN II

To understand how the church ended up undivided and yet divided,
with all the tensions between tradition and modernity vibrating inside
its walls, it helps to tell a story about the last fifty years of Catholic history.

So let's tell three.

Once, more than fifty years ago now, there was an ecumenical council
of the church. Its goal was to reorient Catholicism away from its nineteenth-
century fortress mentality, to open a new dialogue with the Protestant
churches and non-Christian religions and secular ideologies that it had once
flatly condemned, and to prepare the church for an era of evangelization and
renewal.

It was not intended to be a revolutionary council, but then again it wasn't
supposed to happen at all: It was an idea that came to Angelo Giuseppe Ron-
calli, the kindly Italian elected in 1958 after eleven ballots as John XXIII,

and he set the council into motion over the doubts and objections of many Vatican conservatives.

Even once conceived and announced, though, those same conservatives assumed that they could control it, channel its energies into a ringing affirmation of Catholic doctrine and not much more. But the church's bishops, once assembled, had other ideas. With a new generation of theologians whispering in their ears, and perhaps the Holy Spirit as well, they rebelled against stage management by Vatican insiders, and followed the pope's admonition to "throw open the windows of the church" and let in the outside air.

What ensued in Rome between October of 1962 and December of 1965 was an epochal event, a true turning point in the history of the faith. The council's documents repudiated anti-Semitism, they embraced democracy and religious liberty, they opened the way for a renewal of the church's fusty, antique Latin liturgy, they made ecumenical dialogue with other Christians and other religions possible for the first time. But more than all that, they changed the church's self-image, replacing a vertical conception of the church as a priest-dominated hierarchy imposing rules and regulations with a horizontal conception of the church as the blessed, holy, spirit-discerning People of God.

This change was the real "spirit of Vatican II," invoked by reformers ever after. It promised a more democratic Catholicism, a church more in tune with the consciences of individual believers, a church defined not by rigid doctrinal pronouncements but by constant dialogue—with other faiths, with the modern world, and within itself. The "spirit of Vatican II" promised a church for spiritually mature adults, rather than a "pray pay and obey" multitude clacking their rosaries and fretting about a stray Friday meatball. And its reforms were greeted with great joy and enthusiasm, the true fruits of the Holy Spirit, as a wave of renewal rippled across the Catholic world.

But then, tragically if perhaps inevitably, there was a backlash. Pope Paul VI, elected as John's successor midway through the council's sessions, tried to allow space for further innovation, but he also gave in to his fears, and the pleadings of conservatives, when he reaffirmed the church's ban on artificial contraception in the encyclical *Humanae Vitae* in 1968. For countless Catholic couples this prohibition—justified by an abstruse natural law theology divorced from lived experience—was a betrayal of the council's promise, and a permanent wound for people unable to reconcile their lived experience with the official doctrines of the church. The hierarchical church went one way, the People of God went another, and from that breach came a widening division between Rome and the reality of Catholic life.

Then came John Paul II. An admirable figure in many ways, an inspiring voice for freedom in his native Poland, he was also a reactionary on doctrinal matters, determined to rip up two decades of grassroots experimentation and centralize power in the Vatican once more. With the help of Joseph Ratzinger, the German theologian turned *panzer kardinal*, he doubled down on increasingly untenable pre–Vatican II positions—no to contraception, no to married priests and female priests, no to communion for the divorced and remarried, no to same-sex love, no to in vitro fertilization, no and no and no. He made the Western culture war over abortion and same-sex marriage the measure of Catholic orthodoxy, stifled or silenced brilliant theologians and pastorally minded bishops, and promoted yes-men in their place. Worse, he promoted or protected men who tolerated the abuse of minors while turning a blind eye to the obvious link between mandatory clerical celibacy and pedophilia, between the church's cramped sexual vision and the perverted behavior of far too many priests.

His successor, Ratzinger-turned-Benedict, was in many ways even worse: a great theologian in his way, perhaps, but as pope just another reactionary, except this time a liturgical stickler without charisma or the common touch. His appointments were even more hopelessly conservative than his predecessor's; his careless rhetoric inflamed the Muslim world; his attempted reconciliation with Latin Mass traditionalists led to scandal when he lifted the excommunication on a Holocaust-denying bishop; his attempted cleanup of the sex abuse scandal again refused to touch the problem's roots in clericalism and hierarchy and sexual repression. Nothing in his papacy became him like the leaving of it: His stunning 2013 resignation was the kind of revolutionary gesture that the church so badly needed, and worth more than anything else he had said or done as pope.

So across these thirty-five years, the thirty-five years of John Paul and Benedict, the People of God suffered, they drifted, they dissented, and increasingly they simply decamped. The church had not modernized sufficiently, it had squandered or stifled its moment of renewal, it had refused to listen to the *vox populi* that was also, most likely, the *vox dei*. So why should anyone be surprised that in the West, at least, pews stood empty and large numbers of Catholics, baptized and confirmed, barely practiced the faith anymore? It was obvious what the Holy Spirit had intended to happen after the 1960s, obvious how the church needed to adapt to the newfound maturity of its members, obvious that Vatican II should have led to an ongoing transformation, a permanent reform. But all this had been stifled by the fears of a few old men in Rome, by conservative diehards in the laity, by a fear of change that was more suited to a church of Pharisees than the church of Jesus Christ.

So the church's revolution, well begun fifty years ago, stood sadly unfinished as the conclave met in 2013 to elect Benedict's successor. And the church waited, after years of unnecessary stagnation, for a new movement of the spirit, a new John XXIII, a new birth of freedom for the People of God.

That's one story. Now let's tell another.

Once, fifty years ago now, there was an ecumenical council of the church. Its goal was to reorient Catholicism away from its nineteenth-century fortress mentality, to open a new dialogue with other churches and religions, and to prepare the church for an era of evangelization and renewal.

The council turned out to be more reformist than anyone expected going in. A rising generation of bishops and theologians—many of whom would decisively influence the pontificates of John Paul II and Benedict XVI— took control of the process early, and their labors brought about a necessary reconciliation of Catholicism and liberal democracy, an important repudiation of anti-Semitism, a widening of the church's intellectual horizons and a recovery of its ancient patrimony, and a welcome shift away from thundering anathemas to a more missionary spirit.

But the council's reforms were limited in scope. Nothing in its deliberations and documents were meant to rewrite doctrine or Protestantize the faith; instead, essential Catholic truths—from the authority of the pope to the nature of the sacraments to the evils of divorce—were consistently reaffirmed. Vatican II was an adaptationist moment for the church, not a revolutionary one. Between 1962 and 1965, Catholicism changed so that it might remain essentially the same.

Unforunately the world was changing even faster, the council's sessions coincided with an era of social upheaval and cultural revolution in the West, and the Church's hoped-for renewal was hijacked by those who favored a simple accommodation to the spirit of the late 1960s, and the transformation of the church along liberal Protestant lines. Soon two parties developed: a liberal-turned-conservative party that followed the actual documents of the council and sought continuity with the Catholic past, and a hijackers' party loyal to a nebulous "spirit" of the council that just happened to coincide with the cultural fashions that came in in its wake.

This second party had its way in many Catholic institutions—seminaries, religious orders, liturgical conferences, Catholic universities, diocesan bureaucracies—for many years. In the hands of the hijackers, the Council's call for liturgical reform became a license for aesthetic vandalism, its ecumenical spirit was invoked to downgrade Catholicism and treat it as just one church among many, its optimistic attitude toward modernity was bent into a blessing for the sexual revolution, and its call for a more empowered laity was used to undercut the importance of religious vocations, the sacraments, the mass, the very stuff of Catholic life. At every level of the church, Catholic distinctives were dismantled, downgraded, and dismissed in favor of a generic feel-good spirituality, a "Catholicism Lite" that was supposedly better suited to the modern age.

The results were, overall, disastrous: collapsing mass attendance, vanishing vocations, a swift erosion of Catholic identity everywhere you looked. Told that everything was suddenly open for debate, that the church no longer believed as it once had, that the centuries-old rituals and rhythms of the faith were just superstitions standing in the way of an allegedly grown-up (but actually secularized) Christian faith, ordinary Catholics drifted from the church. And the faster the alleged "spirit" of the Council worked itself out, in parishes and schools and religious orders, the faster Catholic numbers fell away.

At first, the papacy did little to stem this tide. Paul VI issued *Humanae Vitae*—and then failed to defend it or urge his bishops to champion it, confirming the impression that the church no longer took its own teachings seriously. As the faithful departed, he murmured and fretted and caviled, but mostly he accepted the hijackers' power over Catholicism's intermediate institutions, their swift transformation of the church's language and liturgy and life.

But at last, in 1978 a pope was elected who belonged to the party of continuity, who rejected the hijacking of the council, who carried its true intentions forward while proclaiming the ancient truths of Catholicism anew. Like his right-hand man, Joseph Ratzinger, John Paul II had supported the reforms of Vatican II; indeed, the only four bishops who were actually excommunicated under his papacy were the council's reactionary critics. But he also recognized that reform had turned into revolution, and necessary change had given way to vandalism. And so he set out, in effect, to reclaim the church *for* the church—to make it clear that Catholicism wasn't simply going to dissolve into a generic postmodern spirituality, that its core teachings were still in place, that it was possible to be Catholic and modern, that the gospel was still the same yesterday and today.

This reclamation project was a difficult one, resisted and balked by "spirit of Vatican II" Catholics. But their Catholicism Lite had a fatal weakness: It failed to reproduce itself, failed to inspire new vocations, failed to win converts, failed to keep children in the faith, failed even to produce children in the first place. And as the hijackers aged and began to (literally) die out, the Catholic witness of the pope and his successor gradually inspired the kind of renewal the council fathers had hoped for: a generation of bishops, priests, and laity prepared to witness to the fullness of Catholicism, the splendor of its truth.

This generation faced many challenges, including the scorn of an increasingly secularized Western elite and the dragging anchor of the sex abuse crisis—which was unfairly blamed on conservative Catholicism and clerical celibacy when in reality it had flowered during the sexual chaos of the 1960s and 1970s. But the John Paul II model, even amid a sea of troubles, was the only available path to Catholic flourishing. The continued decline of the church's liberal wing confirmed it; so did the collapse of the liberal Mainline Protestant churches that Catholicism Lite aspired to emulate; so did the rapid growth of a theologically conservative Catholicism in Africa and the church's continued fade in the home territory of "spirit of Vatican II" Catholicism, Northern Europe.

By the time Benedict resigned and the conclave gathered to elect his successor, then, it was clear that this generation owned the Catholic future, that the liberal alternative had been tried and failed, and that the church of the twenty-first century would embody a successful synthesis—conservative but modern, rooted in tradition but not traditionalist—of conciliar and preconciliar Catholicism, the church of two thousand years of history and the church of Vatican II.

The two stories I've just sketched are the master narratives of liberal and conservative Catholicism in the West. The first one is probably better known, because it's also the master narrative for most secular observers and critics of the church. But the second one has been deeply influential among many of the church's most devout members, and it's the narrative that's guided many of the choices made at the highest levels of Catholicism over the last three decades.

These stories are not easily reconciled, and as my sympathies lie more with the conservative side it's impossible to be fully impartial in assessing their respective strengths. But to understand the situation of the church in the age of Francis it's important to attempt a synthesis.

So let's tell a third story, and try to make it true.

Once, fifty years ago now, there was an ecumenical council of the church. Its goal was to reorient Catholicism away from its nineteenth-century fortress mentality, to open a new dialogue with other faiths and churches, and to prepare the church for an era of evangelization and renewal.

But from the beginning there was deep disagreement over what kind of reform was desirable and possible, and this disagreement ended up written into the documents of the council. For all its future-oriented rhetoric, Vatican II came to clear conclusions only when it looked backward. It dealt directly with problems (the church's relationship to democracy, to religious liberty, to Judaism) that belonged to the crises and debates of the nineteenth and early twentieth centuries. But when it looked forward it turned vague and prolix, with many generalizations about the state of modern man and his unprecedented situation and the need for the church to think and act and evangelize anew, but rather less that amounted to a concrete, specific agenda for such action.

It certain ways this vagueness was a matter of timing. The council began its deliberations at a moment of optimism about the church's institutional strength, its internal cohesion, its capacity to deal successfully with the challenges of the modern age. It closed its sessions in 1965, with the birth control pill newly invented, the divorce revolution just beginning, second-wave feminism just gearing up, and gay rights still the most marginal of causes. In this sense it simply began and ended too soon to address the issues that broke across Catholicism and Christianity with the sexual revolution, and the distinctive crisis that subsequently swept over the church.

Here Vatican II partially resembles not the great councils of the Catholic past, but one of the failed ones: Fifth Lateran, the last council before the Protestant Reformation, which looked backward toward fifteenth-century debates and promoted reforms that were insufficient to address the storm that began just seven months after the council's closing, when Martin Luther went to Wittenberg.

But it wasn't just timing. There was also an essential lack of consensus, from the first, on how far the church could change, what kind of a new agenda could serve the Catholic future without betraying the Catholic past. This tension was evident in the words of John XXIII himself, when he opened the council with this exhortation:

> What instead is necessary today is that the whole of Christian doctrine, with no part of it lost, be received in our times by all with a new fervor . . . that this doctrine be more fully and more profoundly known and that minds be more fully imbued and formed by it. What is needed is that this certain and unchangeable doctrine, to which loyal submission is due, be investigated and presented in the way demanded by our times. For the deposit of faith, the truths contained in our venerable doctrine, are one thing; the fashion in which they are expressed, but with the same meaning and the same judgment, is another thing. This way of speaking will require a great deal of work and, it may be, much patience: types of presentation must be introduced which are more in accord with a teaching authority which is primarily pastoral in character.[1]

This whole of Christian doctrine . . . certain and unchangeable . . . with the same meaning and the same judgment . . . In the debates that followed Vatican II, conservative Catholics could cite these words and many others like them as proof-texts for their argument that the council had not changed anything essential, and anything that hadn't changed explicitly should still be held as "certain and unchangeable" by Catholics the world over, in 1995 or 2015 no less than 1945.

But then: *. . . investigated and presented in the way demanded by our times . . . a great deal of work and, it may be, much patience . . . types of presentation must be introduced . . . a teaching authority which is primarily* *pastoral in character* . . . In these words, and others like them, liberal Catholics heard clear permission to effectively reshape the church's teachings, to press to the edge of what Catholic dogma permitted—and beyond?—if so doing seemed like the way to reach the modern mind. (Indeed, so fraught were these interpretative battles that some liberals later claimed—almost certainly incorrectly—that John XXIII had not actually spoken the phrase "with the same meaning and the same judgment," and that it had been inserted into the official record later by a fearful conservative editor.)

Because the Council had many authors, and because many of those authors were themselves uncertain about what could be changed, both of these readings of its documents were in some sense intended by Vatican II. Not by accident but by design—albeit the design of a hive mind rather than a singular intelligence—there was a tension between the letter and the spirit of the council, between what was explicitly altered and what was only implied. Sometimes (on religious liberty, in particular) there seemed to be a plainly revised teaching, but even where there wasn't there was a new language, and the apparent retirement of older phrases and rhetoric and forms. And this linguistic shift inevitably suggested a new teaching, to those who wished to have one, even as it stopped short of offering one outright.

So in the wars that followed, both interpretations of the council, both stories of what it was intended to accomplish, could stake a claim to carrying on the legacy of Vatican II. And then as the power dynamic shifted and then shifted again within the church, both sides could nurse a reasonable sense of betrayal, shock, and disappointment when their interpretation lost ground or failed to be generally accepted.

When the "spirit of Vatican II" was interpreted to mean that altars should be stripped and nuns should lose their habits and guitars should replace Gregorian chants and confession should be neglected and political interpretations of the gospel should be privileged over moral exhortations and the words "mortal sin" and "hell" and "purgatory" should vanish from sermons and annulments should be granted for practically any cause and seminaries should relax about sexual activity among priests-to-be because

Catholic sexual ethics were in a period of creative flux . . . well, amid all these experiments and more, conservatives could reasonably accuse liberals of a kind of radicalism, because the documents of Vatican II did not license anything like this.

But then when the Vatican under John Paul II and Benedict XVI began disciplining bishops and policing theologians and criticizing Catholic colleges that seemed to stray too far from orthodoxy; when it condemned the most famous manifestation of the post–Vatican II social gospel, liberation theology; when it ordered visitations of seminaries and religious orders to make sure that their pedagogy and spirituality were doctrinally correct; when it cracked down on sacramental abuses (group confession, communion for remarried divorcées) and reasserted teachings that had seemed flexible in the 1970s (the intrinsic evil of certain sinful acts, the "gravely deficient" status of non-Catholic Christian faiths); when it declared that certain questions raised by the sexual revolution, including questions where vast numbers of Catholics now differed with the church, were not open for debate; when it sought to restore more antique language to the liturgy and rein in local experiments . . . amid all this pushback, all this reaction, liberals could understandably complain that this wasn't the church that had been promised them, that the Vatican was effectively withdrawing permissions that had once been extended and changing its mind about how much of John XXIII's "patience" should be shown to people trying to be Catholic in a complicated new world.

From the point of view of the church's unity, though, it's notable that neither the period of liberal ascendance nor the conservative reaction that followed pushed the church's divisions to the point of outright schism. Because the liberal era took place under a flag of "pastoral experiments" that Rome tolerated but rarely officially endorsed—and because on the major question where the papacy explicitly weighed in, birth control, the traditional answer was reaffirmed—the conservative side could tell itself that liberalism's ascendance hadn't affected the deposit of faith, hadn't made the papacy contradict itself, hadn't pitched the church into a true theological crisis. (There was a subgenre of conservative commentary in the 1960s and 1970s that assumed

Paul VI simply had bad advisers, that like the tsar in Russian fable he would rein in the liberals if only someone told him what they were doing.) This conservative belief required a line-drawing, a thus-far-and-no-further, that could seem somewhat arbitrary in hindsight. But it was convincing enough to keep most conservative Catholics resentful and anxious but also relatively docile throughout the 1970s, while the traditionalist fringe remained a fringe. And even the main traditionalist splinter group, the Society of Saint Pius X led by the French archbishop Marcel Lefebvre, insisted that they had never intended rebellion, that they remained loyal to the papacy even if the papacy considered them in schism.

Then in the same way, although the John Paul and Benedict eras certainly created a climate in which liberal theologians trod carefully and theological conservatism was seen as the only path to advancement for ambitious bishops, the Vatican's pushback against liberal theology never went as far as the old campaigns against modernism in the pre–Vatican II church. Liberal Catholics weren't purged or provoked to open rebellion, their hold over many Catholic institutions was weakened but not broken, and their personal identification with the church was strained but not severed. Precisely because the John Paul/Benedict reaction wasn't a comprehensive war on modernism, because it took the form of exhortations and a conservative tilt in appointments and sporadic disciplinary action rather than an attempted top-to-bottom housecleaning, it wasn't that hard for many liberals to draw a distinction between "the Vatican" and the real church (or between "the hierarchy" and "the People of God," to use post–Vatican II language) and to treat the entire post-1978 era as a kind of temporary conservative coup, in which they had lost the levers of power but hadn't lost anything permanent. After all, what one coup could accomplish another could eventually undo.

So for all the real radicalism of the 1960s and 1970s and then the real backlash that followed, overall the post–Vatican II church experienced a kind of uneasy truce. The church's official teaching remained relatively stable once the council's changes were digested, reassuring conservatives in their bedrock assumption that the church's essentials have to endure for the faith to be called Catholic. At the same time, everyday life within most Western Catholic institutions made a lot of room for dissent and disagreement, enabling liberal Catholics to feel reasonably at home in the church while they waited for Rome to finally see the light.

This combination satisfied neither side. But it gave both sides incentives to live together, to remain within the fold, to avoid putting too much stress on the church's internal contradictions, to steer clear of decisive breaks. And the uneasy truce also allowed both theories of Catholicism's relationship to modernity to effectively be put to the test at once, on a scale that allows for conclusions to be drawn about their viability, their ability to actually deliver on their promise of renewal for the twenty-first-century church.

The first conclusion is that the liberal path really did lead very easily to dissolution and decline. This idea was a conservative talking point, yes, and it came in various caricatured forms, and there were plenty of exceptions to the general rule . . . but over years and decades, the sociological evidence was striking, consistent, and difficult to escape. More liberal religious orders and dioceses were less likely to produce the vocations necessary to sustain themselves. (Two mid-1990s surveys by the sociologists Roger Finke and Rodney Stark found that "religious orders retaining the more traditional demands had far more members in formation programs" and that traditional dioceses had about four times as many ordinations as the most liberal counterparts.)[2] More liberal Catholic universities and colleges were more likely to secularize and shed their Catholic identity entirely. Conservative Catholics had more children than their more liberal brethren, part of a consistent pattern across faith traditions (Orthodox Jews were more fecund than Reform Jews, conservative evangelicals had more kids than Mainline Protestants, and so forth), and the children of conservative households were more likely to retain their faith. In their 2014 survey of "Young Catholic America," the sociologist Christian Smith and his coauthors found that Catholic teenagers from more conservative Catholic households were more likely to practice their faith regularly into adulthood than Catholic teens from more theologically liberal households.

So too at the level of countries and cultures. In the heartland of "spirit of Vatican II" Catholicism, the Northern European nations whose theologians contributed so much to the council's liberal voice, the church's collapse was swift, steep, and stunning. Over the course of two generations, much of German and French and Belgian and Dutch Catholicism turned into Potemkin churches, rich in art and finery and historic buildings but empty of numbers, vitality, and zeal. In the swath of Latin America where liberation theology was supposed to bring Catholicism closer to the masses, the masses turned instead to Pentecostalism, choosing a mix of frank supernaturalism and prosperity-gospel preaching over a gospel of political liberation. Meanwhile in Africa, the church was resilient and growing even amid war and misery and persecution—and African Catholicism was far more theologically conservative than in the fading Catholic West.

These patterns were already obvious during the 1970s, when liberal ideas and experiments were at their peak. The institutional collapse of the Catholic Church in the West—the exodus from seminaries, the sudden drop in mass attendance, the swift erosion of Catholic distinctives across a number of fronts—happened before the years of John Paul II and Joseph Ratzinger. "Why Conservative Churches Are Growing," Dean Kelley's well-known sociological study, was published in 1972, and though much of his argument focused on the gains of conservative Protestant denominations, Catholicism was featured as a prime example of a church losing ground as it liberalized.

Disappointment over *Humanae Vitae* probably played some role in these trends, as liberals often argued. But it can't have been the decisive factor, since Protestant churches and denominations that went much, much further than the post–Vatican II Catholic Church in accepting the cultural revolution of the 1960s—churches that accepted not just contraception but divorce and abortion and later same-sex marriage; churches whose theology became so open as to render all creedal definitions irrelevant—hemorrhaged members even faster. The Episcopal Church in the United States, which more than any other body seemed to resemble the church that liberal Catholics wanted to experiment their way toward, was the particularly depressing case study: After fifty years spent racing toward the vanguard of every social change, it entered the twenty-first century a graying sect, split by schism and declining toward extinction.

These trends fed into—indeed, built—the master narrative of conservative Catholicism. As liberal Catholicism faded and liberal Protestantism collapsed, conservative Catholics began to take it as a given that liberalism in religion meant demographic suicide. They developed a kind of modest triumphalism about their own resilience, their wisdom in resisting liberalism's siren song. By the late 1990s, when John Paul II began talking about the twenty-first century as a "new springtime" for Catholicism, most of the church's conservatives assumed that their families and parishes and orders and institutions were the only possible seedbed for that spring.

But this conservative triumphalism was not modest enough. Because the second conclusion we might draw from the trends of the last fifty years is that conservative Catholicism was a preservationist enterprise more than a dynamic one. It limited decline without producing impressive new growth. It was more successful than the church's liberal wing—but only comparatively. And sometimes the difference between their respective trajectories was only a matter of degree.

Most of the trends noted above, vocations and retention rates and more, gave an edge to the conservatives but showed a common diminution regardless of theology, or at best a partial recovery under John Paul II and Benedict. If the church tended to weaken faster under liberal leadership or in liberal cultural climes, as in Germany or the Low Countries, it could weaken or even collapse in more conservative regions and situations as well. Twenty years after Vatican II there seemed to be more strength in Italian Catholicism or American Catholicism or Irish Catholicism—all more "conservative"

Catholic contexts, in different ways—than there was in the German or Belgian or French churches. But the church's position in Ireland declined thereafter, hastened by various awful abuse scandals, the belated arrival of the sexual revolution, and the secularizing effects of Ireland's economic boom. In Italy the shift wasn't as precipitous, but there too (as almost everywhere) economic growth led to increased secularization, the nation's birth rate was soon among the lowest in Europe, and the generation born in the 1980s was less Catholic than any prior Italian cohort. The American church, meanwhile, owed much of its continuing demographic robustness to Hispanic immigration; among white and native-born Americans, across the John Paul II era, mass attendance continued its post-1960s slide.

Nor did the papal reassertion of Catholic teaching do much to close the post-1960s gap between what the church taught (on sexual ethics, especially, but on other matters as well) and what many post–Vatican II Catholics believed. The inconsistent and lapsed dissented from church teaching more than frequent churchgoers, but even among regular massgoers there was a persistent split in the West—about fifty-fifty on divorce and later same-sex marriage, about eighty-twenty in favor of the acceptability of contraception. The division didn't go away when the Vatican began reining in the church's liberals, and neither did the widespread post–Vatican II sense that one could be a good Catholic without fulfilling duties (attending mass every Sunday) or holding beliefs (the real presence of Jesus in the Eucharist, the bodily resurrection of the dead) that the church insisted were nonoptional.

Here the conservative conceit that dissenters would eventually drift away completely or die off gave theological liberalism too little credit. The promise of some kind of reconciliation between Catholicism and late modernity, sexual modernity especially, had a persistent, entirely understandable appeal. Many Catholics might pass from theological liberalism into secularism, but enough remained Catholic to matter, and many people raised with a rote or repressive form of faith continued to find in the church's liberal wing a sense of openness, mercy, and relief. Likewise the tribal pull of Catholic ancestry, while too weak to maintain a robust Catholic culture, nonetheless left many people with a strong sense of the church as *their* church regardless of their disagreements with its leaders, and so they persistently declined to give up the territory they held within it. This was a reality that frustrated theological conservatives, who wondered why liberal Catholics didn't simply join the Episcopal Church or some similar body where their convictions were actively embraced. But religion is always experienced tribally and communally as well as doctrinally, so the conservative frustration was intellectually understandable but ultimately obtuse.

Thus theological liberalism remained influential despite its weaknesses, retained despite doubts and rediscovered as often as it seemed to wane. Meanwhile, conservative Catholicism struggled to find a way to escape its defensive crouch, to define itself not just in factional terms but as Catholicism in full. It held a core of believers—a crucial core, without which Catholicism's trajectory would have followed the Protestant Mainline all the way down—and maintained a counterculture to support them. But it also had many of the faults to which countercultures are heir.

It remained institutionally weak, despite its close association with the papacy. Many of the legacy institutions of Western Catholicism, the diocesan bureaucracies and national committees and prominent universities and charitable organizations, never reconciled themselves to the John Paul II era, or they went along with it halfheartedly, awaiting a different era and a different pope. So conservatives found themselves dependent on a hodgepodge of small colleges and publishing houses and start-up religious orders, which in turn bred both insularity and vulnerability. The conservative intellectual scene sometimes felt like an endless round of reaffirmation and polemic, overdependent on appeals to John Paul's encyclicals, and lacking the sense of aesthetic possibility that traditionally defined Catholic literature, philosophy, and art. And like many self-selected communities it seemed to lack a critical mass of, well, normal people—as John Zmirak, a traditionalist gadfly, pointed out in a reflection on the lifetime he had spent inside the conservative subculture:

It isn't normal for the Church to consist just of saints and zealots, as-cetical future "blesseds," and Inquisition re-enactors. Faith is meant to be yeast that yields a hearty loaf of bread. But since 1968 there has been nothing left to leaven, and we find ourselves eating yeast. . . . The last time I was at the Catholic Marketing Network, which includes all the leading companies in the orthodox Catholic market, most of the attend-ees seemed to be people who'd bought their own booths—so the whole day was spent watching vendors try to sell each other their stuff. ("I'll trade you three copies of *The Secret of the Rosary* for one of those 3-D Divine Mercy holograms.")[3]

This self-enclosure and embattlement also meant that conservatives were slow to grasp the scope of the sex abuse crisis (because they were slow to trust the media outlets that reported on it, and loath to criticize a hierarchy that they needed on their side), and fatally slow to recognize the vipers and con men and false mystics in their midst. ("It's such a pleasant surprise to find a fellow orthodox Catholic," Zmirak noted, that there's always a tempta-tion "not to ask too many more questions—for instance, about the person's qualifications, talent, or temperament.")[4] A figure like Marcial Maciel, the Mexican-born founder of the Legionaries of Christ, who built one of the more apparently fruitful conservative religious orders only to be revealed as a bigamist, drug addict, and pedophile, could have seduced his way to power in any environment. But the embattled conservative-Catholic subculture's eagerness for Success Stories made it that much easier for him to flourish.

The same weakness was apparent when conservative Catholicism en-gaged politically, especially in the United States. In theory it retained the ideological unpredictability appropriate to a universal church, with intellec-tual heroes who belonged to no party or clique. (Two of the most influential philosophers for younger conservative Catholics were Elizabeth Anscombe, a Wittgenstein disciple who defended *Humanae Vitae* and also denounced Harry Truman as a mass murderer for his use of the atomic bomb; and Alas-dair MacIntyre, whose *After Virtue* was a seminal critique of modern moral thought and whose views on political economy were socialist.) But by necessity, given its own sociological weakness, when it engaged politically the church's conservative wing did so first as an ally and then as a client of right-wing parties, which required downplaying portions of the Catholic inheritance that made a poor fit with right-wing ideology.

This posture, and the attempt to make the complexity of Catholic social teaching fit inside a right-wing box, often alienated people—Catholics or potential Catholics—whose religious imaginations balked at the idea that God required them to vote for George W. Bush. And the ever-tighter link between tradition-minded Catholicism and conservative political operations was one reason among many that the conservative Catholicism of the John Paul II era did not turn out to be a particularly effective missionary force.

There was a great deal of rhetoric about the "new evangelization," and Catholicism still attracted a certain kind of convert. But in the West far more believers lapsed than entered, while around the world (with, again, a partial African exception) the church's growth was driven more by demographic momentum than conversion, and Catholic missionary efforts were lapped by Protestants in Latin America and East Asia. In Western cultural debates, the church's language of natural law—which claimed to be based only on reason, not revelation, and thus offered a common ground for all people of goodwill—only seemed to persuade the already converted. No matter how it couched its positions, the church lost argument after argument about marriage, family, sexuality, euthanasia—and eventually found itself in a rearguard battle to protect its own liberties from secular encroachment. Politically, sociologically, and theologically, the faith remained as much on the defensive after decades of conservative reassertion as it had during the years of liberal experimentation, and there seemed little prospect of a change.

So the story of the post–Vatican II church is best understood not as a story of a promising renewal betrayed by the hierarchy (the liberal version) or a temporarily hijacked renewal recovered by John Paul II (the conservative vision).

Rather, it's a story of shared failure and persistent troubles, in which the idea of renewal was constantly invoked but rarely evident—at least on a scale commensurate to the challenges the church faced. Liberal Catholicism's failure was starker, but neither faction in the church's civil war could claim to have delivered Catholicism out of crisis. Neither could claim that their interpretation of the council had led to anything like the renewal or new springtime or new evangelization that had been promised. Instead, their long wars ensured that the church turned inward, litigating its divisions rather than preaching the gospel to the world.

More liberal Catholics, more alienated from the papacy and the church, sometimes had a clearer appreciation of this failure than conservatives. The wisest among them were willing to entertain critiques of how liberalization had run aground in the 1970s. But even conservatives who revered John Paul and admired Joseph Ratzinger's determination to protect the faith from fashionable currents could see by the 2010s that papal leadership was insufficient to the church's challenge, and that something new was required if Catholicism was not to be permanently divided and adrift.

Whatever the new vision might be, it would need to somehow transcend the wars of Vatican II, to claim a Catholicism that wasn't limited by the essentially political labels attached the post-conciliar combatants. It would need, perhaps, a fiercer attachment to orthodoxy and tradition than the reformers of the 1960s and 1970s had shown, but also a more capacious view of the Catholic teaching and a less partisan self-understanding than the conservative Catholic counterculture displayed. It would need a new aesthetic vision (or, counterculturally, an older one) for the digital age; new forms of community for an age of individualism and isolation; new intellectual horizons for where secularism seemed exhausted, incoherent, and yet still largely unchallenged. It would need new lines of engagement with modern attitudes and mores—or perhaps it would need to leave the post–sexual revolution West to work out its own issues for a time, and discover the Catholic future in China's underground churches, in the bloody borderland between African Christianity and Islam, in the contest with evangelicalism and Pentecostalism for the soul of the developing world. In either case, it would need to draw from the now global church, to escape the debates that French and German theologians had begun by discovering what Nigerian or Brazilian or South Korean Catholicism had to offer the universal church.

The limits of the papal office, limned in the last chapter, meant that such a renewal seemed unlikely to be handed down from above. Writing in the *Atlantic* upon Ratzinger's election as Benedict, the Catholic writer and biographer Paul Elie wisely remarked that "much of what is best in the Catholic tradition has arisen in the shadow of an essentially negative papacy, and much of what is worst has occurred when popes overplayed their role."[5] He was addressing a liberal audience, but the message was appropriate for conservatives as well, at the time accustomed to John Paul II's charisma and global presence, and too quick to imagine that the pope would always be the first and best champion for orthodoxy, vitality, and renewal.

Because historically that was not usually the Catholic way. As Elie suggested, the church in ages of crisis and torpor alike has again and again found renewal from below—from Benedict and his monks in Rome's twilight; from Saints Francis and Dominic in the High Middle Ages; from Catherine of Siena in an age of schism; from English converts in the Victorian and Edwardian eras; and on. There was no reason to think that the landscape of *after* "after Vatican II" would be different. In the early years of the twenty-first century, there was no way to know who would renew and reshape the post–John Paul II, post–Benedict XVI church. But one assumption seemed safe: The most important figures in the Catholic future would not be their successors on the papal throne.

Three

A POPE ABDICATES

The pope whose resignation Benedict XVI imitated, to the astonishment of both his inner circle and the world, was born Pietro Angelerio in Sicily in the early years of the thirteenth century. Ascetic from a young age, he joined the Benedictine order at seventeen and then retreated into a hermit's life, albeit one not so isolated to prevent him from founding a religious order to share its privations with him. Nor was he too isolated to intervene in a deadlocked papal election, which had left the throne of Peter vacant for almost two years after the death of Pope Nicholas IV in 1292. In the summer of 1294, with the world still pope-less, the aging Pietro—known widely as "Peter the Hermit"—sent a letter to the fractious cardinals, threatening them with divine retribution if they continued to debate and delay.

So the cardinals, perhaps assuming that a vengeful God might also have a sense of humor, elected the hermit as the pope.

It was a clever idea but not a good one. Pietro demurred and tried unsuccessfully to flee. Once installed under the name of Celestine V he proved to be incompetent, unable to handle the duties of the office and essentially ruled by Italy's dominant potentate, the Neapolitan king Charles II. After less than a year, the seventy-nine-year-old Celestine issued his one consequential decree, declaring a papal right to resignation, and then availed himself of the option, planning to return to an anchorite's existence.

But it was not to be. Benedetto Caetani, the powerful cardinal who had helped shepherd Celestine into retirement, was elected as his successor. Wary of leaving a second pope wandering the countryside, Caetani contrived to have Celestine placed under house arrest in Rome, where he died ten months later.

For the church it was a consequential succession. Caetani, who took the name Boniface VIII, was everything his predecessor was not—ambitious, political, and imperious. His decade as pope was frantic with activity: He established the tradition of the Roman Jubilee, in which pilgrims were promised time off purgatory if they made a pilgrimage to Rome; this became a long-standing tradition of the church, invoked most recently by Pope Francis in his Jubilee Year of Mercy. He issued a new codification of canon law, the *Liber Sextus*, which canonists consult to this day. And in the papacy's most famously immodest act, he issued the papal bull *Unam Sanctam*, in which the papacy's medieval assertion of temporal power reached its greatest height, with the sweeping claim that it is "absolutely necessary for salvation that every human creature be subject to the Roman pontiff."[1]

What Boniface decreed in theory could not be vindicated in political reality. His interventions in the fractious politics of Italy were mostly ineffective, with papal interdicts and excommunications regularly ignored up and down the peninsula. (One of the few well-executed forays earned him literary obloquy: Boniface helped overthrow Dante Alighieri's Florentine faction while the poet himself was in Rome pleading his side's case.) His long war with Philip IV of France over the taxation of the French clergy, the conflict that prompted *Unam Sanctum*, turned into a disaster. After Boniface excommunicated the French monarch, an army led by Philip's advisor entered Italy and seized the pope. In a famous—if perhaps apocryphal—scene, one of Philip's Italian allies demanded Boniface's resignation, the pontiff refused, and the nobleman slapped him across the face. Whatever the details, he was clearly beaten, and died of a fever a month later.

His more pliable successors eventually moved the papal court to Avignon in France, beginning a longer crisis that led to the Great Schism. They also allowed the French king and his allies to accuse the late Boniface of heresy and force a series of trials, in which the question of whether a pope could *be* a heretic was raised but never settled. An ecumenical council, the Council of Vienne, failed to reach a formal verdict—but Dante used his *Inferno* to place Boniface in hell. And when Celestine was canonized, again at the urging of Philip IV, Dante dissented—or so many of interpreters in his *Commedia* suggest, by identifying Celestine with one of the ghostly figures the poet sees hovering in the antechamber of hell: "I saw and recognized the shade of him / Who, through cowardice, made the great refusal." [2]

Over time, though, the mess that Celestine had created was forgotten, and what remained was the image of a holy man renouncing power unfairly forced on him. As the centuries turned and the popes came and went without imitating his abdication, Celestine became part of Catholicism's folklore— the saint who returned to his hermitage (though he didn't), the only pope to ever resign (though there had been a few others), a figure often remembered but never emulated by his overburdened successors.

Celestine's body lies entombed in the Basilica Santa Maria di Collemaggio in Aquila, close to the center of the Italian peninsula. In 2009 there was a terrible earthquake in the city; three hundred people perished, the basilica was badly damaged, but Celestine's remains were preserved.

Visiting Aquila during the rebuilding, Benedict XVI left a gift in the saint's glass casket: the woolen pallium he had worn during his papal inauguration. And three years later, on an ordinary Roman morning, in a statement to a stunned collection of cardinals, the former Joseph Ratzinger announced that he was following his sainted predecessor's example.

• • •

Benedict was always destined to be a less popular pontiff than John Paul. He was more introverted and academic, less political and charismatic, with a craggy face that evoked the Emperor Palpatine and a last name redolent of Teutonic villainy. The years he had spent as the Polish pope's doctrinal watchdog had saddled him with an inquisitorial reputation, and the press was never particularly interested in any other portrait.

But Benedict didn't need to be popular to be successful. He was elected in 2005 with a twofold mandate: first, to serve long enough to make sure that his predecessor's theological agenda took deep root, and second, to clean up the corruption that had festered, in the Vatican and in the wider church, under John Paul's soaring-above-the-details style of governance. The sermon Ratzinger preached to the cardinal-electors before the conclave that elected him was famous for its line criticizing "a dictatorship of relativism that does not recognize anything as definitive and whose ultimate goal consists solely of one's own ego and desires,"[3] a clear attack on secular liberalism (and some forms of liberal religion) that fit neatly with his reputation as orthodoxy's bulldog. But his sermon also stressed what he called "the filth within the church"—a reference not to the sex abuse scandal alone, most likely, but to the web of Roman corruption that had helped enable and protect abusers while lining the pockets of various cardinals and their coteries. His initial papal homily's supplication—"pray for me, that I may not flee for fear of the wolves"[4]—likewise suggested a man determined to clean house, and not merely enforce a conservative theological line.

It was this combination of purposes, not his doctrinal conservatism alone, that made Ratzinger's election possible—along with the sense that after years in Rome he knew the territory better than a reform-minded outsider might, and that he was incorruptible enough to handle the necessary work. And once installed as Benedict, the new pope behaved as if he understood well the limits of the conservative-Catholic master narrative, the extent to which John Paul II Catholicism was a weaker force than some of its apostles wanted to believe.

He had always been more pessimistic than John Paul, less confident in the constant invocations of renewals and springtimes. In one of his more famous public utterances, in a 1996 interview with the German journalist Peter Seewald, he suggested that "maybe we are facing a new and different kind of epoch in the church's history, where Christianity will again be characterized more by the mustard seed, where it will exist in small, seemingly insignificant groups that nonetheless live an intense struggle against evil and bring good into the world—that let God in."[5]

As pope his rhetoric was less apocalyptic than in the Seewald interview, and pitched to a wider audience, not just a faithful core. He constantly urged his fellow Europeans to look anew at their civilization's Christian roots; he issued an encyclical on the global economy that included a long section on ecology; he traveled almost as much as John Paul and worked on the diplomatic opening between Cuba and the United States that his successor brought to fruition.

But his expectations for evangelization were clearly more limited than his predecessor's, and on some level he saw himself tasked mostly with equipping the faithful for a long period as a "creative minority" within a post-Christian West. To that end he tried to welcome as many tradition-minded Christians as possible into the Catholic fold—opening a door for conservative Anglicans to come in with a liturgy that wove together their Book of Common Prayer with the Roman rite of the mass, officially reinstating the pre–Vatican II Latin Mass for any parish that wanted to celebrate it, pursuing a reconciliation with the traditionalists in the Society of Saint Pius X, whose leaders John Paul had excommunicated but whose community was thriving even so. He elevated bishops and cardinals who were cut from this creative-minority cloth, many of them more traditionalist (especially liturgically) than those chosen by John Paul II. And he spent less energy fighting the battles of Vatican II or offering exhortations on political issues like abortion or euthanasia. Instead, he sermonized constantly on Scripture, the saints, and the sacraments, and his great projects were encyclicals on God's love and the theological virtues, and a scholarly but accessible trilogy, published under his pre-papal name, on the life of Jesus of Nazareth.

Little of this theological work received much secular media coverage, but it didn't seem intended to grab headlines. It felt more like Ratzinger/Benedict was trying to create a deposit of material that his mustard seed church could draw on in the difficult generations to come.

Meanwhile, he also pursued the promised housecleaning, beginning with Marcial Maciel, who had been protected under John Paul but whom Benedict banished to a monastery in one of his early acts as pope, with an investigation of the corrupt cleric's order swiftly following. But after that bold start the new pontiff chose to move quietly and cautiously. He took an important step toward financial reform by subjecting Vatican finances to reviews by the international agency Moneyval, with the aim of putting the church's city-state on the "white list" of countries that are fighting money laundering. But the entrenched power centers in Rome were maneuvered around rather than demolished, and while Benedict eased a number of bishops into early retirement, there were no public defenestrations of hierarchs who had protected abusive priests, no confrontations with the powerful cardinals who had taken Maciel's money. Nor was any formal juridical mechanism established for removing corrupt or enabling high-ranking prelates. Predator priests the Vatican bureaucracy could and did sanction and defrock, and the system, centralized by Benedict, worked more effectively and at a faster pace than under John Paul II. But the cardinals and archbishops who covered up their crimes were safe unless the pope intervened directly—and Benedict was loath to wield his power so overtly.

Whatever the merits of this cautious strategy, events overtook it. A new wave of sex abuse revelations hit the church in 2010, touching Ratzinger's own past (as archbishop of Munich, he or his deputies had allowed an abusive priest to return to ministry) and overwhelming his record of reforms with horror stories from the 1980s. The hostile coverage was unfair to Benedict, in a sense: Whatever his failings in Germany he had been one of the few Vatican figures who tried to address sex abuse before the revelations from America made the issue impossible to ignore. But the unfairness coexisted with a rough justice, since he *had* left the men who had fought his 1990s-era efforts (such as Angelo Sodano, dean of the College of Cardinals, a prime recipient of Maciel's cash) in positions of honor and authority, and some of them were "wolves" by any reasonable definition, and still running around the sheepfold years into his pontificate.

As with the sex abuse issue, so with the entire challenge of ruling the church. The media often spun Benedict's role as sinister, but in reality he seemed overwhelmed—and more so as he aged—by the task of changing the way the Vatican worked, of dragging its operations into the digital age and its governance out of the Medici era. He relied on friends like Tarcisio Bertone, the Italian cardinal and his secretary of state, who were widely regarded as incompetent or self-dealing. He stumbled into controversies that a simple Google search in the press office might have avoided, as when he lifted the excommunication of four Society of Saint Pius X bishops without anyone thinking to mention that one of them, Richard Williamson, was a Holocaust denier. And he failed to back up his own appointed reformers when the going got tough: Archbishop Carlo Maria Viganò, assigned by Benedict to work on the Vatican's finances, was outmaneuvered by the forces of the status quo, cut loose by Bertone, and then shipped off to America as the papal nuncio.

The abandonment of Viganò was one of the revelations from the Vati-leaks scandal, which broke in 2012 when Benedict's own butler smuggled out documents detailing internal Vatican machinations and handed them over to an Italian journalist. The butler claimed to be acting out of a sense of loyalty to the pope, a desire to expose how badly his subordinates were serving him. In the (understandably) conspiracy-minded Italian press, though, the leaker was seen as a patsy for the "wolves" in the curia, whose fear of reform made them eager to embarrass the pontiff and divide his inner circle. It was at this point too that the term "gay lobby" began to circulate in accounts of Benedict's Vatican, describing something that was less an ideological pressure group than a kind of network of men with shared sexual secrets, and thus a shared interest in maintaining Rome's status quo.

Either way the leaks were another blow, after years of scandal and hostile media coverage, and it fell amid health problems—a pair of strokes, reportedly—that no doubt reminded Benedict of how John Paul II's public death from Parkinson's had left the church's governance paralyzed for several years. Who could blame him for thinking of the Celestine precedent, the Hermit Pope's still-on-the-books decree permitting resignations? His seven years as pope had been an extended trial. His brother, Georg, had heart problems; a close friend, Manuela Camagni, one of the four consecrated lay women in the papal household, had been killed in a car accident. He had not completed his intended housecleaning, but perhaps that mission should be pursued by someone younger, with more energy, in full health. The Vatileaks investigation had been closed, and the archbishop charged with handling it had delivered Benedict a thick dossier on internal intrigue and corruption—issues of clerical sexual misbehavior, gay and straight, included. Surely this could be handed on to someone better equipped to act on it. If the church needed a turn of the page, a generational shift that left the wars of Vatican II behind, it could begin immediately.

This was the explanation he offered in a post-resignation interview with his longtime interlocutor, Seewald. There was talk of a conspiracy, of blackmail, of political pressure, but no compelling evidence of such a thing has emerged (and not for want of searching by Pope Francis's critics), and the pope emeritus was dismissive: It was quite the reverse, he suggested. He acted in a moment of relative calm, with the Vatileaks scandal at least partially resolved. "The moment had—thanks to be God—a sense of having overcome the difficulties and a mood of peace. A mood in which one really could confidently pass the reins over to the next person."[6] And his motivations, he insisted, were primarily about good governance, about making sure the papacy could truly serve the church. As much as "the office enters into your very being," still "the Pope must do concrete things, must keep the whole situation in his sights, must know which priorities to set, and so on. . . . Even if you say a few of these things can be struck off, there remain so many things which are essential, that, if the capability to do them is no longer there . . . now's the time to free up the chair."[7]

He also added that he timed the announcement with a prosaic purpose: There was a papal trip to Rio de Janeiro scheduled for the next World Youth Day, in early 2013; he was worried that he was too compromised to make the journey. A doctor had told him not to fly over the Atlantic, and he felt that a new pope should be given time to be elected and take office and then plan for the event. "Otherwise I would have had to try holding out until 2014,"[8] he said, but Rio made it seem unreasonable and unfair. So it was the practicalities of the papal schedule that set in motion a once-in-a-millennium decision.

Still, as clean as this logic may have seemed, as much as Benedict tried to reduce his decision to the practical and ordinary, the pope must also have been conscious of the extraordinary step he was taking, and its inevitable repercussions for the office, his successors, and the church.

Though it reached back to the Middle Ages for its precedent, Benedict's resignation was nonetheless his most radically modern decision as pope. The public statement that an aging, ailing, dying pope could not fully exercise the office of Saint Peter was an implicitly secularizing act, one that undercut the traditional image of the pontiff as a spiritual father and elevated in its place the popular but not particularly Catholic image of the pope as the globetrotting do-gooder CEO of Catholicism, Inc. The resignation added to the already potent perception that the best way to judge the Catholic faith's truth claims is to look at whether the Vatican seems to be running smoothly, whether the pope is managerially competent, whether his approval ratings are robust. And it weakened the aura of sacrifice that shadows the pomp and powers of the papacy, the sense that the most powerful man in the church is giving his life for the church, the feeling that the Vicar of Christ no less than any martyred missionary can stand as an embodiment of Dietrich Bonhoeffer's dictum: *When Christ calls a man, he bids him come and die.*

Not for nothing is the room in which the new pope prepares to greet the crowds called the "Room of Tears." A new CEO has rather less for which to weep.

Benedict's subsequent decision to take the invented title pope emeritus, and the confusing suggestion from some of his intimates that he continued to exercise some part of the papal ministry in retirement, seemed like an attempt to walk these implications back. And, indeed, they were only implications; nothing in canon law or doctrine had been altered. Bishops retire, so why not the pope? Popes had resigned in the past, however distant, why not again?

But of course so much of Benedict's career, as Ratzinger and then as pope, had been spent fighting over the implications of Vatican II, not just its explicit words—over the ways that a door once opened could lead to more doors, more shifts, even a new paradigm. A papal resignation after centuries without one was a Vatican II in miniature, a perfect example of the kind of ambiguous, "this changes nothing/everything" adaptation to modernity whose interpretation liberals and conservatives had spent fifty years fighting over.

And now the most conservative of recent popes had delivered them yet another field of battle.

None of which proves that Benedict made the wrong choice, from his own perspective or any other. The papacy has to deal with the world as it is, the image of the pope-as-CEO is inescapable even if theologically problematic, and the need for good governance is particularly pressing in the age of the mass-media panopticon. It's not as if the exercise of the Petrine ministry hasn't changed since the days of Celestine and Boniface VIII, and a conservative Catholicism that sought to avoid any further alteration, lest the trauma of the 1970s return, would risk becoming fossilized with its convictions. At a certain point the post–Vatican II church had to be stable enough for a pope to do something unexpected without the whole edifice crumbling anew.

After three decades of conservative popes, thirty years of restoration, it was not unreasonable to hope that this moment had arrived.

Such must have been Benedict's core belief: That whatever the failures or limits of his internal cleanup effort, his more important and long-standing project—the post–Vatican II course correction, the turn from theological liberalism, the reassertion of Catholic distinctives, Catholic truths—rested on a firm-enough foundation to survive the shock of his abdication. There was no Great Refusal here, from his perspective. Unlike poor Celestine, who had abdicated after less than a year, Ratzinger/Benedict had been in Rome for decades, his institutional influence was immense, and he had given his last full measure of devotion to ensure that his predecessor's project, and his own, would outlast its critics and their foes.

As the conclave gathered to elect his successor, there was a strong case that he had succeeded. Whatever conservative Catholicism's weaknesses and limitations, the rising generation of priests was more likely to embrace the vision of the church that he and John Paul had championed, and the ranks of cardinals included many men who had been picked because they seemed to share his mind. Of course the next pope would be different, of course the church needed change. But at the highest reaches of Catholicism theological liberalism had been marginalized, and there was no reason to think that it would suddenly return.

In that sense, Benedict's legacy seemed secure. He was not fleeing or despairing. He had fought the good fight, he had finished the race, he had kept the faith. And unlike his predecessors, he would get the chance to see what providence had in mind for the drama's next act. So he made his decision, announced it, let the shock ripple through the cardinals and the church. For himself, there was no turmoil. He was at peace.

That night, by interesting coincidence, a bolt of lightning struck the Vatican.

Four

THE BERGOGLIO
SURPRISE

In the second half of the 1990s, well before Benedict's papacy, a small group of cardinals and bishops began holding informal meetings in St. Gallen, Switzerland. The attendees belonged to the dwindling liberal faction in the hierarchy: They included figures such as Carlo Maria Martini, the Jesuit archbishop of Milan; Walter Kasper of Rottenburg-Stuttgart, Joseph Ratzinger's longtime theological sparring partner; Godfried Danneels of Brussels, the leader of one of Catholicism's most liberal national churches; and Cormac Murphy-O'Connor of Westminster, the avuncular primate of the English church.

These men, once expected to lead Roman Catholicism through an age of ongoing reform, instead found themselves persistently out of step with John Paul II's agenda, leaders of an opposition rather than a vanguard. They were also men whose churches—especially in Belgium and Germany—were wealthy, influential but increasingly empty. They had experienced the worst of Western Catholicism's long post-conciliar crisis, with its collapse in vocations, church attendance, and belief . . . and this made Rome's refusal to entertain their preferred reforms seem particularly frustrating.

It was characteristic of the church's effective truce that John Paul himself had given most of them their red hat, elevating them despite their disagreements with his restorationist approach. He had remade the hierarchy in his image (or so it was assumed), but very gradually, with lots of deference to the men who had risen through its ranks under Paul VI. It was also characteristic of the truce that as cardinals these men did not usually argue openly with the pope. After *Humanae Vitae*, in the late 1960s and early 1970s, some liberal bishops—in the Netherlands and Canada, particularly—had seemed to be opening up arguments with Rome, moving toward explicit dissent on birth control. But that had tapered off or been suppressed, and under John Paul the liberals argued instead for a theological big tent, a doctrinal decentralization, in which the Vatican would simply step back from certain debates—debates like contraception and divorce especially, but also debates over syncretism in Asia and Marxism in Latin America—and let local churches and local bishops find the equilibrium that suited their situation.

This was the practical implication of a complex theological argument between Kasper and Ratzinger over whether local churches or the universal church had priority in Catholicism. Kasper, with many liberals, suggested that the entire church would flourish if Germans were allowed to figure out what kind of Catholic message worked in Germany, Nigerians in Nigeria, and so on all across the diversity of a global faith.

Of course there was an underlying assumption that what worked in Germany would be a more liberal theology, that as Nigeria developed and modernized it would also need a more liberalized theology, and so eventually there would be a kind of "spirit of Vatican II" cascade that brought the entire world, the entire People of God, into the broad sunlit uplands of a thoroughly modernized church. But as high churchmen in the age of John Paul II, the St. Gallen group rarely made that argument explicitly. They were more likely to cast themselves as champions of "collegiality"—the idea, elevated with characteristic ambiguity in the documents of Vatican II, that the pope governed the church in cooperation with local bishops and national churches—who felt that under John Paul and Benedict too much power had been centralized in Rome, that the pope held too many reins and gripped them all too tightly.

The group would later be described as a "mafia"—jokingly by Danneels, more critically by alarmed conservatives. But as conspiracies go its first major effort was ineffective. As John Paul's health declined across the early 2000s and the next conclave loomed, the St. Gallen group failed to find a plausible candidate or build a bloc of supporters capable of challenging Ratzinger for the succession. Martini was the group's brightest light, the most *papabile* of the West's dozen or so most progressive cardinals, but by the time John Paul died in 2005 Martini was ill with Parkinson's, and in any event he was seen as too liberal by most of the cardinal electors. In the conclave's first ballot, while Ratzinger was collecting forty-seven of the necessary seventy-seven votes, Martini reportedly received just nine.

At that point the St. Gallen mafia had to back another faction's horse: Jorge Bergoglio, the Jesuit archbishop of Buenos Aires, who had received ten votes, mostly from the Latin American electors. But Bergoglio was hardly the liberals' ideal candidate. He had a somewhat conservative reputation, and Martini, his fellow Jesuit, supposedly disliked him. And he did not seem to necessarily welcome their support. He gained ground over the conclave's second and third ballots, reaching forty votes, enough to keep Ratzinger below the two-thirds threshold. But the Argentine was clearly uncomfortable in the anti-Ratzinger part, and after the fourth ballot he apparently asked his supporters to back the German cardinal instead, in effect making Ratzinger the pope by acclamation.

That defeat seemed to ring down the curtain on St. Gallen. The group ceased meeting formally, Martini passed away (in his dying interview, he described the church as "two hundred years out of date" [1]), Murphy-O'Connor aged out of the ranks of voting cardinals, and Walter Kasper almost followed him. Had Benedict's resignation been offered a month later, his longtime rival would have been eighty, the age at which cardinals lose the right to vote. It was likely that Benedict was aware of this, and perhaps there was even a kind of graciousness in the timing—a gesture of conciliation to what seemed like a defeated foe. After all, one vote hardly seemed to matter, given the weakness of the liberal faction, the aging of its leadership, the absence of a plausible papal candidate who embodied "spirit of Vatican II" Catholicism the way the late Martini had.

Or so it seemed to most savvy Vatican-watchers. Wishful thinkers in the secular press might talk up the possibility of a liberalizing pope, but this was John Paul and Benedict's College of Cardinals, and as divided as the wider church might be the men wearing red hats mostly embodied theological conservatism. Which is why the most plugged-in conclave coverage in early 2013 focused more on the nuts and bolts of Vatican governance—the Vatileaks scandal, the dossier on curial corruption, and the question of whether a pope might be elected who could go to war with the Vatican bureaucracy.

When it came to specific candidates, the handicappers picked out two Ratzinger allies, Angelo Scola of Milan and Marc Ouellet of Quebec. There was talk that an alliance of curialists and Latin Americans might elect Odilo Scherer of São Paolo, who had spent many years in Rome and was seen as the "business as usual" candidate, backed by the aged but still influential Angelo Sodano. But as the cardinals gathered and the pre-conclave maneuvering began, it was clear that most of the voters wanted an energetic reformer, someone who could curb the (mostly Italian) power of the Vatican's court, and succeed as a manager where Ratzinger/Benedict had fallen short.

Which was where—unbeknownst to most observers—the remains of St. Gallen found an opening. Precisely because of theological liberalism's weakness within the conclave, its seeming marginalization in the College of Cardinals, the liberals' argument for collegiality and decentralization seemed less threatening to conservatives than it might have under different circumstances. Thus it resonated with the many cardinals frustrated with the incompetence of the Ratzinger-era Vatican. So long as they weren't being asked to elect a Martini-like figure as pope, the idea of a pontiff who released some reins seemed attractive; so long as the theological legacy of Benedict and John Paul seemed secure, there was surely room to loosen things up a little bit.

In the run-up to the conclave, then, a number of cardinals listened with fresh ears to figures like Murphy-O'Connor and Kasper, who canvassed the electors not on behalf of one of their own dwindling group, but on behalf of a figure whose theological views seemed to place him close to a conclave's middle, whose personal austerity offered a sharp contrast to the mode of living common among certain Vatican insiders, and whose background and biography seemed well suited to opening the next chapter in Catholicism's history, and to leading a post-European church.

They were canvassing on behalf of Cardinal Bergoglio.

The arc of Bergoglio's life and career follows a literary script: youthful success, defeat and exile, unexpected vindication and ascent. The grandchild of Italian immigrants to Argentina, devout from an early age and committed to the priesthood after a teenage epiphany, Bergoglio entered the Jesuits in 1958, when he was twenty-two, just four years before the Second Vatican Council opened in Rome. His formation was lengthy (Jesuits spend more than a decade in training) and initially old-fashioned in its rigors; the Jesuit order in Buenos Aires, as elsewhere, did a great deal of its work educating the national elite. But by the time he took his final vows and became a Jesuit in full, in 1973, the reforms of the council and the turbulence that followed had transformed his order, and divided it as they had divided the wider church.

The Jesuit spirit, the genius of the order, has often inclined its members toward extremes. In some contexts—the early Reformation era, the nineteenth century—the Jesuits have seemed hyper-Catholic, terrifying in their fervor, the shock troops of the papacy. During the Reformation they were Rome's spies, missionaries, and martyrs in Elizabeth's England; in

Catholic-ruled countries they were the church's fiercest anti-Protestant enforcers (a Jesuit sermon touched off the Saint Bartholomew's Day Massacre); and in the contested areas of Central and Eastern Europe their schools and sermons won back populations drifting toward Luther and Calvin. Their independence and zeal were feared not only by Protestants but by ostensibly Catholic monarchs and secularizing, centralizing states, which forced their temporary suppression in the late eighteenth century and sought to restrict their work thereafter. From Protestant Norway to revolutionary Mexico, Bismarck's Germany to James G. Blaine's Ohio, wherever Catholicism was feared or attacked or embattled the Jesuits were cast as the most distinctive danger, the tip of Rome's spear and the heart of its conspiracy. And the order played its part, defending papal privileges even as they vanished or were stripped away, taking a throne-and-altar view of Catholic politics even as thrones were toppled, and leading the war against modernism within the church as the nineteenth century gave way to the twentieth.

Yet in other situations—as missionaries in culturally alien contexts, as confessors to the powerful and privileged, as chaplains to the thoroughly modernized and sexually liberated—the Jesuits have sometimes seemed borderline heretical, deliberately relativistic, a church unto themselves. The two aspects of the order's reputation are in tension but also linked to one another, because they're both rooted in the missionary impulse, the desire to do whatever is necessary in order to propagate the faith. That daring has led Jesuits to martyrdom at the hands of Protestant queens and Mohawk chieftains and Marxist revolutionaries. But it's also inclined them to treat doctrine strategically and instrumentally, to make theological leaps and downplay moral absolutes when they threaten to impede conversion.

In missionary territory this means that Jesuits have often embraced what's called "inculturation," a refashioning of the Christian message so that it makes a better fit with the preexisting habits and customs and theological instincts of Japanese peasants or Chinese mandarins or the Tupi-Guarani Indians of Paraguay. This tendency has frequently put them at loggerheads with other religious orders (particularly their longtime rivals, the

Dominicans) working in the same areas, as in the debate over the efforts of Matteo Ricci, a brilliant Jesuit priest in seventeenth-century China, who was attacked for adopting Chinese concepts into his preaching and permitting converts to continue to venerate their ancestors. Ricci and his fellow Jesuits argued that this was a modest accommodation necessary to win converts, while their critics insisted that they were cheaters and compromisers who had fatally watered down the faith.

In more comfortable contexts, meanwhile, like the French court under Louis XIV, the Jesuits have been accused of watering down the moral content of Christianity in order to keep people in the faith. In the seventeenth century, this meant telling the pleasure-loving upper classes of a secularizing France that just because they kept a mistress or fought duels or frequented prostitutes or earned an awful lot of money from dubious commercial enterprises they need not have a particularly guilty conscience, nor think of themselves as anything but good Catholics who happen to have a few very normal human flaws. The great Jesuit-Jansenist controversy of the late 1600s, a battle whose relevance for our own era will be discussed in a later chapter, turned on just this issue of Jesuit moral flexibility, with Jansenist priests and pamphleteers hammering Jesuits for salving the consciences of an effectively pagan aristocracy, while the Jesuits answered by accusing the Jansenists of being cruel Calvinists without a trace of genuinely Catholic mercy.

That Matteo Ricci is currently a candidate for canonization and the Jansenists, not their Jesuit foes, were ultimately condemned as heretics tells you something about the importance of Jesuit flexibility within the church. But it also tells you something important that Catholicism has never before had a Jesuit as pope.

In the aftermath of World War II, perhaps chastened by how the church's reactionary impulses had sometimes cleared a path for fascists, the Jesuits were in the process of swinging from their fierce nineteenth-century conservatism to a new, more liberal experimentalism. And by the late 1960s, many Jesuits believed that the Second Vatican Council had ruled decisively in favor of this new experimental style—not least because Jesuit theologians had played a major role in the council's liberalizing turn—and given their order a mandate for a new kind of missionary adaptation. But instead of a Protestant Europe or an ancestor-venerating China, they needed to adapt to a civilization in which secular ideologies seemed like Catholicism's chief competitors—individualism among the Western bourgeoisie, Marxism among intellectuals and workers and the world's wretched and exploited. Thus the widespread Jesuit tendency after Vatican II both to relativize and politicize Catholic teaching—to play down commandments that conflicted with the West's post–sexual revolution lifestyle (much as Jesuit confessors had done with the duels and mistresses of French courtiers centuries earlier), while playing up the social teaching of the church to compete with Marxist-Leninist utopianism in the developing world.

In Latin America the emerging big idea for how to compete with communism was liberation theology, which promised a synthesis between gospel faith and political activism, with Jesus's Sermon on the Mount as a blueprint for social revolution instead of *Das Kapital*. Or alongside *Das Kapital*, more aptly, since many theologians believed that they could baptize Marxist ideas the way that Thomas Aquinas had baptized Aristotelian philosophy. Bergoglio's provincial, the head of the Jesuits in Argentina, Ricardo O'Farrell, supported this program, backing priests who wanted to live as political organizers among Argentina's poor, and ordering a rewrite of the Jesuit curriculum in which sociology crowded out theology, and Hegelian dialectics replaced Thomism.

But O'Farrell soon found himself dealing with Argentina's version of the larger post-conciliar crisis, in which the adaptations favored by reformers were followed swiftly by institutional decline. Under his leadership vocations plummeted, the order lost members and morale, and more conservative Jesuits were in revolt. In the summer of 1973 he stepped aside, and his superiors turned to the younger generation. At just thirty-six, the promising Father Bergoglio was elevated in his place.

Where the order's numbers were concerned he made a success of things. Vocations rebounded, the society stabilized, and he won many ad-mirers among the men formed under his leadership. But he made enemies as well: A fellow Jesuit told one of Bergoglio's biographers that as provincial "he generated divided loyalties: some groups almost worshipped him, while others would have nothing to do with him, and he would hardly speak to them."[2] Some of his fiercest critics were on the order's theological and politi-cal left. Radical priests felt that their revolution had been betrayed, liberation theology's adherents felt undercut and marginalized, and a coterie of Jesuit academics fretted that Bergoglio's program for Jesuit formation—which re-stored some of the traditional elements abandoned by O'Farrell, including a focus on Catholic history and the Ignatian spiritual exercises—was too reac-tionary, too pre–Vatican II. Or simply too pious: One liberal critic marveled that Bergoglio encouraged students to "go to the chapel at night and touch images! This was something the poor did, the people of the *pueblo*, some-thing that the Society of Jesus worldwide just doesn't *do*. I mean, *touching images* . . . what is that?"[3]

His leadership also coincided with Argentina's 1976 military coup and the subsequent "Dirty War," during which left-wing Jesuits were targets for the junta's thugs. Bergoglio was accused of complicity in the arrest and torture of two priests, a charge that seems mostly baseless; indeed, he seems to have labored behind the scenes to save people (not only priests) in danger of joining the ranks of the "disappeared."

But he did not attack the Dirty War publicly, and the Jesuits under his leadership kept a low political profile as well. The entire Argentine church was a compromised force during the junta's rule, and Bergoglio probably couldn't have played the kind of public, prophetic role—as a vocal critic of the regime—that the martyred Archbishop Oscar Romero played in El Salva-dor. But some in the order blamed what they saw as his conservatism for the absence of a clear Jesuit witness against the junta's crimes.

These critics eventually gained the upper hand. After Bergoglio's term ended in 1979, the order's leadership swung back to the theological left, and many of his policies were altered or reversed. A decade later, after an unhappy period in which the Argentine Jesuits were divided into pro- and anti-Bergoglio camps, he was exiled from the leadership, sent to a Jesuit residence in the mountain town of Córdoba, and essentially forgotten.

That exile lasted several years, and ended when John Paul II's choice to be archbishop of Buenos Aires, Antonio Quarracino, plucked Bergoglio to serve as his auxiliary in 1992. The rescue made everything that followed possible, but it also seemed to complete the former provincial's break with his own order; indeed, the Jesuit general allegedly delivered a harsh critique of Bergoglio's fitness to Quarracino, which the archbishop ignored. Over the next twenty years, which included many trips to the Vatican, Bergoglio never set foot in the Jesuit headquarters in Rome.

Told this way—conservative Jesuit fights post–Vatican II radicalization, ends up shunned by left-wing confreres, gets rescued by a John Paul appointee— the story of the future Francis's rise and fall and rise sounds like a case study in the conservative master narrative, and his ascent like *The Making of a Conservative Pope*.

But Bergoglio's positioning was more complex than this. After his emergence from exile and his appointment in Buenos Aires, especially, his course was ambiguous. He was an austere figure as archbishop, wary of the press—he gave almost no interviews—and he clashed frequently with Argentina's left-wing president Cristina Fernández de Kirchner. He accused her (accurately enough) of cronyism and corruption, and she attacked him as the embodiment of "medieval times and the Inquisition" when he opposed the same-sex marriage law that she pushed through in 2010. But he also had a distant relationship with many of his city's conservative Catholics, especially in the upper-class neighborhoods where pre–Vatican II Jesuits had been tutors to the young Argentine elite. He preferred to minister in poorer areas, imitating the radical priests he'd once clashed with over Marxism. Nor was he really much of a "culture warrior," to borrow the American phrase: He was quick to criticize local priests who seemed too strict or punitive (for instance, those who refused baptism to babies born out of wedlock); his war with Kirchner obscured an attempt at political compromise on same-sex marriage (he tried, unsuccessfully, to broker a civil unions alternative); he stressed ecumenism and dialogue and "encounter" (a favorite word) with other Christian groups and other faiths; and he scandalized traditionalists by not only befriending Pentecostalists but participating in their prayer services. In a telling moment, his spokesman criticized Pope Benedict's 2006 address on faith and reason in Regensburg, Germany, which sparked riots around the Muslim world with a (gentle) critique of Islam's relationship to philosophy, for setting back the cause of Muslim-Christian relations. It was a small indicator of the daylight between the Benedict papacy and Bergoglio's own style, and it led to some tense moments with Vatican conservatives.

Had he changed, somehow, during his years in exile? His biographers differ on this question. The British writer Paul Vallely has argued that the young Father Bergoglio was basically a pre–Vatican II traditionalist as provincial, and then, in exile, experienced a kind of theological and political conversion to his critics' point of view. This is a fascinating idea, but perhaps too psychologically pat, and Vallely's evidence is interesting but thin. He makes much, for instance, of the older Bergoglio's tendency to criticize retrospectively his youthful self's too hasty or overly authoritarian decision-making. ("You can do a great deal of harm with the decisions you make," he once told an interviewer.[4]) But this self-criticism could be more about style than ideological substance. And Vallely and his sources are too fond of false dichotomies, in which it's supposed to be surprising, a sign of some radical interior change, that a theological conservative could be pastoral or want to spend time among the poor.

The alternative explanation emerges from Austen Ivereigh's biography, *The Great Reformer: Francis and the Making of a Radical Pope*, the best and richest account of Bergoglio's life, which proposes a stronger continuity between the young provincial of the 1970s and the archbishop in Buenos Aires. To begin, Ivereigh argues that the younger Bergoglio was never a real traditionalist, never an enemy of Vatican II, never a foe of renewal or reform.

Instead, he was trying to heed the warning of Yves Congar, the great mid-century Catholic theologian, that "true reform" must always be safeguarded from "false" alternatives—reforms that become too radical, that move too quickly, that abandon necessary things in the quest for revolution. In this sense, his battles with radicals and liberals in his own order should be understood as an attempt to steer a moderate course, one that would reject both extremes and hold the center together. And this moderation, in turn, explains why Bergoglio seemed to change between the 1970s and the 2000s—because the situation in the church had changed. When the theological left was ascendant in the post–Vatican II period, it was natural for him to oppose its excesses. But when the left subsequently went into eclipse, it was equally natural for him to turn a critical eye on the excesses of theological conservatives.

Ivereigh also argues that this quest for "true reform," this desire to steer between traditionalist and radical interpretations, was one of the many ideas that Bergoglio shared with John Paul II and Benedict. Like him, both popes were men of Vatican II, liberals in the context of the council's debates, who tried to rein in radical interpretations of its reforms and emphasize the continuity between the church before and after. Like him, both defended popular Catholic piety and mysticism—what Benedict, as Cardinal Ratzinger, called "the faith of the little ones"[5]—against the condescension of certain theologians. Both, like him, rejected fusions of Christianity and Marxism while offering at best a cheer-and-a-half for capitalism.

But this parallelism shouldn't be pushed too far. Bergoglio's background and worldview also set him apart from his predecessors in several important ways. First, as an Argentine he had a very different experience of globalization than his predecessors did in Europe, one shaped by disappointments particular to his country. Across his lifetime, the Argentine economy was one of the world's losers, persistently underperforming and corruption-wracked. During the 1970s and 1980s, inequality and the poverty rate increased in tandem; from 1998 to 2002, while Bergoglio was archbishop, Argentina endured first a panic and then a depression. Where John Paul's and Benedict's shared skepticism of capitalism and consumerism was intellectual and theoretical, for Bergoglio the critique was more visceral and personal. As an archbishop and then a cardinal, there was a pungency to his attacks on malefactors of great wealth, his outrage on behalf of the betrayed and mistreated poor, which was distinctively Latin American and Argentine and quite different from the language in which his papal predecessors spoke.

Second, in the course of his political experience in Argentina he encountered very different balances of power—between the left and the right, between church and state, and within global Catholicism—than the previous two popes had experienced. As much as Bergoglio had clashed with Marxist-influenced Jesuits, the Marxists in Argentina weren't running the police state, as they were in John Paul's Poland and in the eastern half of Ratzinger's native Germany. They were being murdered by it, which made their ideology seem considerably less threatening than the Cold War Marxism that ruled from Moscow or Warsaw or East Berlin. Likewise, the fact that the church in Argentina was morally compromised during the Dirty War had theological implications: It meant that for Bergoglio, the more intense forms of traditionalist Catholicism (including the Society of Saint Pius X, the schismatic group that rejected Vatican II's acceptance of liberal democracy, which has a seminary in Argentina) were associated with fascism in a very specific, immediate way. Finally, coming from the church's geographical periphery himself, Bergoglio had reasons to sympathize with the St. Gallen group's argument that John Paul had centralized too much power in the Vatican, and that local churches needed more freedom to evolve.

Third, Bergoglio was a less systematic thinker than either of his predecessors, and especially than the academic-minded Ratzinger/Benedict—more reliant on ghostwriters, more inclined to down-to-earth and off-the-cuff public rhetoric, and more skeptical of intellectual systems in religion. Where Benedict *defended* popular piety against liberal critiques, Bergoglio *embodied* a certain style of populist Catholicism—one suspicious of overly academic faith in any form, be it liberal or conservative, radical or traditionalist. As his attempt to import the piety of the *pueblo* into Jesuit formation suggests, he had an affinity for the kind of Catholic culture in which mass attendance is spotty but the local saint's processions are packed—a style of faith that's supernaturalist but not particularly doctrinal. And to the extent that his faith did have an intellectual foundation, it was the idea of a popular genius in theology, of the way that the piety and creativity of the faithful could effectively teach and develop doctrine from below.

Finally, whatever his personal relationship to his order, Bergoglio remained a Jesuit-formed leader, with an Ignatian vision of a church perpetually "on mission," perpetually going outward to the peripheries, ever in search of the prodigal, the one lost sheep. This made him, in certain ways, a natural apostle of the new evangelization that both John Paul and Benedict had called for; one of his major projects, the Aparecida Document that Latin America's bishops published in 2007, was praised by many conservatives for its forthright missionary zeal. But again there was a contrast with Benedict, especially in how little stress Bergoglio laid on the internal life of the church, how little both liturgical rules and doctrinal correctness (on contested moral issues, but also theological questions generally) seemed to matter to him compared to the imperative to go out, to encounter, to embrace. If the agenda of the two conservative popes could be summed up as "retrench, restore, and then evangelize," Bergoglio seemed more impatient with the first two impulses, uncertain of their necessity, and focused almost exclusively on the third.

"*Hagan lío!*" he liked to say to young people. It was a colloquial phrase—translated as "Shake things up!" "Make noise!" or "Make a mess!" or even "Raise hell!" And not one that Benedict XVI would ever utter.

Not all of these distinctives were apparent to the cardinals in the conclave, and perhaps a fuller sense of Bergoglio's background and perspective would have changed the outcome of the vote. But perhaps not, because once his candidacy gained momentum, different pieces of his biography seemed to be arranged to suit what different electors wanted to see in him.

The St. Galleners canvassed for him because they saw hints of their own worldview in his focus on poverty and social justice, his seeming weariness with certain culture war battles, and his decentralizing instincts. Conservatives came around to him because they were reassured by what they knew of his wars with left-wing Jesuits, his earthy supernaturalism, his conflicts with the Argentine president. Latin and African cardinals appreciated his non-European, from-the-peripheries perspective. North American cardinals saw a fellow New Worlder and an experienced manager whom they could back against the Italianate corruptions of the curia. And institutionalists and curialists saw a man who didn't know Rome that well, and who was old enough—at seventy-seven, with a missing lung—that if things went badly they wouldn't go badly for that long.

Bergoglio himself was not just a passive receptacle for these various hopes. He had his moment, like Ratzinger with his "dictatorship of relativism" sermon, in the pre-conclave meetings, when each cardinal delivered brief, informal remarks. Bergoglio's words were addressed to a clear problem of the post–Vatican II church, the way in which the post-conciliar civil war had left the church turned inward, locked in theological combat with itself. Such inward focus, the Argentine warned, led to "self-referentiality and a kind of theological narcissism," to a "spiritual worldliness" that cripples true evangelization:

> The Church is called to come out of herself and to go to the peripheries, not only geographically, but also the existential peripheries: the mystery of sin, of pain, of injustice, of ignorance and indifference to religion, of intellectual currents, and of all misery. . . .

> In Revelation, Jesus says that he is at the door and knocks. Obviously, the text refers to his knocking from the outside in order to enter, but I think about the times in which Jesus knocks from within so that we will let him

come out. The self-referential Church keeps Jesus Christ within herself and does not let him out. . . .

Put simply, there are two images of the Church: Church which evangelizes and comes out of herself . . . and the worldly Church, living within herself, of herself, for herself. This should shed light on the possible changes and reforms which must be done for the salvation of souls. . . .

Thinking of the next Pope: He must be a man who, from the contemplation and adoration of Jesus Christ, helps the Church to go out to the existential peripheries, that helps her to be the fruitful mother, who gains life from "the sweet and comforting joy of evangelizing."[6]

The speech, like his candidacy, was a kind of Rorschach test. Conservatives could read it as a natural continuation of John Paul II's vision of a "new evangelization" and a "new springtime," in which the church—having overcome the chaos of the 1970s—could once more take the full Catholic gospel to the world. Liberals could read it as a call to transcend doctrinal obsessions and liturgical fussiness, to return to the engagement with modernity that they felt the last two papacies had interrupted. And anyone caught between the warring factions and weary of the long Catholic *kulturkampf* could read it simply as an eloquent call to leave those battles irrevocably behind—even if the specific details of how to do so might be as yet undiscovered.

The speech did not earn him his majority, but it made him a real contender, a plausible figure despite his age, and probably a widespread second choice. How exactly the voting proceeded in 2013 is a little more uncertain than in 2005, but Ivereigh and Vallely agree that Bergoglio started out with around twenty or twenty-five votes—presumably a mix of Latin Americans and liberal-leaning Europeans, as in 2005. Angelo Scola was the leader vote-getter, but not by much: His prickly personality had made enemies, and he was betwixt and between—too reformist for the taste of the Italian curialists, but too Italian for the cardinals who wanted to elect a real outsider. Meanwhile, Odilo Scherer's candidacy was a nonstarter, tainted by its association with the Vatican curia; Marc Ouellet won votes as a conservative alternative to Scola; and some Americans voted for Timothy Dolan of New York, probably as a placeholder while they tried to figure out their final choice.

By the second ballot it was clear that Scola had a ceiling, and Bergoglio had the momentum. Scherer pushed his supporters toward his fellow Latin American, a number of Americans swung Bergoglio's way, and some of the anyone-but-Scola European cardinals did as well. By the third ballot, it was Scola and Ouellet and Bergoglio, and the Argentine was well ahead, with at least fifty votes.

Had Bergoglio been seen as a liberal, or even—to borrow the subtitle of Ivereigh's biography—a potentially "radical pope," many Ratzingerian cardinals would have presumably aligned against him at this point, with either Ouellet or Scola giving way to the other, or both giving way to some dark horse. But only the most traditionalist electors, the Ratzingerian group's rightward flank, seemed worried about his ideology and theology. Raymond Burke, the American head of the Apostolic Signatura, the Vatican Supreme Court, and an apostle of the Latin Mass, may have made some effort to rally an anti-Bergoglio front. But he was isolated on the conclave's right, and all the momentum ran the other way.

Momentum in a conclave has a theological element. Does the Holy Spirit actually pick the pope? Ratzinger, ever interested in theological precision, had answered in the negative as head of the Congregation for the Doctrine of the Faith: The Spirit might *guide* a conclave, he suggested, but given the low moral character and catastrophic governance of certain pontiffs, it had to be the case that electors sometimes resisted that guidance. (He left unexplored the possibility that the Spirit had picked certain popes to chastise the church.) But theological niceties aside, and notwithstanding the grubby realities of papal politics, all or almost all of the men who entered the Sistine Chapel that week believed themselves to be discerning God's will through the voting process. And after three ballots, that process, and with it perhaps the divine wisdom of the Holy Spirit, seemed to be pointing toward the cardinal archbishop of Buenos Aires.

So it was that at least one of his rivals—some say Ouellet, some Scola; perhaps both—imitated Bergoglio's gesture in the 2005 conclave and urged their supporters to back the voting leader. On the fourth ballot Bergoglio fell just short of the seventy-seven, and then on the fifth the vote became a landslide: He finished with more than ninety-five of the one hundred and fifteen votes.

Bergoglio seemed at peace—so his fellow cardinals said, so he later said himself. When he passed the necessary seventy-seven, the cardinals stood and applauded. The Brazilian cardinal Cláudio Hummes, a Franciscan, took him by his shoulders, kissed him, and said: "Don't forget the poor."

The words resonated, apparently. He turned them over in his mind, and when asked the traditional question, "What name do you take?" he answered Francis, "in honor of Saint Francis of Assisi."[7]

Just as there had never been a Jesuit pope, there had never been a pope named Francis. Indeed, Bergoglio was the first pope in 1,200 years to take a new, un-roman-numeraled name. A small gesture, but still a radical one. And a sign of things to come.

Five

THE FRANCIS AGENDA

First there was the hotel. On his first day as supreme pontiff, the new pope circled back to his Vatican hotel, where he picked up his luggage, thanked the staff—and paid his own bill.

Then there was the newspaper. A few days into his pontificate, he put in a call back to Argentina, to the family-owned kiosk that had delivered the newspaper to his residence, to cancel the delivery and thank them for their service. "Seriously," he told the disbelieving vendor, "it's Jorge Bergoglio, I'm calling you from Rome." [1]

Then there was the car, the residence, the outfits. The new pope would travel in a Fiat, not a black Mercedes. He remained in the Casa Santa Marta, the (admittedly spacious) Vatican guesthouse where the cardinals had been quartered during their votes, rather than moving into the papal palace. He dressed simply, in papal white, eschewing the capes and hats and other flourishes that Benedict had favored. He wore a small cross, not a large one. He traded in the pope's traditional red shoes—red for the blood of the martyrs, not fashion, though the press didn't know that—for ordinary black ones.

Then came the first papal press conference, on a plane back from World Youth Day in Rio, Francis's triumphant return to Latin America just four months after his election. Famous in Argentina for almost never granting interviews, the former Jorge Bergoglio took the microphone and delivered a freewheeling performance, riffing on financial reform at the Vatican, praising the greatness of Pope Benedict, humbly downplaying his own humility (he stayed in the Casa Santa Marta because the papal palace was too lonely, not because it was too fancy, he told the journalists), reaffirming the church's position on abortion and same-sex marriage but also suggesting that these things were well known and didn't need to be constantly addressed . . . and then, in the turn of phrase heard round the world, answering a question about a "gay lobby" in the Vatican by saying that "if someone is gay and is searching for the Lord and has good will, then who am I to judge him?"[2]

Then there were the papal phone calls—cold calls, mostly, to people who had written to him, but who often (and understandably) thought they were being pranked. To a single mother, who had resisted her boyfriend's pressure to have an abortion, Francis promised to baptize her baby. To a man whose brother had been murdered in a gas station robbery. To a man who had just been released from prison after a twenty-year sentence for murdering his parents. To a traditionalist critic of Francis's style, who was struggling with cancer; Francis thanked him for his criticisms and promised to pray for him. To a group of Spanish nuns, who weren't there to take the call; Francis chided them, jestingly, for being out of the convent when he was trying to get in touch.

Then there were the gestures, the images, the iconography of the new pontificate. Francis washing the feet of teenage prisoners, including two young women, at a Holy Thursday mass held in a Roman prison. Francis beaming in the midst of crowds. Francis carrying his own bags onto planes and buses. Francis being hugged by a small boy onstage in the midst of a papal audience, while two cardinals tried to coax the child away with sweets.

Francis being embraced by a child with cerebral palsy. Francis going to confession, publicly, inside Saint Peter's Basilica, kneeling at the confessional in white. Francis embracing, and blessing, a man disfigured with boils.

Then in September of 2013, there was the interview, a wide-ranging conversation in the Jesuits' Italian magazine, *La Civiltà Cattolica*, with the editor, Father Antonio Spadaro, which was published without the Vatican press operation even knowing it was coming. It was in this conversation the pope used one of his most arresting images—suggesting that he wanted the church to resemble "a field hospital after battle," in which the most important thing is to bind up open wounds, to use mercy as a medicine, before offering the patient a meticulous blueprint for full health. The hospital image was part of an expansive, often moving vision of Catholic evangelization . . . but also one presented, rather explicitly, as an alternative to what Francis called a "restorationist" or "legalist" focus on the church's moral teaching, its doctrinal distinctives. No names were mentioned, and of course many conservatives reached for alternative readings, but it was hard not to read the pope's criticisms of "those who today always look for disciplinarian solutions . . . who long for an exaggerated doctrinal 'security' . . . who stubbornly try to recover a past that no longer exists" as a partial rebuke of the church's conservatives, or at least of the Benedict/John Paul/restorationist master narrative that they had long embraced.[3]

The world took notice. The press took notice. And the narrative was established. Francis the reformer. Francis the media sensation. Francis the people's pope. Francis, the great liberal Catholic hope.

But was he really? This was the great debate of Pope Francis's honeymoon period, with Catholics and non-Catholics alike lining up to argue over where the new pontiff stood, whether the changes he seemed to represent were real or just a media concoction, whether he could really be claimed for the liberal side in the Catholic civil war.

The case for Francis's progressivism was straightforward. It was clear early on that one of the broadest teaching themes of his pontificate would be dear to the hearts of Catholics who leaned toward the economic left. From his first apostolic exhortation to his choice of photo ops, Francis laid a constant stress on economic issues, on the church's social teaching—and more specifically on the crimes of the rich, the corrupting influence of money, the plight of the unemployed, the immigrant, the poor.

The specific content was not always different from previous papal statements on economic subjects; the Vatican has always regarded "Anglo-Saxon" capitalism with some skepticism, and it was none other than Joseph Ratzinger who once remarked that "in many respects democratic socialism was and is close to Catholic social doctrine."[4] But Francis returned to these issues more often, and his sharp tone and vivid imagery—his frequent references to the "throwaway culture" of modern capitalism, his condemnation of "an economy that kills," his pungent description of money as "the dung of the devil"—seemed like a deliberate strategy, intended to grab attention, to spotlight these issues more than others, and to challenge the press's (never accurate, but well-entrenched) image of a church exclusively interested in sexual morality. Indeed, Francis made this last intention more or less explicit: In the plane press conference, the *Civiltà Cattolica* interview, and other forums, he seemed to endorse the view that the church had become too sex-obsessed under his predecessors, too finger-wagging about sexuality and marriage and abortion, even as he moralized sweepingly about the plight of migrants, the despoliation of the environment, the wickedness of war.

Then there were the new pope's appointments, his choice of personnel. These were not uniform, but the overall pattern was hard to miss. In keeping with his identification with the Catholic peripheries, the emerging developing-world church, Francis appointed more non-Europeans to the College of Cardinals, and in his choice of bishops and archbishops he made many unexpected picks, reaching well down the ladder of episcopal promotion to pluck men who had a reputation for being pastoral, for having (as he liked to say) "the smell of the sheep."

But he also favored men from the church's progressive wing. Figures who had lost influence across the John Paul and Benedict pontificates, like Honduran cardinal Óscar Andrés Rodríguez Maradiaga, were invited into the pope's kitchen cabinet, a cluster of cardinals that was supposed to advise him on curial reform. In Europe the old guard of St. Galleners regained influence over episcopal appointments in their countries, while Benedict appointees were sidelined or effectively demoted within the Vatican bureaucracy. Cardinal Burke, the alleged leader of the last-ditch anti-Bergoglio opposition at the conclave, was a prominent example: The Vatican's highest-ranking American under Benedict, Burke was removed from his position on the Congregation for Bishops, the body that selects most of the world's bishops, and then (somewhat later, as we shall see) cashiered as head of the Apostolic Signatura. Meanwhile, many of the bishops plucked from obscurity by Francis and his advisers turned out to be "pastoral" in a style familiar from liberal Catholicism's 1970s heyday—from Blase Cupich, a critic of the American hierarchy's focus on abortion, who was lifted from Spokane to become the archbishop of Chicago, to Nunzio Galantino, bishop of a tiny diocese in Italy's boot and Francis's surprise pick to lead the Italian bishops conference, who urged his fellow prelates "to listen without any taboo to the arguments in favor of married priests, the Eucharist for the divorced, and homosexuality."[5]

That "listen to the arguments" credo applied outside the hierarchy as well, where the Francis era brought the swift rehabilitation of figures who had been disciplined or marginalized in the preceding decades. Timothy Radcliffe, the former head of the Dominican order and a prominent advocate for Catholic recognition of gay relationships and second marriages, received an admiring email from the pontiff's aides and then later a (minor) Vatican appointment. Francis received Gustavo Gutiérrez, one of the godfathers of liberation theology, in a private audience and he was later welcomed as a key speaker at a Vatican event. Father Sean Fagan, an Irish priest ordered to cease publishing after he wrote extended critiques of church teaching on contraception, masturbation, divorce, and homosexuality, had his freedom to write restored by the Congregation for the Doctrine of the Faith after a personal intervention by the pope.

At the same time, Francis often seemed to be carrying on a discussion with himself on theological matters, floating controversial ideas in a much more casual fashion than any modern pope, conducting phone conversations and even interviews that the Vatican press office had to explain were not, *not*, part of the official papal magisterium, and breaking not just with protocol but with church law (as in the Holy Thursday foot washing, which was previously supposed to be confined to men, in imitation of the twelve apostles) in order to make a vivid and inclusive gesture.

So the arguments that certain conservatives marshaled for total continuity between Francis and his predecessors—that the media was taking his public comments out of context, that they were twisting his words to fit their own "good pope, bad pope" narrative—were themselves a case of special pleading. Yes, the media had a narrative to push; yes, some of Francis's public gestures mirrored moves his predecessors made to less fanfare or acclaim; yes, some of his headline-grabbing comments (on the compatibility of Catholic doctrine and evolutionary theory, say) only got attention because certain reporters have no real clue about what Catholicism teaches. But overall the media were not deceived in thinking that the new pontiff differed from his predecessors in substance as well as style. The early days of the Francis era were a rare case in which secular journalists grasped the significance of something happening in Rome more quickly than many pious Catholics.

There could be no real doubt, a year or more into his pontificate, that the new pontiff saw his papacy as a corrective to the John Paul and Benedict years, a swing of the pendulum especially away from the Benedictine vision of the church. There could be no question that Francis intended a more experimental and adventurous papal style, a less rigorous approach to public teaching on faith and morals, and a form of evangelism that sought common ground between Catholicism and some late-modern lifestyles instead of sharpening the contrasts. The only question was how far the new pope intended the pendulum to swing.

• • •

Here the church's conservatives could initially take comfort. First, neither the pope's hostile attitude toward global capitalism nor his progressive tilt on issues like migration and climate change threatened any kind of doctrinal rupture within the church. At most, they injected a Latin American perspective into a discussion dominated by Europeans and North Americans, and threatened a particularly American marriage of conservative Catholicism and free market ideology, which given the state of conservative politics in America perhaps deserved a period of papal challenge and self-critique. Or they threatened to disrupt conservative narratives that really had mistaken political differences for theological ones—as in the case of Oscar Romero, the Salvadoran bishop gunned down by a death squad, whose canonization had been slow-walked by Vatican conservatives because Romero was an icon of the Catholic left, even though the slain bishop's faith seemed orthodox. When Francis beatified him in 2015 (after Benedict had unblocked the process), there were the expected hosannas from the church's liberals, but there were also some interesting reflections from conservatives, who acknowledged that they had conflated Romero with the Marxist-leaning theologians who had praised him, that they had let the church's culture war blind them to his sanctity.

So long as doctrine didn't seem to be in question, then, a papal agenda that elevated figures like Romero and emphasized a commitment to the global poor seemed to have the potential to straddle, rather than worsen, some of the church's internal divides. Indeed, it promised to highlight, usefully, the ways in which those divides aren't necessarily as binary as the language of "left" and "right" suggests. Many theological conservatives in the developing world were natural economic populists, and they appreciated the way that Francis talked about globalization, the free market, and the environment. A theology of ecology, a call for a more just distribution of global wealth—here a St. Gallen European liberal and an African conservative could find common ground.

So long as the pope didn't claim that Catholic teaching absolutely required Venezuelan socialism or a Danish tax rate, his rhetoric was well within the bounds of the church's social doctrine, and from a political perspective many of his words were as compatible with a crunchy, "small is beautiful" conservatism as with social democracy. His implicit targets were Ayn Rand and Joel Osteen, not Russell Kirk or Edmund Burke, and unlike the left-wing Jesuits he feuded with in the 1970s, there seemed no danger that Francis was about to go full Marxist, or demand that the catechism include an official Catholic blueprint for how to run a welfare state.

Unlike those 1970s-era Jesuits too, there was nothing obviously secularized about Francis's initial style, no sense that he envisioned the church as a political operation devoted primarily to redistributing wealth on earth. Indeed, his first sermon as pope had warned against exactly this danger: "If we do not profess Jesus Christ," he told the cardinals who had elected him, "we may become a charitable N.G.O., but not the Church, the Bride of the Lord."[6] He was devotional in his piety, emphatic about the importance of the sacraments and saints, sometimes apocalyptic in his themes—he frequently recommended Robert Hugh Benson's dystopian novel *Lord of the World*, a favorite text of pessimistic conservative Catholics, and there were more public mentions of the devil than one heard from Benedict. Rather than replacing the breviary with social action or the mass with consciousness-raising sessions, his chief desire seemed to be to welcome as many people as possible back into liturgical life, the confessional, and the communion line.

He was also careful at first to disavow any sort of explicit moral or doctrinal revolution, even when his more incautious words seemed ambiguous or unsettling to conservatives. He might think the church talked too much about abortion or same-sex marriage, and he might appoint men who seemed to feel the same—but he repeatedly insisted that he had neither the intention not the capacity to alter the church's teachings on those issues. His "who am I to judge?" comment, however different in tone from the usual Vatican language on same-sex attraction, could be read as a simple restatement of the catechism's stress on the equal dignity of gay people, the importance of not reducing any sinner to his sin. He was inclined to reinterpret *Humanae Vitae* in anticolonial terms, stressing the ways that Western models of population control had been imposed, with cruel consequences, on indigenous populations, but there was no sign that he planned to jettison the document. He seemed to have little interest in reopening a debate on women's ordination. And so on.

What he did seem to have in mind, on the first year's evidence, was less a revolution than a rebalancing—a shift in the papacy's public rhetoric, and a shift in its approach toward liberal and lapsed Catholics, premised on the idea that a more explicitly welcoming church would win more converts, keep more believers in the pews, and bring more drifting Catholics home. He wasn't putting more liberal Catholics in charge of defending doctrine or overseeing the church's liturgical life. Gerhard Müller, a Ratzinger ally and a rare German conservative, remained in charge of the Congregation for the Doctrine of the Faith—Ratzinger's old office, the former Inquisition, which took the lead in elucidating and enforcing the church's doctrinal commitments— and later Robert Sarah, a tradition-oriented Guinean, was placed in charge of the Congregation for Divine Worship. Rather, Francis seemed to be trying to use the church's progressive wing pastorally, by putting them on the front lines of evangelization, where in theory their greater sympathy for modern currents would make them more compelling witnesses, or at least less likely than a finger-wagging traditionalist to be preemptively tuned out.

Nor were his progressive appointments necessarily all *that* liberal, by the standards of the secular world or liberal Protestantism. Their inclinations were evident enough in what they emphasized and what they didn't say: You could read an awful lot of Blase Cupich sermons without finding anything that would make a Democratic Party functionary the least bit uncomfortable. But unlike some of the priests whom Francis allowed to be rehabilitated, most of his picks for bishoprics weren't outspoken advocates for doctrinal change. Instead, in the style of St. Gallen, they offered calls for dialogue and decentralization, and absent some kind of papal permission it was hard to imagine any of them questioning church teaching outright.

Thus one could argue, at least at first, that these appointments were actually more "moderate" than "liberal," and that Pope Francis was just trying to rebuild a Catholic center rather than pushing the church toward revolutionary change.

This was the argument advanced by the veteran Vatican journalist John Allen in his early book on the Francis pontificate, *The Francis Miracle*, which described the new pope as "moderate in the extreme," and attuned to the preferences of Catholicism's vast middle rather than its liberalizing wing. Through his appointments and his public rhetoric, Allen argued, "Pope Francis can change the Church significantly without altering a single comma in the catechism."[7] And that change of emphasis alone, he suggested, might be enough to begin rebuilding Catholic unity, since even more liberal Catholics don't always "expect the Church to overhaul its teaching, understanding that the weight of tradition in Catholicism is too strong to make that realistic."[8] Rather, they hope for a welcoming church, and that's what Francis was offering—"a Church that not long ago seemed to be growing more rigid, all of a sudden loosening up, embracing a more merciful and understanding attitude toward those who don't share its ideas."[9]

In this interpretation of his role, where John Paul and Benedict had regarded themselves primarily as custodians of Catholic truth against relativizing and liberalizing trends, Francis was positioning himself as a mediator between two equally dangerous extremes within the church—one liberal to the point of being radical, the other overly traditionalist. In his first papal letter, *Evangelii Gaudium*, "The Joy of the Gospel," he argued that contemporary Catholicism faces two great temptations:

One is the attraction of gnosticism, a purely subjective faith whose only interest is a certain experience or a set of ideas and bits of information which are meant to console and enlighten, but which ultimately keep one imprisoned in his or her own thoughts and feelings. The other is the self-absorbed promethean neopelagianism of those who ultimately trust only in their own powers and feel superior to others because they observe certain rules or remain intransigently faithful to a particular Catholic style from the past. A supposed soundness of doctrine or discipline leads instead to a narcissistic and authoritarian elitism, whereby instead of evangelizing, one analyzes and classifies others, and instead of opening the door to grace, one exhausts his or her energies in inspecting and verifying.[10]

In this passage the "gnostics" are (implicitly) the church's theological liberals, the "self-absorbed promethean neopelagians" are its doctrinaire traditionalists. In other words, Francis was nodding to Benedict's and John Paul's constant concern about religious individualism, about the dangers of a purely do-it-yourself form of spirituality and faith, while also arguing that the opposite temptation was a major problem for the church as well. From the new pope's perspective the dictatorship of relativism, in Benedict's famous phrase, could not be confronted by doctrinal rigor alone. Worse, the rigorists could be as closed to grace as any liberal, any doubter, any heretic, any member of the church of the Almighty Self.

This distinction was the interpretative key to Francis's dialogic rhetoric on doctrine, it seemed, which one could also frame in terms of the various groups that Jesus encountered in the New Testament. In his conflicts with 1970s-era left-wing Catholics, Jorge Bergoglio had seen the equivalent of first-century Judaism's Hellenizers and revolutionaries, ready to either water down or politicize the faith just as many Jews had been in their response to the Greco-Roman world. In the secular world the new pope saw plenty of scoffing Romans, quick to dismiss Catholicism as a dangerous and destabilizing superstition and to answer religious claims with Pilate's "what is truth?"

But among conservative and traditionalist Catholics, where John Paul and Benedict had seen the seeds of a renewed and vigorous church, the new pope saw a great many Pharisees and scribes.

Most Catholic conservatives, of course, found this analogy unpersuasive. To be sure there were legalists in their ranks; to be sure there were stone-throwers and nostalgists and bigots; to be sure the temptation toward self-righteousness was ever-present, ever-real. But looking at the big picture, it seemed unfair to treat their beleaguered subculture—the homeschooling families raising five children on a modest budget, the young men joining the priesthood in a world that sneered at celibacy, the clusters of Catholics praying the Rosary at abortion clinics, the elderly parishioners sacrificing to keep eucharistic adoration going—as if it shared in all the authoritarian faults of the church in Franco's Spain or Eamon de Valera's Ireland. Especially since it was this subculture that in many cases had kept Catholicism in the West going, kept it from sharing Mainline Protestantism's fate, kept parishes from closing and seminaries from emptying, kept the church's schools from going under and the church's charities from becoming simple clients of the government, kept the church's scandal-plagued bishops from becoming generals without an army.

And all this without any of the cultural support that what Francis called the gnostic temptation could count on! Because after all that gnosticism, that theological liberalism, wasn't just the worldview of a faction in the Catholic Church; it was the worldview of the entire mainstream post-1960s culture, backed up by the may-the-Force-be-with-you spirituality of Hollywood blockbusters, the mass-media assumption that dogma and doctrine were always cruel and imprisoning, the endless array of spiritual-but-not-religious bestsellers (from *The Celestine Prophecy* to *Eat Pray Love* to *The Da Vinci Code*), and then the ever-expanding moral individualism of courts and bureaucracies and universities. Whereas the traditionalist temptation found its fullest expression in . . . what? The Society of Saint Pius X? The occasional young-fogy parish priest? Cardinal Raymond Burke? Were these the self-absorbed promethean neopelagians Francis had in mind—and if so, couldn't he see how culturally weak they were?

This conservative reaction was reasonable, but it was also a somewhat Western-centric perspective. In the developing world matters could be very different. In parts of Latin America and the Philippines a more clericalist style of conservative Catholicism did retain cultural and political clout, abortion and marriage laws rooted in Catholic teaching could be applied harshly, and in the new pope's home country and elsewhere the hierarchy was not so very far removed from a close association with authoritarian power. In Catholic Africa, meanwhile, there was no ascendant sexual revolution or dominant cultural liberalism as yet: Instead, the continent's popular culture and its political elite often demonized and persecuted gay people, with the church sometimes abetting those efforts and often standing to one side.

So perhaps, in the Francis era, conservative Catholics in the West needed to recognize that in a global church the pope might need to correct conservative excesses even when those excesses weren't particularly present in Europe and America. And maybe there was a further way for them to take what seemed like unkind criticism from the Vatican, a way for the usual conservative docility to papal pronouncements to be applied. Maybe they were playing, or had fallen into, the role of the elder brother in Jesus's parable of the prodigal son—the loyal son who stayed in his father's house working while his younger sibling went into the wider world and squandered his inheritance. When the younger brother came home and his father ran out to meet him, the elder brother was resentful, angry, eager to see his erring sibling condemned instead of feasted. This desire was only human, and it did not detract from the loyal service the older son had given: "You are always with me," his father reassured him, "and all that's mine is yours." But how would the story have been different if the elder brother rather than the father had gone out to meet the returning prodigal, wearing all his grievances on his sleeve? How would it have gone for the family if the face of mercy had been a face of self-righteous disappointment instead?

From one perspective, the perspective of a self-critical conservative trying to assimilate the new pope's critique, that was part of what had happened to Catholicism during the long John Paul II/Benedict restoration. The church's face had become an elder brother's face, virtuous but unwelcoming, devout but unforgiving. Something essential had been preserved and saved, yes, and the people who had done the preservation were, indeed, often heroic in their piety and service. But as preservationists tend to do, they adopted a siege mentality about everything and everyone outside their inner circle—which meant that the church's gaze, when turned upon the wider world, was defined more by an elder brother's anxieties than by a father's forgiving warmth.

Whereas the Francis style, even if it risked muddying the clarity of doctrine, was potentially more attuned to the complexities of the church's relationship to the liberal, the dissenting, and the lapsed. First, it correctly recognized, as some conservatives did not, that these groups weren't about to fade away or disappear. They were all baptized Catholics, all the responsibility of the church's pastors, and if many were fully prodigal many others still were under the church's roof—still intensely practicing their faith, still sacrificing for the church even if they rejected various teachings and felt disappointed that Rome didn't see their point of view.

If Catholicism in the West could have collapsed without the resilience of its conservative subculture, a church that consisted only of the conservative subculture would be a rump, with not only its prodigals but many of its churchgoers and schools and charitable works shorn away. It might come to that eventually, depending on how wide the gulf between secular liberalism and the church became. But such a catastrophe was something to avert and not expect. For the time being the church had to act as if all its baptized souls were still reachable, and where its message wasn't reaching them then perhaps the problem wasn't just their dissenting spirit, but also the attitude of the messenger and the style of the message.

Moreover not every form of "liberal" Catholicism is identical or interchangeable. Certainly there are lapsed or dissenting Catholics who wouldn't be fully satisfied until a pope celebrated a same-sex nuptial mass under the baldacchino in Saint Peter's. But as Allen had argued, there were others who were simply alienated by a too frequent conflation of conservative theology and conservative politics, or who believed that the church could change its tone even if it couldn't change its teaching, or who found the church's "no" to all artificial elements in sex and reproduction hard to understand or follow without necessarily expecting the rule to be eliminated. (This last group, it should be noted, included the many *conservative* Catholics the world over who didn't practice natural family planning.)

Then finally there were the many Catholics (I know them, you probably know them, anyone who goes to mass or inhabits a Catholic family knows them, sometimes I am even one of them) who might sensibly be classified as persuadable rather than liberal, because their relationship to their faith was simply changeable, in that very human way—fluctuating with their moods and interests, their relationships and state of life, the last magazine article they read and the sermon they heard on Sunday, and the charisma and credibility of the church's leaders.

It was this last group, perhaps especially, to whom Francis's deliberately exaggerated critiques of clericalism and pharisaism might be pitched. These critiques were unfair to many conservative Catholics in their implication that a weak conservative subculture somehow had the same vices as a church enthroned and powerful in Counter-Reformation Spain. But they clearly spoke to an image, a stereotype, that many people (Catholic and non-Catholic) still carried in their minds when they thought about the church. For real evangelization to begin anew, perhaps that pre–Vatican II image needed to be somehow formally disavowed, discarded, laid to rest—and who better to do that than the pope himself? Maybe it took a Roman pontiff disavowing and critiquing clericalism to distance the church from that stereotype, to finally shatter Catholicism's authoritarian image, and to persuade people to look at Catholic Christianity anew.

Especially if that pope was not a secularizer, not a lukewarm bureaucrat, not a U.N. functionary in a white biretta, but a clearly Christian figure, with all the intimations of transcendence his position should entail. This was the real potential promise of Francis for conservatives, once his agenda and inclinations were established: That in ushering an unexpected springtime for liberal Catholicism, he would also model a way of being Catholic and modern that left certain failed 1970s progressive experiments behind. In creating a new and stable Catholic center, in reintegrating the best elements of liberal

Catholicism into a new post–Vatican II synthesis, he might also decisively ring down the curtain on more radical ideas of where the church should go—like those espoused by the longtime papal critic Garry Wills, say, who greeted Francis's election with a book, *The Future of the Catholic Church with Pope Francis*, which argued that in the long run the church's understanding of natural law, its opposition to abortion, the sacrament of confession, and the priesthood itself were all destined for the same fate as the Latin Mass.

If Francis-era Catholicism could make the Willsian sort of effectively Protestant liberal Catholicism look completely out of date—if it could engage with questions of social justice without seeming to reach naively for political utopia—if it could be ecumenical without being iconoclastic, modern without being anti-supernatural—if it could open a door to the doubting and struggling and dissenting while also reaffirming the basic stability of doctrine—if it could build a Catholic future without being hostile to the Catholic past—well, at the end of all those "ifs" lay the promise of a new Catholic center, a style of faith that might be "moderate" but never lukewarm, a church that still had its divisions but had managed to finally transcend the 1960s, and move into a new era rather than fight the same old civil war.

In the secular media's response to Francis, its initial fascination and then for a time its near-obsession, you could see the promise that this kind of message offered. Some of this excitement was ideologically motivated, reflecting the desire among many moderns—many journalists especially, judging by how the church of John Paul II and Benedict was covered—for the Catholic Church to change to fit the liberal consensus, for the last bastion of premodern religion to accept the modern vision of enlightenment. Some of it was less about a newfound desire for conversion than a newfound hope that Catholicism might be poised to convert to liberalism's implicit faith, that the progressive vision of history's arc might be vindicated in the Vatican itself.

But there was more to it than that. It wasn't just the famous "who am I to judge?" that went viral; it was the entire iconography that Francis manifested early on, which amounted to a living *imitatio Christi*, an imitation of Christ, visible in everything from his personal austerity to the children crowding around him to his physical intimacy with the captive, the suffering, the deformed.

In a truly post-Christian society, the kind of pagan landscape that many conservative Catholics feared the West had become, would Francis's representation of Jesus's ministry have so fired the public's imagination? Likely not: In an actual de-Christianized society, as in ancient Rome or Hitler's Germany, the weak and disabled and deformed would probably be considered inferior, unclean, subhuman. A leader who embraced them would be tainted, not elevated, by the gesture.

So the enthusiasm for Francis was an indicator that the pessimistic streak in conservative Catholicism, the view of Benedict XVI that the church was destined to spend a long time as a beset minority or a faithful remnant in a secularized West, might be a bit too pessimistic. Instead, the opportunities for religious witness might be broader than a simple narrative of Christian decline would suggest, and beneath the layers of self-assurance and superiority, contemporary secularism might actually be weaker than it looked.

The enthusiasm for the new pope was also a sign that Catholicism still loomed larger in the Western world's psyche than any other religious tradition, that Lenny Bruce's line about how "there's only one '*the* Church'" still had force. Whether the pope's outreach ultimately worked or not, it suggested that neither sex abuse scandals nor Vatican misgovernment nor the gulf between church teaching and Western mores had induced modern man to simply forget about the Catholic faith. Even in the twenty-first century, it turned out, many millions of people—including even that most jaundiced of demographics, the secular press—could still be inspired by an antique religious organization and its aged, celibate leader.

Which was, at the very least, a beginning. And if the new pope could keep his church together, if his new Catholic center held, perhaps it could even lead to something more than that—perhaps even to the renewal long expected by liberals and conservatives, but long denied to both.

If.

Six

THE MARRIAGE
PROBLEM

In February of 2014, just under a year after Francis's election, the cardinals gathered again in Rome for a consistory, a council in which new cardinals are given their red hats and discuss various topics with the pope. The subject of this particular consistory was the church's teaching on the family, and the new pope asked a member of the St. Gallen faction, one of the liberal cardinals who had canvassed for his candidacy, to deliver the keynote address.

The cardinal was Walter Kasper, Ratzinger's old intellectual rival. He had recently written a book on the theology of mercy, and his remarks to the cardinals took up this theme. Much of the address was a restatement of Catholic teaching on marriage and sexuality and the challenges that the sexual revolution posed to Catholic faith. But in the crucial passages Kasper proposed a crucial change: In the name of mercy, the German cardinal argued, the church should consider creating what he called a "penitential path" that would allow divorced and remarried Catholics to receive communion.

This had long been an important cause for Kasper, and the first experiment that he imagined a more decentralized Catholicism should allow. In 1993, he and two other German bishops had written a pastoral letter, read in many German pulpits, which proposed that the general rule prohibiting remarried Catholics from receiving the Eucharist might not apply "in complex, individual cases," and suggested that pastors and confessors should have the discretion to decide whether a given second marriage should bar someone from communion.

The 1993 letter prompted a rebuke from Rome, where Ratzinger was then in charge of the Congregation for the Doctrine of the Faith. The rebuke was not surprising, since it was only a little over a decade since John Paul II had issued the apostolic exhortation *Familiaris Consortio*, which urged pastoral mercy, kindness, and accompaniment for divorced Catholics, but also stated that "the Church reaffirms her practice, which is based upon Sacred Scripture, of not admitting to Eucharistic Communion divorced persons who have remarried."[1]

These words notwithstanding, it was understood that many priests did admit remarried Catholics to the Eucharist, and that many bishops—in Germany and elsewhere in the West especially—tacitly approved. But this was de facto, not de jure, and as a matter of church teaching the rule remained firm, even as other controversies—gay rights and same-sex marriage above all—emerged to eclipse the divorce debate.

It was still eclipsed in Francis's early days as pope. Just a week into his pontificate, he had praised Kasper's book on mercy, and in his famous in-flight press conference coming back from Rio he seemed to indicate an interest in the remarriage issue, offering a positive-seeming mention of Eastern Orthodoxy's practice on divorce, which allows second (and even third) marriages under a special, penitential rite and after a temporary abstention from communion. But the furor over gay priests and "who am I to judge?" over-shadowed these remarks, as did other interviews, other controversies, across Francis's first year as pope.

The issue surfaced again in the fall of 2013, when the Vatican doctrinal chief, Gerhard Müller, wrote an article for the Vatican daily *L'Osservatore Romano* reaffirming the church's rule. Cardinal Óscar Rodríguez Maradiaga, part of the pope's kitchen cabinet, swiftly criticized Müller for being too black-and-white in his thinking. ("The world isn't like that, my brother," said Rodríguez Maradiaga.)[2] This kind of cardinal-versus-cardinal clash was unusual, but it was still just a skirmish, and when Kasper rose to speak at the consistory, the issue that he came to raise was still a layer or two deep in the Catholic consciousness—present, potent, but not yet a major flashpoint.

In his remarks, Kasper began by assuring his fellow cardinals that he did not intend to make it one—that he did not intend to question "the indissolubility of sacramental marriage and the impossibility of a new marriage during the lifetime of the other partner," that he wanted no part of a "cheapened mercy" offered without change or cost.[3] But then he went on to the same theme he had taken up twenty years before. Perhaps, he suggested, just as in Vatican II the church had shifted in various ways to accompany a changing world, there were ways in which the church's teaching on marriage and the sacraments could—well, not change, exactly, but adapt. Perhaps there could be, alongside a general rule, a "narrow path" for "the smaller segment of the divorced and remarried," the spiritually serious among them, who might do penance for their first marriage's failure and then return to communion. Perhaps, somewhere "between the extremes of rigorism and laxity," a "new perfection" of pastoral practice could be found.[4]

Many, indeed most, of the assembled cardinals reacted skeptically to these perhapses. But it was Kasper, not they, who had been asked to speak. And slowly it would become clear that his elevation was not a mere gesture to the St. Gallen faction. The pope intended the German cardinal's speech as the first step in a dramatic progression, which would soon become the most important and most contested front in his crusade to change the church.

The Catholic Church's teaching on marriage begins with the Gospel of Mark, likely the oldest of the gospel narratives. Jesus is teaching a crowd in Judea, and the Pharisees appear with a testing question: "Is it lawful for a man to divorce his wife?" Jesus answers by asking them about the law of Moses, and they remind him that "Moses allowed a man to write a certificate of divorce and to send her away."[5] At which point Jesus, as elsewhere in the gospels, makes the law more demanding, more radical, more transcendent:

- And Jesus said to them, "Because of your hardness of heart he wrote you this commandment. But from the beginning of creation, 'God made them male and female.' 'Therefore a man shall leave his father and mother and hold fast to his wife, and the two shall become one flesh.' So they are no longer two but one flesh. What therefore God has joined together, let not man separate."
- And in the house the disciples asked him again about this matter. And he said to them, "Whoever divorces his wife and marries another commits adultery against her, and if she divorces her husband and marries another, she commits adultery."[6]

From the first, this vision of marriage's indissolubility, its one-flesh metaphysical reality, was crucial to Christianity's development and spread. It was sociologically important, because it made such a stark contrast with the sexual landscape of ancient Rome. It taught the fundamental equality of the sexes in a world defined by patriarchal power, it offered a metaphysical view of human sexuality in a world where ideas about (elite, male) sexual expression were interwoven with prostitution and slavery, and it promised permanence and protection to the women and children set aside by the ease of Roman divorce. But more than that it was theologically important, because Saint Paul's vision of human marriage as "a mystery" connected to Christ's relationship to his church was embedded deep into the church's liturgy, its theology, its self-understanding as the "bride of Christ" destined for "the wedding feast of the lamb."

Much later, in its wars with Protestantism, the Catholic Church would be accused of abandoning the Bible in favor of invented traditions, man-made doctrines. But in the case of marriage the church has cleaved to the plain text of Mark's gospel (and the very similar passages in Matthew and Luke), while most other Christian communions have found reasons to soften the New Testament's demands. The Orthodox churches came to accept divorce and remarriage, albeit with the provision that remarriage be penitential rather than sacramental, because of pressure from the Byzantine throne to unite canon law with Roman law, which provided various grounds for divorce. (The desire of certain Byzantine emperors to marry twice was not incidental to this process.) The Protestant churches initially made limited allowances for remarriage, sometimes based on a line in Matthew's gospel where Jesus seems to make an exception for cases of "sexual immorality" (a phrase that varies with the translation). Over the intervening centuries, and especially after the sexual revolution, the exception became more general. Today both conservative and liberal Protestant communions accept that a second marriage can be as valid as the first.

But not the Church of Rome. Consistently across the centuries, it taught that if a first marriage was valid, a second marriage was not just wrong but actually an impossibility, because the first marriage, the real marriage, still bound the spouses in a single flesh. Consistently across the centuries, the church taught that the exception in Matthew's gospel allowed for separation but not a second union. Consistently across the centuries the church taught that remarriage after divorce placed people in a state of public adultery, a state that excluded them from communion unless they either separated or avoided having sex with their second spouse. And consistently across the centuries, the church insisted that this teaching, hard as it might seem, was not an impossible demand. The highest ideal proposed by the New Testament, the holiest state of life, was celibacy, while marriage was for ordinary sinners—and even the most ordinary of men and women could unite in a true one-flesh union, whose metaphysical reality would endure despite their failings and their sins.

This view, the long-standing Catholic view, has a solid claim to being the view of the earliest Christians. In the second-century book *Shepherd of*

Hermas, one of the first manuals of Christian morality, we find the Catholic reading of Matthew's exception: In the case of a wife's adultery, the husband is allowed to "put her away, and remain by himself," but he is urged to hope for her repentance and return, and if he remarries instead "he also commits adultery."[7] Similar interpretations appear in many church fathers' writings on marriage, and in early councils and synods across the Mediterranean world. In a few cases (some Frankish synods in the eighth century, notably) the possibility of remarriage is allowed. But the preponderance of early rulings point to a firm view of indissolubility, and the prominent papal interventions of the first millennium do as well. Indeed, for the most part when the Christians of the early church debated the possibility of second marriages, the issue was marriages contracted *after the death of the spouse*, which some ascetic Christian sects taught were impossible as well.

In the second millennium this preponderance of evidence gave way to the clarity of firm doctrinal definitions—some issued in the Middle Ages, some in the Reformation and its aftermath, and some during the social revolutions of the present day. Again and again, ecumenical councils—famous ones like Trent, forgotten ones like the Second Council of Lyon—declared that the church cannot accept either the Orthodox compromise or the Protestant alternative. Again and again, popes insisted on the principle of indissolubility, the impossibility of second marriages, against royal desires and local adaptations alike. Again and again, a link between the sacrament of marriage, the sacrament of confession, and the sacrament of communion was reaffirmed.

The church's obdurance on this point came at a cost, and not only in our own phase of modernity. It made missionary work more challenging in practically every cultural context. It made reunion with the Eastern churches, and then later the Protestant churches, that much more difficult. (When certain Eastern churches reconciled with Rome in the nineteenth century, their profession of faith included an affirmation of marital indissolubility even in cases of adultery.) It brought the church into conflict with the royal houses of Europe; in the reign of the much married Henry VIII, it helped make martyrs of Thomas More and John Fisher, and in the process lost much of the English-speaking world for the Catholic faith. And then finally it became a major problem for contemporary Westerners as civil divorce became easier, and then a very ordinary fact of life.

But the teaching's resilience, its striking continuity from the first century to the twentieth, is also a study in what makes Catholicism's claim to a unique authority seem plausible to many people, even in a disenchanted age. Two thousand years after Jesus of Nazareth had answered the Pharisees' worldly, reasonable position with an absolute demand, the church that claimed him as its founder still held to his scandalous words: *What therefore God has joined together, let not man separate.*

Of course alongside this striking continuity there was adaptation, compromise, and change. The church taught that while a valid marriage between two Christians could never be undone, for "natural" marriages—marriages between non-Christians, be they pagan or Jewish or Muslim or something else—various exceptions could apply. One of Saint Paul's letters was invoked, for instance, to permit a non-Christian marriage to be dissolved if one party wished to convert to Christianity and the other spouse did not. As the church's missionary efforts expanded to polygamist societies in the Age of Discovery, converts with multiple wives were often allowed to remain with their favorite spouse rather than their first wife. Then as mixed marriages proliferated in the nineteenth and twentieth centuries, the church extended the Pauline exception to include nonsacramental marriages in which one spouse but not the other was a baptized Christian; if they divorced and one or the other subsequently wished to become Catholic and marry in the church, their prior marriage could be dissolved with Rome's approval.

Then in addition to these exceptions there was the vexing issue of what sort of union constituted a valid marriage, and what role the church had in overseeing and affirming that validity. For centuries most marriages in the West were made by the couple alone, sometimes with a priest's blessing but quite often not. In the Middle Ages clandestine marriages proliferated, made by couples seeking to escape arranged unions and parental control. The church recognized such unions, but in a world of shaky record keeping and limited communication technology, who was really married to whom could be a matter of debate. The line between betrothal promises and marriage vows could be blurry, a man could get away with bigamy by decamping for a distant town or country, and so on.

Protestant reformers made much of the inevitable scandals, and Counter-Reformation Catholicism responded by instituting new requirements for validity: a priest's presence, two witnesses, written records. But even these requirements were only imposed by some bishops in some countries, and it wasn't until 1908 that canon law officially applied them to Catholics anywhere in the world, giving us the form for a valid Catholic marriage that the church still requires today.

But if the requirement for a priest and witnesses is now clear, other rules for what makes a valid marriage have become more ambiguous over the last fifty years. Traditionally a marriage could be deemed spurious, invalid, null for a relatively narrow list of reasons—the age of the parties, a failure to consummate, consanguinity, preexisting religious vows, the compulsion or blackmail of one of the parties. But with the divorce revolution the question of what constituted true consent began to be interpreted more liberally, with psychological factors—immaturity, ignorance, a lack of real commitment, a lack of openness to children—increasingly stressed as impediments to a true marriage, and reasons for the church to declare a broken union null and allow the parties to marry someone else.

This expansive approach to annulments was pioneered in the post-1960s United States, where a large, efficient, and relatively accessible set of tribunals made the process more available than elsewhere in the world. After Vatican II certain dioceses became famous as "annulment factories," and by the Benedict era the United States accounted for a staggering 60 percent of annulments worldwide.[8] From one perspective, this made America a cautionary tale, a capital of laxness and de facto "Catholic divorce." From another it suggested that the American system was a model for how the church should adapt to post-sexual revolution realities, and that the many countries and regions where the annulment process remained opaque, corrupt, or unavailable would benefit from the American example. (The second perspective was not confined to the church's liberals: Not a few conservative Catholics assumed that between secularism and the sexual revolution, large numbers of Westerners were essentially incapable of entering into a real marriage.)

Either way, there was a global patchwork in how the church approached the validity of its flock's marriages, and also a patchwork of pastoral responses to remarried Catholics who wished to receive the Eucharist *without* an annulment. In Western countries especially such Catholics generally had little difficulty finding a liberal-leaning pastor who would bless the reception of communion. In highly mobile societies they had little difficulty finding parishes where their marital history was unknown. And since in many post-Vatican II parishes confession lines were short and communion lines long there was little in the way of social pressure or convention to reinforce the church's teaching.

At the same time, though, there were plenty of places—including in Pope Francis's Latin America—where the traditional Catholic stress on receiving communion worthily kept not only the remarried but also the merely divorced away from the altar. And everywhere some divorced Catholics simply didn't know or understand the church's teaching and thought that divorce alone barred them from receiving the Eucharist.

Meanwhile, secularization and the sexual revolution had also multiplied the number of baptized and confirmed Catholics who married outside the church—in secular spaces, beaches and courthouses and so on, without a priest to preside and record their nuptials. Often these couples didn't realize that their marriages were considered invalid by the church, or that if they divorced without ever having the marriage blessed by a priest they could then remarry without an annulment. If they were irregular massgoers many of them didn't care, and might receive communion in the same spirit as a Christmas-and-Easter churchgoer attends church—as a nod to their Catholic heritage, undertaken out of familial or cultural habit, in a spirit of casual participation rather than defiance or respect.

Faced with this complicated patchwork of beliefs, practices, and motivations, the early-twenty-first-century church resembled in certain interesting ways the church of the Middle Ages—with a formal teaching on marriage impressively unaltered from the New Testament, but undermined or challenged by a mixture of uncertainty, ignorance, cultural complications, and doubts about what definition of marital validity should count.

But there were two crucial differences. First, in much of the modern world the ambient secular culture was more hostile to the church's formal teaching on divorce's impossibility, and to Christian sexual morality more generally, than any part of the medieval or early modern world had been. (Even in pursuit of Anne Boleyn, Henry VIII insisted that all he wanted was an annulment, not a divorce.) Second, the speed of travel and communication meant that everyone everywhere was more aware of these tensions and complications, and so there was much more pressure—as always in late modernity—on the pope and on the Vatican to do something about it.

Which is where Cardinal Kasper's proposal entered in. According to the German cardinal, and to the many voices soon raised in his support, he was proposing a modest and necessary response to the mess created by swift cultural change, and a perfect example of what Pope Francis meant when he envisioned the church as a "field hospital," binding up wounds rather than passing judgment. If in certain countries the church already erred on the side of mercy in granting annulments, if in many places priests winked at the rules for receiving communion, why shouldn't Rome take account of both those realities, cut away the thickets of bureaucracy surrounding the annulment process, and give priests a simple pastoral program for reconciling the remarried? If the church's teaching on indissolubility could survive easy annulments and remarried Catholics receiving communion from accommodating priests, why couldn't it survive the church actively liberating priests and parishioners from hypocrisy and disobedience, and letting them do with clean consciences what many of them were doing anyway?

It was also strongly implied that this would be a partial solution to the hemorrhage of churchgoers in the West, giving not only the remarried themselves but many lapsed Catholics in their circles—family, friends, and so on—a reason to regard the church as less intolerant and more forgiving, and consider making a return. The general liberal assumption that rigid rules had driven Catholics from the church was given a particularly vivid illustration by the issue of divorce: In the case of remarried Catholics, the church was explicitly denying them the fullest form of communion, so it wasn't surprising that they would deny the faith or drift from it. And then there were their children: If the parent did attend mass and did follow the church's rule and abstain from the sacrament, their offspring might grow up with a sense that their family was somehow only sort-of Catholic, that their mother or father was not fully loved by God.

Conservatives, as ever, had their doubts. They doubted that rigidity was the real driver of secularization, noting the sharp decline within Protestant denominations that had accepted divorce and remarriage years ago. But they also pointed out that mercy for the remarried and their children would not be the only message sent by the change that Kasper proposed. What of the suffering children from a first, now broken marriage, who would now have even the church itself seem to bless their family's breakup? What of the wavering, laboring couple trying to keep their marriage together in hard times, who would see their remarried neighbor go to communion and wonder why they should continue with the struggle? Many Catholics ignored the church's teaching, yes, but overall it still seemed to have an effect on people's willingness to make a marriage stick—American Catholics still had lower divorce rates than Protestants and nonbelievers,[9] while in Latin America divorce rates were far lower than in the Protestant nations of the West.[10] Wouldn't a compromise risk that modest but real achievement, undercutting Catholic marriages already challenged in many other ways? As ever in any proposed reform, wasn't there a danger that the desire for what it would immediately accomplish—mercy and welcome for a particular group of Catholics—was obscuring the long-term consequences for Catholic families and children, which might make the shift far less merciful than it seemed?

More cynically, conservatives also wondered about issues specific to Kasper's Germany, where the church remained extremely wealthy—with about $6 billion in income annually—thanks to a "church tax" levied by the state on every baptized Catholic even though most no longer attended mass. The lapsed could evade the church tax by disaffiliating, and more and more Germans were doing so every year, threatening the funding base of the institutional church—a threat deemed so grave that the German bishops had threatened Catholics who disaffiliated with excommunication. Against this backdrop, the German zeal for mercy seemed notably selective, and the Kasper proposal looked like it might have some unspoken financial motivations, as a gesture intended mostly to soften lapsed German Catholics' hostility sufficiently to keep them from checking a tax form box that would cost the church its revenue.

But these were all pragmatic, sociological, and political considerations. The deeper problem was doctrinal: Whatever its immediate practical effects, from the conservative perspective, Cardinal Kasper had fastened on the one reform that the church could *not* contemplate—at least not without falling into self-contradiction and performing an auto-demolition on its own claim to authority. The church's teaching on marriage could survive widespread hypocrisy and disobedience, because all of the church's teachings could survive widespread hypocrisy and disobedience. That was the nature of Christian morality, that all would sin and fall short, and that particular societies would sin and fall short in particularly pervasive ways. The church could be latitudinarian and tolerate such messiness, or it could move to impose a more stringent discipline and strive for a more perfect uniformity, or it could do both at once depending on the culture and the circumstances. But what it could not do was break faith with its own tradition, declare that the ontological reality of a marriage didn't matter under specific extenuating circumstances (like a stable second marriage with kids), and teach that what the church and Jesus Christ considered adultery was also, somehow and in some cases, not.

This, to conservatives, was the path that Kasper was urging on the church. Under his proposal, Catholics would be told by Rome that even though their first marriage might well have been a real marriage, even though it could well have constituted an indissoluble reality, they could still live with and sleep with someone who was not their husband or wife in good conscience, without any need to promise amendment when they went to confession or fear sacrilege when they went up to receive communion. The Kasperian argument might hedge by talking about the discretion of pastors and a case-by-case approach and the importance of avoiding scandalous behavior, but the rule it established was clear: What the church considered to be objectively real was not necessarily binding, what the church considered a serious, public, ongoing sin did not necessarily require repentance in the confessional, and what Jesus said about marriage no longer necessarily applied.

Also, all of Kasper's hedges were likely to be swept away eventually if his position carried the day. The standard pattern in the post–Vatican II church was that some innovation was introduced as an exception for rare occasions or special circumstances—for instance, permitting communion in the hand instead of on the tongue, or allowing cremation rather than burial at Catholic funerals—and then became the rule, because cultural pressure and imitative behavior overwhelmed any halfhearted resistance at the parish level, and the "spirit of Vatican II" was taken to require the shift. In the case of remarriage, because the stakes were higher the cultural pressure would inevitably be more intense, almost everyone would expect that the new path should be available to them, and the individual pastor would be left in a near-impossible position if he tried to defend the church's teaching case by case.

Moreover, even if the individual pastor were sufficiently conscientious to attempt a rigorous discernment process, he was probably overburdened already—the church since the 1960s being, after all, a church with too few vocations for its flock. Alternatively, if he was the sort of rather less conscientious pastor who held confessions for just thirty minutes every week (in Cardinal Kasper's Germany, almost half of the priests, according to a church study, had not gone to confession themselves in the past year[11]), the idea that he would throw himself into intensive spiritual direction for the remarried—let alone that he might actually tell some of them no at the end of a discernment process—beggared belief.

More likely, once a "penitential path" was instituted and approved, it would become more like a penitential *act*: Express appropriate contrition for the failure of your officially Catholic marriage and then go to communion with a clean conscience for the duration of your civil one. This change would effectively reverse the formal Catholic teaching that divorce was sometimes necessary but remarriage remained impossible; instead remarriage would be acceptable so long as you were sufficiently sorry for your past divorce. With that as the standard practice, only the most scrupulous of Catholics would bother with the longer and more uncertain process of annulment, only the most obsessively self-scrutinizing would consider abstaining from communion. For everyone else, the Catholic view of marriage would be effectively transformed into something more Orthodox or Protestant or secularized: lifelong marriage as the notional ideal, but second marriages—celebrated civilly, but perhaps eventually with some kind of informal blessing from the pastor as well—as a morally acceptable second-best.

This change alone would raise serious questions about the continuity and coherence of what Catholicism taught, not to mention the infallibility of the pope doing the teaching. But there was also no reason why the transformation would stop with the issue of divorce and remarriage. In comments following his address to the cardinals, Kasper explicitly suggested that the church's teaching on marriage required exceptions because it was too hard for the "ordinary Christian" to follow,[12] and because the obligations that people undertook when they entered second marriages (to support their spouse, to care for the new union's offspring) could not be set aside without doing new damage, opening new wounds. This argument was reasonable in worldly terms, but it was a revolutionary one from the perspective of traditional Catholic moral theology.

The Catholic position on personal morality, defined against Protestant challenge in the sixteenth century, was that the grace necessary to persevere in virtue is always available to ordinary Christians. Therefore God's law is never impossible to follow, whatever costs obedience appears to impose. This doesn't mean that the law isn't hard to obey, or that sins can't be dramatically mitigated by circumstances, or that the underlying situation doesn't affect the scale of human guilt. But it means that the church—and, as confessors, its priests—cannot tell people that they are *free* to sin because God is understanding, or that their personal burdens make it *impossible* to do otherwise, or that a serious sin might be the *right* choice under a lesser-of-two-evils calculus. Forgiveness is absolute if repentance is sincere, but nobody can ever be told that God simply accepts their sin for the time being, that they can be—to borrow the language of Martin Luther—*simil justus et peccator*, at once justified and sinning. For the church to imply as much, to suggest that for the ordinary Christian the moral law is an aspiration rather than an obligation, would be dereliction of its basic duty to tell people the truth about their situation. It would not be mercy but a lie.

If this traditional Catholic view were officially altered or dismissed, if the church began to teach instead that in some cases and for some people the moral law is unreasonably hard to follow and concessions must be made, then that shift would have obvious implications well beyond the specific question of adultery and remarriage. After all, many different situations involve entanglements and obligations and commitments that are difficult to escape. The soldier who commits war crimes because his superior expects it and he faces death or court-martial otherwise, the loan shark who rips off the poor because his family's livelihood depends on it, the politician who takes a bribe because everybody else is doing it and there's a greater good involved in his continued public service . . . all of these cases and countless others take place in contexts that make sin seem a necessary evil, virtue a near-impossibility.

Needless to say Cardinal Kasper's intention was not to license bribery or war crimes. His implicit idea, common to liberal theologians since the sexual revolution, seemed to be that sexual sins are at once more distinctive and less serious than others, and that the obligations imposed by irregular relationships have more positive elements than the obligations imposed by, say, a corrupt boss or a brutal sergeant or a rancid political culture.

It is not clear that this distinction holds up under scrutiny. (The father who starts a new family may hurt his legitimate children more than a bribe-taking politician hurts the common good.) But even if you accepted that somehow this new teaching, this view of the moral life's sometimes impossible demands, would only apply to sexuality and marriage, its implications would still ripple outward and change much more than just how the church regards divorce.

For instance: If the obligations involved in a second marriage need to be accommodated by the church, why not the obligations of a polygamous marriage—where similar promises are made, similar entanglements are present, and children are just as (if not more) likely to be involved? In Africa, especially, where the definition of marriage is contested along rather different lines than in the West, a consistent application of Kasper's proposal would all but necessarily open the door to accommodating people in polygamous unions—especially since many of the women in such unions are plainly in a more difficult, more sympathy-inducing position than men or women in a second marriage in the West, with fewer rights and freedoms and less capacity to break away and keep their children if they do. A church that hesitated to ask too much of "ordinary Christians" in the rich, egalitarian West would be obliged, for both consistency and decency's sake, to make similar accommodations for Christians in contexts shaped by African marital traditions and Islam. A church that welcomed adulterers to communion in Germany or America would have no good reason to withhold the sacraments from polygamists in Nigeria or Kenya.

Nor would it have a clear reason to withhold them from sexually active same-sex couples either, especially those who exchange vows and raise children and make a life together. Given the deeply rooted nature of homosexuality, its probable biological origin in most cases, gay Catholics have a reasonable argument that church teaching asks something harder of them than it does of divorced and remarried Catholics, who after all are at least allowed to marry *one* person whom they love. So a church that no longer took its own teaching on adultery seriously but still drew the line at sodomy would be undercutting its claim to having a sexual ethic that's consistent rather than just homophobic. It would be telling gay Catholics to bear a cross that it had just declared was far too heavy for most straights—an untenable position, ultimately, and a bigoted-seeming one in the meantime.

Nor, for that matter, would such a church have reasons to draw lines around certain nonmarital romantic heterosexual relationships either, given that those can involve as many moral and emotional commitments as a second civil marriage, and in many late-modern societies quite often involve kids as well. The logic of the Kasper proposal could be applied to any stable, entangling commitment that fell outside the norms proposed by Catholic sexual teaching. All could be seen as cases, like divorce and remarriage, where the church's teaching needed to be redescribed as an ideal rather than a commandment, and where a premodern theology of absolutes needed to give way to a modern theology of situations.

Conservatives tended to suspect that might be the point, that Kasper's proposal was designed to be a depth charge, released to shatter the edifice of Catholic moral teaching on sexuality and allowing creative rebuilding in the rubble. Whether this suspicion was fair depended on which of the various points of view enfolded into progressive Catholicism you were talking about. There were supporters of the Kasper proposal who genuinely believed that it made at most a modest change in church discipline and who regarded the foregoing argument as so much slippery-slope nonsense. There were others for whom the change was obviously meant as an entering wedge in a broader transformative campaign. There were others still who genuinely hadn't thought that far ahead, since one style of liberal Catholicism takes a certain pride in not knowing exactly what it wants—it's open to the movement of the Spirit in history, and whatever comes, comes.

But no matter its immediate consequences, there was no doubt that if adopted Kasper's proposal would be a major turning point. Most intra-Catholic debates since the Second Vatican Council had turned on the question of how much the church could change, how much "development of doctrine" was actually possible. The papal answer had been clear, reaffirming not only specific teachings and disciplines but also the moral theology underpinning them, denying that "development" could ever lead to real reversal. John Paul's 1993 encyclical *Veritatis Splendor*, in particular, had been an extended rebuke to the idea that modern complexities made moral absolutes archaic, and a straightforward condemnation of the many Catholic theologians who argued the spirit of Vatican II required accepting situation ethics.

But here, in Kasper's proposal, was a chance to vindicate the progressive reading of what Vatican II had made possible, and prove that the interpretation of the Council advanced by the last two popes was provisional rather than binding.

After all, if a rule rooted in Jesus's own words, confirmed by dogmatic definitions and explicitly reconfirmed by the previous two popes, linked to Reformation-era martyrdom and bound up with three of the seven sacraments, could be so easily rewritten . . . well, then what rule or teaching could not?

Thus remarriage and communion was a place where conservatives felt they had to draw a line. But more than that: It was an issue where a defeat would threaten to radically alter their own understanding of the Catholic faith. For a pope to contradict his predecessors so flagrantly, to break with a tradition so deeply rooted and recently reaffirmed, was supposed to be literally impossible—precluded by the nature of papal infallibility, prevented by the action of the Holy Spirit, and unimaginable given the premises that conservative Catholics brought to these debates. Indeed, if a pope could bless communion for some adulterers using premises explicitly rejected by his immediate predecessors, it would suggest that the Orthodox and Anglicans were closer to the mark in their view of church authority than the Catholics—that the pope might be a fine symbol of unity, but that as the last word on faith and morals his authority had been rather exaggerated for at least a thousand years.

This possibility made the Kasper proposal different from most of the other ways that a pope of Francis's inclinations might seek to liberalize the church. His leftward forays on economics, migration, and the environment might annoy some conservative Catholics, in the United States especially, and likewise his tendency to downplay issues like abortion. But there was no question that they fell within the realm of normal papal rights. His off-the-cuff theological speculations might seem to flirt with heterodoxy on occasion, but because they were off-the-cuff speculations rather than a formal teaching, their implications were necessarily limited. And there were certain changes he could make (allowing priests to marry, say) that would displease some conservatives without making them question his authority or their own beliefs about the church. These included changes in the precise realm Kasper was addressing, the realm of remarriage and divorce: If Francis simply took steps to expand the American approach to annulments to the global church, conservatives might think it unwise or overly lax, but they would also accept that such a reform would be within his authority as pope.

But the remarriage and communion issue was far more fundamental, and thus the Kasper proposal far more fraught. Indeed, the issue of divorce was more fundamental than other vexed issues where conservatives believed the authority of the church to be at stake: more scripturally rooted than the prohibition on artificial birth control, more directly linked to Christ's own words than the prohibition on same-sex intercourse, and more consistent in its historic application than the church's response to modern bioethical and end-of-life controversies. It was, in many ways, the basalt slab upon which every other Catholic sexual teaching rested—the indissoluble sacramental character of marriage was the reason for everything else the church asked of Catholic Christians where sex was concerned, for everything (from premarital sex to masturbation) that it labeled a grave sin.

Ironically this is probably why Kasper's speech, and the brief wave of publicity it generated, did not seem to immediately trouble many conservative Catholics. It wasn't just their faith in an unchanging magisterium at work; it also simply seemed outlandish to imagine that a pope with so many different irons in the fire (including the issue that he had been elected to address, the internal reform of the Vatican and curia) would decide to create a full-scale theological crisis so early in a promising pontificate. Given that so much of his purpose as pope seemed to involve transcending old controversies, urging the church to face outward and leave off its ceaseless civil war, was it likely that Francis would decide to reignite a battle from the 1970s and 1980s? No, conservatives told themselves, probably this had been an olive branch to liberals on an issue where the pope had no intention of directly following their advice. Or perhaps it was a case of Francis trying to mediate between conservatives and liberals—letting the liberal wing of the church make its case, and then doing some reform around annulments that would annoy rigorists but remain a theologically acceptable compromise.

They were wrong, understandably but badly so. But it would take some time for that to become apparent. One consistory speech did not a crisis make, and while doubts stirred among conservatives, the full revelation was still eight months away.

Seven

TO CHANGE
THE CHURCH

H ow does one change an officially unchanging church? How does one
alter what is not supposed to be in your power to remake? One answer: Very carefully, and by overwhelming consensus.

That's the answer suggested by the experience of the Second Vatican
Council, which in its ambiguities did not officially touch Catholic doctrine
but certainly seemed at times to tiptoe very close. Nowhere was this tiptoeing
more fraught than on the issue of religious liberty, where reformers wanted
to accept and bless American-style church-state relations, even though
the church had long insisted that governments should grant special privileges to Catholicism, with non-Catholic religions tolerated but not granted
equal status. So the council had to find a formula that would reconcile the
nineteenth-century papacy's thundering denunciations of religious freedom
with the 1960s-era church's desire to make its peace with religious pluralism

and leave the age of throne-and-altar (or dictator-and-altar, in the instance of Franco's Spain and other cases) Catholic politics behind.

This could not be accomplished without controversy, and the first pass at the document that became *Dignitatis Humanae,* the council's declaration on religious freedom, was pulled from the council floor on a late November day in 1964, amid objections from conservative bishops to the substance of the text. The council's reformers protested, asking Pope Paul VI to put the text to an open vote. They had a majority on their side, but on what John Courtney Murray, the Jesuit intellectual who had built the case for the religious freedom shift, dubbed his personal "*dies irae*" (day of wrath), the pontiff decided to table the matter for another year, till the council's final session.

In the delay Paul VI showed prudential wisdom. The text was massaged to include more vocal affirmations of tradition, it was debated and wrangled over and finally brought up for a vote at the end of 1965, with the pope's own weight clearly behind it. This time it passed not just easily but overwhelmingly, by 2,308 votes to 70.

Ever since, Catholics have argued over how much the document actually changed Church teaching and whether its claim to continuity was plausible. Some answered no: One of the dissenting votes was Marcel Lefebvre, who went on to found the semi-schismatic Society of Saint Pius X. But because the consensus behind its passage was so overwhelming, the doubts and difficulties never provoked a crisis or threatened a major schism; the Lefebvrite break was small and happened later, and across the civil wars of the John Paul II era many of the church's conservatives claimed ownership of *Dignitatis Humanae* as eagerly as liberals.

Ecumenical councils are the only situation where Catholic teaching gets put to a vote (albeit one subject to papal approval), and the opportunities they present do not come along often. But after Vatican II, Paul VI established a permanent synod of bishops, a group of several hundred chosen from around the Catholic world that was supposed to meet semi-regularly to advise the pope. Synods did not technically have any doctrinal authority, and under John Paul II and Benedict their role was strictly circumscribed. But to the church's liberals in those years, "synodality" seemed to offer an attractive alternative to what they viewed as papal centralization and intransigence— a decentralized, dialogic process whereby questions could be kept permanently open for debate. And that process could also provide a mechanism for changing the church's answers to some questions, since if the bishops were perceived to be speaking together, a pope could rely upon that consensus to shield a high-stakes move from criticism—in the same way, if not through the same process, that the 2,308–70 vote protected *Dignitatis Humanae* from its critics.

But as the Francis era dawned, an irony faced pro-synodality liberals. The long pontificates of John Paul and Benedict had made the church's bench of bishops more conservative, and often especially so in the developing world "peripheries" that Francis wanted to empower. So a synodal church would not automatically be a liberalizing church. To be an instrument of change, the synodal process would need careful steering, the bishops involved would need to be selected carefully and then nudged, and the pope himself would have to make his desires clear without making them official.

Which, during the months when conservative Catholics were reassuring themselves that he had no intention of touching anything doctrinal around marriage, is what Pope Francis and his inner circle set out to do.

In October of 2013, a few months before Cardinal Kasper's address to the consistory, the Vatican announced that a synod on "the vocation and mission of the family in the Church and in the contemporary world" would be held in two parts across the next two years—in 2014 the first, "extraordinary" synod would set an agenda that a second, larger, "ordinary" synod would take up in 2015.

The pope entrusted the task of organizing the process to a new-hatted cardinal, Lorenzo Baldisseri, who had served as secretary of the conclave that elected Francis; as his deputy the pope appointed Archbishop Bruno Forte, a noted Italian theologian with a progressive bent. Across the spring and summer of 2014, as Kasper traveled and spoke and dropped hints that Pope Francis agreed with his proposal on remarriage and communion, Baldisseri made it clear that Kasper's ideas would be on the synod's agenda, and implied his own support for them. There was talk of the need to "update" the church's teaching, dismissive references to the antiquity of John Paul II's *Familiaris Consortio* (it was, after all, more than a generation old), and a promise that the pope wanted an open, freewheeling debate on subjects that previously had been closed. To that end the synod organizers circulated a questionnaire to lay Catholics inviting criticisms of the church's approach to family issues, and they selected theological experts to advise the synod whose opinions had heretofore placed them close to dissent.

Meanwhile, the pope sent more direct signals. His silence alone was one: The fact that he was permitting Kasper and Baldisseri to speak as they did indicated that he favored an airing of their arguments, and implied that he favored something close to their conclusions. So did one of his "private" interventions—a phone call to an Argentine woman married to a divorcée who had written to him asking his advice on whether to receive communion; the press reported that his answer was "yes, go." (The Vatican spokesman's only comment was that private phone calls "do not in any way form part of the pope's public activities," and "consequences relating to the teaching of the church are not to be inferred.")[1] So did the essays that began appearing in the Jesuit journal *Civiltà Cattolica*, run by his friend and increasingly vocal ally Father Spadaro and only published with the pope's approval, which mined Catholic history in search of obscure case studies that might justify a Kasperite reform. So did some of the names that he added to the roster of bishops invited to attend the synod: not only Kasper but Belgium's retired cardinal Godfried Danneels, Kasper's fellow St. Gallener and a longtime advocate for communion for the remarried.

On a matter of less doctrinal significance, everyone would have acknowledged what was happening, what the pope wanted, and not only most bishops but most conservative Catholics would have gone along. But not in this case, not with the doctrinal stakes so obvious and high. So conservatives began to argue publicly against Kasper.

The loudest voice belonged to Raymond Burke, already—from the conclave onward—Francis's most prominent foil. Square of face and body, earnest in the way of his native Wisconsin, with a canon lawyer's preference for the letter of the law and a liturgical traditionalist's piety, Burke would have been a natural opponent of the Kasper proposal under any circumstances. But his early demotion from the Congregation for Bishops and the sense that his days as head of the Vatican's Supreme Court were numbered seemed to give him a latitude that many cardinals lacked. So he became outspoken, helping to organize a book-length volume, *Remaining in the Truth of Christ*, in which he and four other cardinals—including Müller, the Vatican's doctrinal chief—critiqued Kasper's proposal and defended the existing teaching. And the press responded by raising his profile further, albeit mostly by portraying him as a wrong-side-of-history figure out of step with the Franciscan age of mercy.

Burke was far enough out on the traditionalist limb and sufficiently harsh in many of his judgments that Kasper's opponents might have preferred a different spokesman. But his willingness to wade into the fray came at a time when many other conservatives couldn't agree among themselves about *how* to disagree with Kasper—how to frame the argument, how much to appeal to past authority, how much to relitigate matters they thought settled, how to acknowledge the pope's role in elevating the German cardinal's ideas. So in general a kind of rhetorical circumlocution prevailed, in which conservatives simultaneously pleaded their case to the pope while reassuring themselves that he would inevitably rule in their favor, that all the countervailing indicators were just feints or misunderstandings, and that all he wanted was to test them, somehow, in the furnace of an open debate.

But whether that debate would actually *be* open became, after Kasper's proposal itself, the second-most controversial question of the synod process. In September Cardinal Baldisseri was overheard telling his dining companions in a Roman restaurant that interventions from individual bishops would be screened in advance, and anything too rigorist or tradition-minded would be excluded by delay. (This detail and many others were later compiled by Edward Pentin, a reporter for the conservative *National Catholic Register*, in a short book with a vivid title: *The Rigging of a Vatican Synod?*) In the week before the synod the synod managers, Baldisseri and Forte, announced that these interventions would not actually be published, and that the synod's proceedings would be filtered to the public through the Vatican press office. In that same week the opening remarks of the synod's "relator," the conservative-leaning Hungarian cardinal Peter Erdo, were reportedly rewritten to include more quotes from Pope Francis and somewhat fewer from his papal predecessors and from scripture. As the synod opened Burke and his coauthors attempted to circulate their book defending the ban on communion for the remarried. More than a hundred copies passed through the Vatican post office and most were never seen again. At the same time, Burke began giving interviews complaining that the synod was being manipulated to un-Catholic ends, and after a few days other conservatives began noting that the press office's highlights from the synod seemed to suggest a change-oriented, liberalizing consensus that did not exist.

Nor were these anxieties allayed when Pope Francis announced the committee of six prelates who would hash out the synod's final document. All but one were notable progressives, among them Víctor Manuel Fernández, rector of the Catholic University of Buenos Aires, who had been made an archbishop under Francis and was said to be the pope's frequent ghostwriter. (Under Benedict, to then Cardinal Bergoglio's frustration, Fernández had repeatedly been denied a bishop's mitre—perhaps because he was the author, among other notable publications, of a theological work entitled *Heal Me with Your Mouth: The Art of Kissing*.) Nor were they allayed by the tone of the daily papal homilies, delivered in the chapel in his residence at Santa Marta before the synod. They frequently urged the pontiff's hearers to be unafraid of change and newness and a "God of surprises," while warning against "evil pastors" who "lay intolerable burdens on the shoulders of others, which they themselves do not lift a finger to move."[2]

So there was a certain amount of suspicion, shading into paranoia, among the conservative bishops already when the synod reached its midway point. And then all hell—by Vatican standards—broke loose.

On the morning of October 13, 2014, the synod's managers released a so-called *Relatio post Disceptationem,* a "Report After the Debate," which was supposed to summarize the proceedings thus far and set up the small-group discussions that would lead to the writing of the synod's final document. No prior *relatio* had ever attracted much attention, but this one did: Journalists, both Catholic and secular, were stunned by its language. A "pastoral earthquake," wrote veteran Vatican watcher John Thavis.[3] "It feels like a whole new church," tweeted the liberal *National Catholic Reporter*'s Josh McElwee.[4] The world's headline writers agreed: By the time the bishops designated to meet the press that day emerged for their press conference, newspapers around the globe had announced that Pope Francis's church was galloping toward change.

Those changes encompassed the Kasper proposal for the remarried, which the *relatio* implied that many of the assembled bishops had endorsed, and went beyond it, suggesting that the church should change its attitude toward gay couples ("accepting and valuing their sexual orientation") and unmarried couples ("recognizing positive elements even in . . . imperfect forms"), and treat nonmarital relationships as potential seedbeds for spiritual growth rather than emphasizing their sinfulness.[5] Gone was the language of mortal sin and moral absolutes; gone were phrases like "adultery" and "living in sin." The idea that the *relatio* proposed instead, the Vatican journalist John Allen wrote soon after, seemed to be a kind of "lifestyle ecumenism"[6]—in which, much as the post–Vatican II church had sought to recognize the virtues of non-Catholic churches and denominations, the twenty-first-century church would recognize and celebrate the virtues of second marriages and second unions and cohabitation even as it continued to teach that they fell short of Catholicism's official marital ideal.

The *relatio* did not push the logic of Kasper's proposal all the way to its conclusion: It only raised the idea of communion for the remarried, not for same-sex couples or the unmarried or polygamists. But it was extended in the direction—toward a larger revolution in Catholic sexual ethics—that the German cardinal's conservative critics had argued his ideas would lead.

The *relatio* shocked many of the synod's bishops. It had been sent to the press before it had even been read to them, and they did not recognize the synod they were attending in the confident proposals of the text. In that day's press conference, the Hungarian cardinal Erdo grew testy at media questions, pointing to Bruno Forte and saying "ask him, he wrote it."[7] (As, indeed, he clearly had—most likely well before the synod even reached its midpoint, given that the *relatio* was dispatched to the press in six translations simultaneously.) Addressing the media the next day, the South African cardinal Wilfrid Napier described the situation created by the *relatio* as "virtually irredeemable," since media accounts had outraced any ability to establish what the bishops really thought.[8]

Napier spoke for most of the synod's African attendees, who—along with the Poles and most of the Americans—represented one of its more tradition-minded blocs. The strong German theological influence on Vatican II had been summed up aphoristically as "the Rhine flows into the Tiber." In the 2014 synod it was fair to say—as Allen put it—that "the Rhine flows into the Tiber—and hits the Zambezi."[9] This African resistance prompted Cardinal Kasper, the day after the *relatio* controversy erupted, to make an unguarded comment to Edward Pentin, in which he complained about the obduracy of figures like Napier and his fellow Africans. The Africans were prisoners of their own societies' totems and taboos, he suggested, and they "should not tell us too much what we have to do."[10]

Pentin published the complaint, Kasper denied saying it; Pentin produced the audio, Kasper apologized. The moment evoked similar controversies in Anglicanism, in particular the very similar comments about allegedly primitive Africans by a very liberal American bishop, John Shelby Spong, during the Anglican communion's agonizing civil war over same-sex marriage.

In the modern Catholic Church, though, high churchmen didn't usually speak that way about each other publicly. But then again neither did they issue demands of the pope, and implicitly accuse their fellow cardinals of flirting with heresy, as Kasper's foe Cardinal Burke did on a daily basis throughout the synod.

Nor did they ask a retired pope to rein in his successor. But after the *relatio* came out a group of conservative bishops reportedly went to the semi-cloistered Benedict, asking him to intervene. He was actually in the process of doing so, in a most oblique way: His collected works were being reissued, and he had gone in and edited out a 1972 article in which, as a young theologian, he had entertained the possibility of communion for the remarried. But this signal as to where he stood was all that conservatives would get; if he was really asked to take an active role in the proceedings, he demurred.

Nor were there usually scenes like the one that unfolded on the synod floor two days after the *relatio*, when the small groups that were supposed to offer amendments released their reports, and were informed by Baldisseri that their comments, like the synod interventions generally, would not be published publicly—leaving the synod managers in control of what the outside world received.

At once bishops rose in protest, led by Napier and the conservative George Pell of Australia, a former rugby player whom Pope Francis had charged with the thankless task of cleaning up the Vatican's finances. Their objections were seconded by more moderate and even liberal cardinals, including two of the church's consummate politicians—the archbishop of Washington, Donald Wuerl, and the pope's secretary of state, Pietro Parolin. When Baldisseri tried to bat down their objection, sustained boos and jeers echoed in the synod hall—a dramatic moment that ended with a nod from the pope himself, present as a silent observer, to indicate that the reports should be published after all.

Seven of the ten published reports contained significant criticisms of the *relatio*. Soon after, in what was taken as a concession to its critics, Napier and another bishop joined the committee drafting the final document. But then came reports of conflict between Napier and Baldisseri, rumors of arm-twisting to induce wavering bishops to vote for the *relatio*'s language, still wilder rumors that the pope intended to dissolve or otherwise disempower his own Congregation for the Doctrine of the Faith—and then the news, revealed in an unusual step by Burke himself, that the outspoken traditionalist had been finally fired from the Apostolic Signatura, and assigned to oversee the Knights of Malta, once a crusading order and now a charitable league run by rich Catholic gentlemen. It was clearly an exile for the Kasper proposal's staunchest critic.

But after all these intimations of conservative defeat, when the final document was released, it looked like a relative victory for their side. The *relatio*'s language was rewritten, the overall rhetoric was more scriptural and less novel, there was more affirmation of church teaching and less "lifestyle ecumenism," the Kasper proposal was simply referred for further study, and the lone paragraph on gay Catholics confined itself to urging parishes and pastors to treat them with "respect and sensitivity."[11] Then in the final vote, which went paragraph by paragraph through the document and asked the bishops to vote "yea" or "nay" on each, even the dialed-back paragraphs on remarriage and homosexuality fell just short of two-thirds support, meaning that under synod rules they wouldn't be included in the final document at all.

Except that they were, by order of Pope Francis himself. And then the pope moved to offer his interpretation of the synod, in a closing speech that seemed to place him in the same role that he had staked out in much of his papal rhetoric—as a kind of mediator between the church's warring factions, neither Burkean nor Kasperite but seeking balance between extremes. That balance, he warned, could only be struck by avoiding various temptations—"a temptation to hostile inflexibility" but also a temptation toward "a deceptive mercy"; a temptation of the "do-gooders . . . the so-called 'progressives and liberals'" on the one hand and a temptation of "the zealous, of the scrupulous . . . the 'traditionalists' and also of the intellectuals" on the other.[12]

Then, noting that "many commentators, or people who talk, have imagined that they see a disputatious Church where one part is against the other," he reminded the bishops that in the end the Holy Spirit guaranteed unity through him, through the pope, "*cum Petro* and *sub Petro* (with Peter and under Peter),"[13] a stronger than usual assertion of his own authority from a pope who often liked to refer to himself as merely the bishop of Rome.

"Dear brothers and sisters," he finished, "now we still have one year to mature, with true spiritual discernment, the proposed ideas and to find concrete solutions to so many difficulties and innumerable challenges that families must confront; to give answers to the many discouragements that surround and suffocate families."[14] And with that the first synod ended.

Afterward no one could quite agree on what had happened. The competing factions each had incentives to downplay the significance of the conflict. The liberals, who wanted the perception of a smooth process unfolding inexorably toward change, tended to suggest that any controversy was mostly media-driven, or the work of a few disgruntled conservatives, or just the work of the cashiered Cardinal Burke. They tended to praise the synod for its openness compared to prior iterations (which was fair, up to a point, since even if the synod was stage-managed it was not as scripted as synods under the conservative popes), to declare that any messiness or tension was just a sign of the Holy Spirit working on hardened hearts, and to insist confidently that wherever the church was going, Pope Francis was fully in control. Their response to conservative vexation mostly took a more-in-sorrow-than-in-anger tone: It was unfortunate that certain of their coreligionists could be so disloyal to the pope, so conspiratorial in their thinking, so alarmist about what were, in the end, very modest reforms that left doctrine untouched. Surely if being Catholic meant anything it meant accepting the outcome of church processes, and trusting they would work out for the best. Why did a few conservative malcontents have so little Catholic faith?

Conservatives, meanwhile, could not but acknowledge the existence of a major conflict, and while the more liberal Catholics talked about the wonderful, spirit-filled working of the synodal process the more conservative

Catholics complained it had been rigged or otherwise manipulated. But many of them still stopped short of drawing the obvious conclusion—that any "rigging" had been conducted with the full approval of the man in charge, and that everything from the design of the synod to the shocking *relatio* to the final decision on which paragraphs to include reflected the pope's own personal intentions, not the freelancing of the men who ran it, Archbishop Forte and Cardinal Baldisseri.

For Catholics, especially American Catholics, accustomed to appealing to papal authority in the Western culture wars, it was just too much to acknowledge that they might be on one side and the Vicar of Christ on the other. So instead there was a pattern in which conservatives accused the liberals, up to and including the synod managers, of betraying Francis's broader intentions for the synod by focusing narrowly on the Kasper proposal, for which there could not be a consensus because it went so clearly against the doctrine of the church. The problem was not the pope himself; it could not be the pope himself. It was just the men around him, whose ambitions had pushed the synod process off the path that the Holy Father himself preferred.

This argument was not really credible, even if it was the only way that some conservative Catholics could reconcile their abiding papalism with the evidence of their eyes and ears. In the period around the synod, as in others during Francis's pontificate, you got a truer assessment from the Catholic fringes, the theological radicals on the left and the Latin Mass traditionalists on the right, where skepticism of the papacy ran highest, than from the more mainstream Catholic experts. You also got a truer assessment from the secular press: They might be biased in Francis's favor and unconcerned with the theological stakes, but their "reformist pope at war with reactionary Vatican" narrative still captured the reality of the church's conflict better than either blithe, "the Spirit is moving" liberals or anxious, "but don't blame the pope" conservatives.

Still, to be charitable, one might say that many liberals and conservatives weren't really talking to the world or to one another in their analyses. They were talking to the pope himself, producing a kind of propaganda with an audience of one. The liberals were trying to confirm Francis in his instincts, to reassure him that the process he had set in motion was supernaturally controlled. The conservatives were trying to correct the pontiff without quite saying so, as a courtier might advise an erring sovereign: *This path you are taking is a mistake, so let us say that your advisers are to blame for it, leaving you free to choose more wisely henceforward.*

In the months following the synod, many conservatives believed that Francis would heed their arguments—that having sought a consensus for his favored changes and met with such resistance, having seen that there would be no Vatican II–style vote for communion for the remarried even with his own men stage-managing the process, he would retreat to the safer terrain of, say, annulment reform, a middle ground between conservatives and progressives and one that didn't threaten any kind of rupture.

By the summer of 2015, six months after the synod, the signs seemed somewhat favorable for that interpretation. None of the rumored reorganizations or purges had yet to come to pass. Burke was gone to the Knights of Malta but conservative figures such as Müller and Pell were still highly placed, and Müller's Congregation for the Doctrine of the Faith went so far as to issue a clarification—with the pope's approval, presumably—that the rules on communion for the remarried were still in effect. The pontiff's rhetoric over the first half of 2015 seemed intended to reassure conservatives: "From the end of the synod," the conservative Vatican reporter Sandro Magister wrote in May, "there has not been even one more occasion on which he has given the slightest support to the paradigms of the innovators," and "he has intensified his remarks on all the most controversial questions connected to the synodal theme of the family: contraception, abortion, divorce, second marriages, homosexual marriage, 'gender' ideology." [15]

Even the dissonant notes encouraged conservatives: When Cardinal Reinhard Marx of Munich, speaking for the German liberalizers, insisted that "the synod cannot prescribe in detail what we have to do in Germany" and "we are not just a subsidiary of Rome," [16] it was taken as a sign that the German bishops felt themselves likely to be on the losing end of the synodal process's ultimate conclusion.

Then for a time the Francis papacy returned to the pattern of his first year: a politically left-leaning pope whom conservatives could still love, a pope of the people whose style fascinated the secular world, a pope who seemed like he might transcend the church's right-left divisions rather than exacerbate them.

He traveled to the Philippines in the winter, celebrating the largest papal mass in history and carrying on his pilgrimage into the teeth of a tropical storm. In the early fall came a successful visit to Cuba and the United States (now headed toward a Vatican-brokered détente), complete with the first-ever papal address to Congress, huge crowds, and a rapturous media response. Both trips had their moments of controversy: A question about overpopulation on the plane ride back from Asia produced a papal crack about how Catholics "don't have to breed like rabbits," which managed to irritate both birth control advocates and fecund traditionalists; conservatives thought Francis underplayed human rights and communism's crimes on his trip to Cuba, and liberals were shocked when he met with Kim Davis, a Kentucky clerk jailed for refusing to sign same-sex marriage licenses. But these controversies were all well within the (admittedly unusual) parameters of the Francis papacy.

In between these pilgrimages the pope released *Laudato Si'*, his first encyclical, a major statement on the environment and ecology filtered through Francis's typical populist style, complete with withering dismissals of the entire Western ruling class and Bergoglian turns of phrase like "the earth, our home, is beginning to look more and more like an immense pile of filth."[17] The Catholic left received it warmly; the Catholic right had more reservations. But overt criticism of its substance was a mostly American phenomenon, and many conservative Catholics made a clear effort to receive the pope's teaching, to accept and digest and wrestle with its distinctive critique of modernity and technology and capitalism even when it seemed to point in political directions they found uncongenial.

There was a similar reaction to the beatification of Oscar Romero, the

Reagan-era Salvadoran bishop slain by right-wing death squads, which took place in this same period. The expressions of "on second thought . . ." admiration for Romero from conservative Catholics, especially in America, felt like a case study in how Catholicism often depolarizes itself after an era of division . . . by including and sifting, you might say, recognizing sanctity in once controversial figures without blessing every idea that those figures' admirers and partisans have embraced.

Finally there were papal moves on child sexual abuse, where Francis had intervened to remove three bishops—one in Minneapolis, one in Kansas City, one in Paraguay—who had moved too slowly to deal with obvious priest-predators, and then in June of 2015 announced that there would be a special tribunal established to deal with the problem of bishops who mishandled abuse cases. It was a step that promised to complete the cleanup begun under Benedict, and it suggested, again, the possibility that Francis's legacy might yet be a unifying one.

But then the autumn's second synod approached, and the pope began making a different sort of move. First, in late summer, came his personal appointments of synod fathers, which amounted to another round of deck-stacking. Each bishops conference around the world had elected delegates to the synod, and many of their choices had a decidedly conservative cast. But Francis, in response, set about adding delegates who were well known for liberal sympathies, including Chicago's Blase Cupich, John Atcherley Dew, the archbishop of Wellington in New Zealand (a long-standing proponent of communion for the remarried), the papal ghostwriter Archbishop Fernández, Father Spadaro of *Civiltà Cattolica*, and (once again) the retired cardinals Kasper and Danneels. Looking at the synod roster, you could see two clear constituencies for Kasper's proposal: the Northern European bishops . . . and Francis's personal appointees.

Then in September, the pope surprised everyone by issuing—on his own, without consultation with the bishops—new guidelines for annulments, which would go into effect on December 8, the beginning of what he had decreed would be a Jubilee Year of Mercy for all the church. These were not only the reforms that had been seen as a potential compromise response to the Kasper proposal—an extension of the American annulment model to the rest of Catholic world, the elimination of a time-consuming second review of the annulment tribunal's decision. They also included a "fast track" option, in which local bishops could approve an annulment petition in less than forty-five days if both parties consented and certain personal factors were involved. Since that list of factors was both varied (everything from a concealed affair to a lack of religious faith to the duration of the marriage) and the papal language vague and open-ended, it seemed to be a permission slip to liberal bishops to expedite most if not all annulment petitions where there wasn't a contesting spouse, effectively making a Catholic annulment easier to get than a civil divorce.

The fast-track option was a major liberalization of the church's rules, the kind of thing that would have been hotly debated if it had been the endgame of the synodal process. So what did it mean that Francis was acting on it unilaterally beforehand? One possibility was that it was a move to turn down the temperature of the synod, to take Kasper's proposal off the table (because the new annulment rules seemed like they would cover a lot of people whom Kasper's path was supposed to help bring back to communion), and create more room for conversation about all the other issues the synod was supposed to be addressing—from marriage preparation to religious education to threats to family life from poverty and war in poor countries and materialism in rich ones. John Allen read it this way: "By implementing the compromise in advance," the Vatican journalist wrote, "Francis has not quite resolved the Communion debate, but he's made it less burning. . . . Whatever people may think of the fine points [of the annulment reform], everyone will be realistic enough to grasp that in the immediate wake of one major reform, it will be a while before the time is ripe for another."[18]

But Allen was wrong. Rather than a preemptive compromise, it turned out to be a shift of the goalposts, removing one potential middle ground by simply handing a victory to the liberalizers, and setting up a synod in which they felt free to push for further liberalization still.

The methods were similar to the first synod. Again the debate would take place behind closed doors, with only summaries of the goings-on released to the press. Again Pope Francis had appointed his own committee to write the final document, which seemed heavily weighted toward progressives. Again there was a controversial text written by Baldisseri and Forte: The so-called *Instrumentum Laboris*, or "Working Document," which summarized the first synod's proceedings in ways that seemed tilted toward progressive conclusions. This time there was talk that the final document would face a simple up or down vote, instead of allowing bishops to vote paragraph by paragraph. There were even rumors that this document, like the midterm report of the prior synod, was already written by the pope's collaborators. This rumor seemed to set up a fait accompli, where wavering bishops would have a choice between voting yes on whatever the committee produced or being seen as casting a vote against the entire synod process—and with it, against the pope himself.

But the conservatives were less surprised than in the fall of 2014, more organized, quicker to move against their opponents. On the first day, Peter Erdo, the conservative Hungarian cardinal-relator whose remarks had been rewritten heavily the prior fall, delivered a long synod-framing address that seemed to forcefully exclude the Kasper proposal from consideration. At the same time, Cardinal Pell delivered a private (at first) letter from thirteen cardinals to the pontiff and to Archbishop Baldisseri, in which they criticized the synod's procedures—the absence of transparency, the problems with the working document, the voting procedures—and then warned against its broader drift, which the cardinals argued could effectively Protestantize the church:

> A synod designed to address a vital pastoral matter—reinforcing the dig-
> nity of marriage and family—may become dominated by the theological/
> doctrinal issue of Communion for the divorced and civilly remarried. If
> so, this will inevitably raise even more fundamental issues about how the

Church, going forward, should interpret and apply the Word of God, her doctrines and her disciplines to changes in culture. The collapse of liberal Protestant churches in the modern era, accelerated by their abandonment of key elements of Christian belief and practice in the name of pastoral adaptation, warrants great caution in our own synodal discussions.[19]

The list of signatories to this warning was striking. It wasn't just figures like Burke or the cardinal-theologians who had joined his book project before the last synod, but a much broader group of powerful, politically active churchmen, some of them considered potential popes. It included Müller, the Congregation for the Doctrine of the Faith prefect—making overt the obvious tension between the pope and his own doctrinal watchdog—as well as Pell and Napier; it also included Napier's fellow African, Robert Sarah, the Guinean head of the Congregation for Divine Worship, an austere figure who had risen from a boyhood in a poor rural village under French imperial rule to become Catholic Africa's most *papabile* churchman. Then there was New York's Timothy Dolan, a gregarious church politico, as well as Toronto's Thomas Collins, Nairobi's John Njue, Mexico City's Norberto Rivera Carrera, and more. The heft of the names suggested a widening division, not just between the pope and a few disgruntled traditionalists, but between Francis and his "cabinet's front bench," as the Canadian priest-columnist Raymond de Souza put it later.[20]

This division did not seem to trouble Francis's inner circle, as they were the ones who first publicized the letter. News of its existence was leaked during the synod's first week to Andrea Tornielli, a papal favorite among the Italian press corps, with the idea being (presumably) that the letter would make the conservatives look disloyal and leave them isolated on the synod floor. However, the existence of the letter was mentioned but not the names of the signatories attached, suggesting perhaps that the papal circle wanted to reveal the fact of opposition (which Tornielli called a "lobby" opposed to "openness"[21]) but not its scope.

If the exact strategy was unclear, it was clear enough what the pope thought about the intervention, since on the second day of the synod (after the letter's delivery, but before it had received any publicity) he offered a noteworthy intervention of his own, chiding the assembled bishops for giving in to "the hermeneutic of conspiracy," which he called "sociologically weak and spiritually unhelpful."[22] The text of these remarks was not published, but the pope's words were clearly intended to be made public, because Father Spadaro quoted it on social media and various Jesuit publications soon confirmed it, making Francis's attack on conspiracy theories the main news from the day's proceedings.

Sticking to their circumlocutory style, many conservative synod watchers portrayed Francis's words as reassuring. After all, they included a promise that nothing was being manipulated, that nothing doctrinal would be changed! But this promise had been issued before, and in terms of the day-to-day working of the synod, the papal intervention was clearly a vote of confidence in Baldisseri's synod management and a dismissal of the cardinals' criticisms. The composition of the final committee remained as it was, and the synod itself continued with its twofold approach to transparency. On the synod floor all questions remained open for debate, the Kasper proposal continued to be elevated, and its conservative critics were accused of preferring a "mummified" synod—sealed in airless stasis by the bandages of tradition—to an open one. (Father Spadaro, whose Twitter persona was basically the reform party's hyperactive id, tweeted an image of a bandaged mummy while chiding Baldisseri's critics.)

At the same time, the debates themselves were kept secret from the wider world. Bishops were allowed to publish their own interventions, but few of the progressives did, and when a Polish archbishop published a summary of what various clerics had actually said on the synod floor, Baldisseri disciplined him for rule breaking. (The summary had included a rather striking intervention from one of Francis's appointees, the Panamanian cardinal José Luis Lacunza Maestrojuán, which urged the bishops to follow the merciful example of the Mosaic law in allowing for remarriage—which amounted to implying that the Pharisees had been right about marriage and that Jesus had been wrong.)

Yet for all of this maneuvering it was still not at all clear that the Kasper proposal had anywhere close to the necessary support. The Australian archbishop Mark Coleridge, one of the more admirably transparent of the liberals (he jousted with conservative critics on his blog), indicated that it would fail by almost two to one if put to a straight up or down vote. So the reform party began raising the possibility that there might be no final document at all, nothing for the bishops to vote on—in effect an open-ended conclusion, which would theoretically maximize the pope's freedom to rule on communion for the remarried as he saw fit, while avoiding a scenario where his handpicked committee wrote a liberalizing document and saw it go down to a shock defeat.

The young Filipino cardinal Luis Tagle, widely seen as a proto-Francis and possible successor, floated this no-document option at a press briefing on the fifth day of the synod, and others soon took it up. It was at this point that Sandro Magister published the full text and list of signatories of the cardinals' letter, a leak that was hard to interpret (given Magister's own conservative leanings) as anything but a spine-stiffening message to other conservative bishops, a signal that their resistance had ample support among the cardinals. Not that all the signatories were happy to see it leaked, especially since Magister had several of the names wrong; Müller compared it to the Vatileaks scandal, Dolan and Napier insisted that it had been well received by the Holy Father (Roman rumors of papal anger notwithstanding), and it became another place where liberal and conservative synod watchers jousted over What It All Meant.

In that jousting the church's John Paul II–era lines of battle continued to be ironically reversed. After years of using "the magisterium has spoken, the case is closed" as an argument ender, conservative Catholics now sided with the reluctant rebels, insisting on the limits of papal power, and generally covering synodal politics with a focus on the politics—a style that implicitly conceded the possibility of the very changes that theologically they considered impossible. Meanwhile, liberal Catholics had suddenly turned ultramontane: They were papal supremacists who found interventions like the cardinals' letter impertinent, absolute believers in the Holy Spirit's tight control of doctrinal deliberation, and firm clericalists when it came to any objections raised to Kasper's proposal or the synod proceedings from outside the papacy and hierarchy.

There was also a striking irony in the contrast between Francis's style—earthy, direct, populist—and the kind of arguments marshaled in defense of his proposals, or Kasper's. Because on the point at issue the conservatives had the simplest, most direct case: This was what the church had always taught, this was what the plain words of the New Testament said, this was how the church's understanding of sin and the sacraments obviously cashed out. Meanwhile, the counterarguments accused conservatives of simplemindedness and unsophistication. In defense of a populist pope who scorned "doctors of the law," liberals claimed that the Kasper proposal's wisdom was something that only (liberal) doctors of theology could understand; in defense of a pontiff who attacked clericalism they complained about not only cardinals but conservative pundits and bloggers and tweeters rushing in where only serious churchman ought to tread.

All that said, these reversals and ironies were mostly on the surface. At a deeper level the lines of division were still the same as they'd been since the 1960s: The liberal side believed the church needed to evolve with modern man (or as Archbishop Coleridge put it during the synod, "history will have its way, however much we try to cling to illusions of timelessness"[23]), the conservative side believed that certain evolutions were a betrayal of the faith once delivered to the saints. The selective ultramontanism of liberals, the sudden conservative rediscovery of the possibility of papal error—these were tactical intellectual shifts, in the service of deeper commitments that remained more or less intact. Thus the ultimate clash distilled a conflict of sincerely held visions, in which compromise was difficult to achieve.

• • •

For the cardinals and bishops trying, nonetheless, to hash a compromise out, as the synod proceeded the leak of the cardinals' letter looked more and more like a crucial turning point—in the conservative side's favor. There was no more talk of a document-free conclusion, and the head counts that leaked from the synod indicated that, if anything, support for blessing communion for the remarried was dropping, from Coleridge's one-third estimate to more like a quarter of the synod bishops. So there was no question of anything like Kasper's original proposal being brought up for the vote. Instead the liberals shifted tacks, returning to the broader idea of doctrinal decentralization, of a "local option" for churches and bishops' conferences, an official tolerance for experimentation without fear of sanction from Rome. This direction seemed to be where the pontiff himself was leaning in a speech two weeks into the synod, in which he talked about empowering national bishops conferences— bodies created after Vatican II, which had a certain prestige but no official teaching authority—and spoke of the "need to proceed in a healthy 'decentralization.'" [24]

But here too the conservatives pushed back, insisting that whatever was meant by decentralization, it could not encompass the crucial points of doctrine at issue in the communion-and-remarriage controversy. The Germans could experiment with some things, perhaps, but not with new rules for the remarried that contradicted John Paul II and the Council of Trent. The universal church simply could not have one teaching on marriage in Berlin and another in Warsaw. And if it tried, the experiment wouldn't work because the center wouldn't hold: The entire modern experience of Anglicanism, where the churches in North America went one way and the churches in Africa another, suggested that doctrinal decentralization simply pulled factions further apart, and led eventually to schism.

Balked again, the reformers now retreated to a third approach: not a formal path back to communion, not a country-by-country decentralization of doctrine, but a pastor-by-pastor, case-by-case approach, which would distinguish the "external forum" of church teaching from the "internal forum" in which priests dealt with individual souls. The "internal forum" had been the rubric under which various bishops had tacitly allowed communion for the remarried during the 1970s, with the idea (then au courant in liberal theology) being that the individual Catholic conscience was competent to decide when and how general moral rules applied. Of course this interpretation of conscience's primacy was hard to square with anything the church had previously taught on the matter, and it was decisively rejected by John Paul II's *Veritatis Splendor* . . . but now what was old was new again, and the goalpost moving of Kasper's proposal plus the pope's own annulment reform meant that this idea could be cast as a compromise, a way for the synod to achieve unity and give the pope some blessing for reform.

But still they did not have the votes for it. Instead, there was a final furious negotiation carried out between the German liberals and their conservative countryman, Cardinal Müller, within the German-language synod group. What they eventually came up with, and what the synod as a whole accepted, was studiously ambiguous language: rich in promises of welcome and integration, but lacking in any explicit statement that the remarried could receive communion. Here's a sample paragraph, from the final document:

> Conversation with the priest, in the internal forum, contributes to the formation of a correct judgment on what hinders the possibility of a fuller participation in the life of Church and Church practice which can foster it and make it grow. Given that gradualness is not in the law itself (cf. *FC* 34), this discernment can never prescind from the Gospel demands of truth and charity as proposed by the Church. This occurs when the following conditions are present: humility, discretion and love for the Church and her teaching, in a sincere search for God's will and a desire to make a more perfect response to it.[25]

Read strictly and literally and through the lens of traditional teaching, the traditional rules for what full participation requires, this was technically orthodox. Read expansively and intuitively and through the lens of what Walter Kasper and the pope desired, it showed a sympathy toward returning the remarried to communion without welcoming them explicitly. Read by a normal person through a neutral lens, it was a turgid, impenetrable endorsement of nothing in particular—which is presumably why 64 of the 250-odd bishops still voted against it, when the document was brought up for the once threatened but ultimately permitted paragraph-by-paragraph vote.

Which made the actual outcome of the synod . . . well, the newspapers were unsure. "Bishops Hand Pope Defeat on His Outreach to Divorced Catholics," the *Wall Street Journal* declared.[26] "Amid Splits, Catholic Bishops Crack Open Door on Divorce," countered the headline in the *New York Times*.[27] In a sense they were both right: Relative to every prior magisterial statement on the subject, the synod's language was ambiguous and unstable. But relative to what the pope had plainly wanted and what conservatives had feared, it was only a shift of rhetoric, not one that touched doctrinal substance.

The pope himself seemed to feel that he had been balked and outmaneuvered, judging from his closing address to the synod, which read more like an outburst than a summation, from a leader angered in defeat. Gone was the evenhanded, balancing speech of the 2014 synod. In its place came a frontal assault on the conservatives who had resisted him. He compared them to the older brother in the parable of the prodigal and the jealous laborers in the parable of the vineyard workers, and that was the kind part. They also stood accused of "a facile repetition of what is obvious or has already been said"; of "burying their heads in the sand" and repeating prohibitions in "language which is archaic or simply incomprehensible"; of using Jesus's message as "dead stones to be hurled at others"; of sitting "in the chair of Moses and judg[ing], sometimes with superiority and superficiality, difficult cases and wounded families"; of giving in to "conspiracy theories and blinkered viewpoints"; and above all of a "fear of love" that had strangled Christian mercy.[28]

His anger was understandable, if not appropriately directed. His two-year synodal project, stage-managed to build a Vatican II–esque consensus behind a major, headline-capturing reform, had ended with the pontiff on the losing side of precisely the processes that he had championed. Along the way, a man who had been elected on the promise to "go out" from a self-enclosed, self-obsessed church, to leave civil war behind, had turned bishops against bishops, theologians against theologians, and raised the stakes in the church's internal conflict to their highest point in decades.

It was not only the conservative combatants who felt shocked that it had come to this. The mood in Rome was paranoid and toxic; the mood within the hierarchy distrustful and disappointed. "If a conclave were to be held today, Francis would be lucky to get ten votes," a Vatican source told the *New Yorker* just before the synod.[29] It was an overstatement then; by the end of that strange October, it was not.

Eight

HIS HOLINESS
DECLINES TO COMMENT

At several points during his pontificate, Pope Francis granted interviews to Eugenio Scalfari, a prominent Italian journalist and noted atheist. Of all the pope's public performances these conversations were among the strangest, because Scalfari did not take notes. Instead, the interviewer, who was eighty-nine at the time of the first interview, published "transcripts" of their conversations summoned up from memory. So while Francis tended to be more adventurous in these conversations than even in his usual off-the-cuff remarks, it was difficult to tell what the pontiff had definitely said, and what the aging journalist had embellished or invented or misinterpreted.

The initial Scalfari conversation, in the fall of 2013, was filled with striking utterances. It had the pope calling proselytism "solemn nonsense," insisting that "there is no Catholic God," suggesting that "everyone has his own idea of good and evil and must choose to follow the good and fight evil as he conceives them," and wandering into faintly New Age pastures: "Our species will end but the light of God will not end and at that point it will invade all souls and it will all be in everyone."[1]

The official Vatican website ultimately withdrew the interview, after briefly publishing it, with a clarification from the press office that "the text was an after-the-fact reconstruction" which had been approved by Francis without it being "clear how closely the pope read it."[2]

This was the sort of modest fiasco that would normally preclude a follow-up interview, but instead the pope spoke to Scalfari again in the summer of 2014. Again there were striking formulations, including a suggestion that some cardinals were guilty of abusing children and a pledge to "find solutions" to the "problem" of priestly celibacy.[3] Again there was a declaration from the Vatican press office that while the "spirit" of the conversation was accurate, "individual expressions that were used and the manner in which they have been reported cannot be attributed to the pope."[4] Then the same dance played out again in the spring of 2015, when Scalfari's text had the pope speculating, heretically, that lost souls would be "annihilated" instead of damned.[5] Once more the press office characterized the interview as "private discussions" whose details could not be confirmed.[6]

By this point it was clear that Francis saw an advantage in this sort of deliberately unreliable communication—whether as a form of freewheeling dialogue with a nonbeliever, a means to communicate very informally to supporters, or simply a way to talk casually without the strictures that an actual interview transcript would impose. So it was not surprising that he returned to Scalfari following the second synod on the family, speaking with him by telephone three days after his blistering closing remarks. The conversation, or at least Scalfari's reconstruction thereof, appeared in the Italian newspaper *La Repubblica* a week later, and it included this response to a question about the pope's intentions for communion and the remarried and the outcome of the synod:

"This is the bottom line result," Francis said (supposedly). "The de facto appraisals are entrusted to the confessors, but at the end of faster or slower paths, *all the divorced who asked will be admitted.*"[7]

Again, of course, the Vatican denied that this quotation was necessarily accurate. But by now everyone sensed that it must be reasonably close to something the pope had said.

That same week the vigorous Father Spadaro, who was increasingly taking on the role of Francis's public theological interpreter—a one-man Congregation for the Doctrine of the Faith for a papacy in conflict with its official CDF—published a wrap-up of the synod in *Civiltà Cattolica*. In his essay, what had appeared to be a setback for the church's liberals—the conservative tone of the document, the at-most-ambiguous paragraphs on the internal form, the absence of any specific mention of communion for the remarried— was reinterpreted as a major victory for reform. All that mattered, Spadaro wrote, was that the document had talked of integrating the remarried, and the traditional teaching had not been formally restated. What wasn't restated was, by implication, potentially defunct. "It is not said how far the process of integration can go," he said of the remarried, "but neither are any more precise and insurmountable limitations set up."[8]

This reading of the synod's report was similar to how progressive Catholics had often interpreted the documents of Vatican II. Whatever was novel was taken to control the text's meanings and implications. Whatever was conservative was assumed to be vestigial. What mattered above all was the direction of movement, pointing to further movements still. This was not the traditional method of interpreting of the church's magisterium, which held that anything novel was supposed to be interpreted in continuity with prior teaching, and wherever there was ambiguity the preexisting tradition remained the rule. But it explained why liberals and conservatives could look at the same texts and draw radically different implications, with the tradition-minded appealing to what the document said, and the progressives seeing vast space for action in what it didn't say.

Now it seemed the pope himself might be one of those progressives. Through Scalfari and Spadaro, Francis appeared to be signaling that he would take the ambiguity of the synod's document and use it to declare a new discipline, in which communion would be granted to the remarried not through any formal penitential pathway but through a permission slip to pastors, who would be urged to admit people to communion without an annulment "case by case," but generously enough to make the answer in each case an all-but-foregone conclusion.

This was not what the synod had voted for, and it promised to empty out the church's teaching on divorce, to make the rule against remarriage strictly theoretical. Much more than anything at Vatican II, it also threatened an immediate crisis for papal authority, because across two synods the church's conservatives had made it clear that they considered such a change to be something—or very, very close to something—that the pope did not have the authority to do.

But now some of those same conservatives, who had briefly been relieved by their apparent synod victory, braced for that crisis to arrive. There were still attempts to insist that all was still stable and settled, that the synods had ratified orthodoxy and that Francis surely would as well. But many conservative observers now acknowledged the obvious. Those who had argued at the synod against communion for the remarried, wrote the Canadian priest-columnist Father de Souza in November, "must be ready for the Holy Father to decide differently. He has steadily prepared the Church for just that. It would be foolish to ignore the signs."[9]

Yet when the papal exhortation finally arrived, five months later, it was not quite what conservatives feared. *Amoris Laetitia*, "The Joy of Love," was the longest papal document in history—two hundred and fifty-six pages, some sixty thousand words. It was at times rich in earthy pastoral insight, at times rote and repetitious and banal. But all eyes turned at once to chapter eight, in which the pope took up the question of Catholics in irregular relationships, and said . . . well, once again no one was quite sure.

Instead of explicitly addressing the controverted questions, the pontiff moved to a more abstract level of moral theology, engaging in a kind of critical dialogue with John Paul II's *Veritatis Splendor* on the question of what constituted mortal sin. (Indeed, several key passages seemed to borrow from an essay that the papal ghostwriter, Archbishop Victor Fernández, had written for a conference on *Veritatis* a decade earlier.) Where the Polish pope had rebuked situational ethics, the Argentine pope piled up lists of mitigating factors that could make an apparent mortal sin less serious. Where John Paul II had insisted that even in difficult circumstances the moral law is never impossible to follow, Francis discussed all the ways in which family turmoil and personal psychology and the exigencies of modern life could make the moral law seem either too hard to comprehend or too difficult to obey. A casual reader, reading the two papal documents together, would have no doubt that Francis wasn't so much developing John Paul's thought as arguing with it.

Some of these arguments didn't directly contradict anything in *Veritatis Splendor*; they just placed a much stronger rhetorical emphasis on existing Catholic teaching concerning the ways that personal circumstances reduced moral culpability. But others seemed to go further, toward a vision of the moral law as either a gnostic mystery or a kind of unfair trap for ordinary mortals—who "may know full well the rule, yet have great difficulty in understanding 'its inherent values,' or be in a concrete situation which does not allow [one] to act differently and decide otherwise without further sin." [10]

This idea was very Kasperian, akin to the cardinal's suggestion that the church's teaching on marriage and sexuality asked too much of the "ordinary Christian." It also came perilously close to contradicting not only John Paul and other recent popes but the Council of Trent in the sixteenth century and countless teaching documents in between. The idea that some circumstances do "not allow" Christians to avoid sin, that God's grace is sometimes insufficient and the moral life sometimes resembles *Star Trek*'s no-win Kobayashi Maru training exercise, would be a serious revision of the church's traditional position—closer to certain Protestant theologies than to Catholic moral teaching as defined and defended by past councils and past popes.

This flirtation with theological revision was serious enough to occasion more than twenty pages of suggested edits from Müller's CDF, which saw the long document late in the process. Not that it mattered, since most if not all of those suggestions were ignored. But the revisionism happened at an abstract and general level, as a broad point about a lot of different moral dilemmas, and not in the concrete form of a particular answer to the particular question of communion for people living in relationships that are publicly adulterous. It was clear that chapter eight of *Amoris Laetitia* yearned in the direction of changing the church's rules for communion, that its logic suggested that such a change was reasonable and desirable. Yet the pope never said so directly, never made explicit what he repeatedly implied, never simply came out and said: *For many of the divorced-and-remarried, the church's law is too hard to follow, the moral dilemmas too extreme, and therefore they cannot be considered to be seriously sinning, and can receive communion in good conscience.*

Although there were two footnotes in the text that came particularly close. One, footnote 329, strongly suggested that it is unreasonable for the church to ask—as John Paul's *Familiaris Consortio* did—a remarried couple raising children together to try to live as brother and sister, without having sex, because in such cases "the good of the children" might suffer from their parents' want of intimacy.[11] The second, footnote 351, was attached to a passage that discussed how pastors might accompany couples living in nonmarital relationships—people who, because "of conditioning and mitigating factors," may not be "subjectively culpable" for their sins, and therefore should be helped to "grow in the life of grace and charity" before their irregular situation is resolved. The footnote elaborated what that help might mean, by saying:

> In certain cases, this can include the help of the sacraments. Hence, "I want to remind priests that the confessional must not be a torture chamber, but rather an encounter with the Lord's mercy." ... I would also point out that the Eucharist "is not a prize for the perfect, but a powerful medicine and nourishment for the weak."[12]

What were those "certain cases" where the sacraments might be given? Well, the strong implication of the papal language was that they included some cases where people continued to live in public adultery. But the footnote did not say so clearly; instead it very deliberately said so unclearly, leaving open the possibility that like prior papal documents those "certain cases" only included people trying to live as brother and sister, trying to be chaste.

Which meant that *Amoris Laetitia* left the church in a bizarre position. After two synods, two years of heated argument and deep division, the pope's great matter came down to a strange question: Could long-standing church discipline and a core moral teaching be rewritten via a suggestive footnote to a deliberately ambiguous papal exhortation? Not just the synods themselves, but decades of debates about how far the church could go to accommodate modernity, how much change could be allowed, were all suddenly distilled into a strange sort of textual parsing. Depending on your interpretation, *Amoris Laetitia*'s drift proved that the pope *could* change what his recent predecessors had taught was unchanging and essential—which would be a church-shaking, revolutionary development! Or else, just as plausibly, its lack of clarity proved that even a pope who wanted to change a major teaching was constrained—by the Holy Spirit?—from doing so.

This uncertainty lent itself, and swiftly, to multiple interpretations of what the pope meant and where the church might go next. There were conservatives for whom relief was the dominant emotion: The pope had not explicitly taught heresy, the gravest crisis had been averted, and the thing to do was hail everything in *Amoris Laetitia* that affirmed orthodoxy and simply ignore its footnotes and ambiguous, arguing–with–John Paul II formulations. On the other hand, there were conservatives (among them Cardinal Raymond Burke) for whom those footnotes and formulations were too dangerous to be ignored, and who therefore pressed the case that *Amoris* was not actually a fully magisterial document, that as a mere apostolic exhortation (as opposed to a papal encyclical) it could be corrected, challenged, or ignored. The first camp seemed to want to talk as little as possible about the contested portions of *Amoris*, and, indeed, complained that people were making too much of them. The second camp began circulating public petitions, signed by various conservative theologians, asking the pope to clarify what he had meant, and affirm the positions that his ambiguities had shadowed with a doubt.

Then there were those middle-grounders who wanted to accept *Amoris* in full while also acknowledging that the footnotes did point to some relaxation of the rules for the reception of communion, and who therefore labored to make that relaxation fit with prior teaching, prior doctrine. This case for continuity was made by several prominent figures linked to John Paul II and Benedict—including Rocco Buttiglione, an Italian philosopher and jurist, and Christoph Schönborn, an Austrian cardinal and theologian assigned to explain *Amoris Laetitia* to the press.

The most compelling idea that Buttiglione, in particular, put forward was that someone could be in a second marriage (or a nonmarital relationship) that amounted to a form of psychological compulsion or constraint, in which threats or blackmail or overt abuse from their partner or spouse made the sin of sexual relations merely venial and not mortal, and therefore not bad enough to require refraining from communion. (The more striking analogy used was to the condition of a prostitute under the sway of a brutal pimp.) It was these kinds of genuinely extreme cases, Buttiglione argued, that *Amoris* had in mind when it hinted at opening communion, and the opening it envisioned was a kind of provisional one for desperate situations, with the sacrament offered to weak Catholics in a kind of emotional captivity who had not yet found a way to escape.

This argument had its merits and its difficulties, but the main issue with it was that it did not imply what liberal reformers actually wanted, and already claimed to have won. It suggested that a remarried Catholic (or a cohabitating Catholic, or a Catholic in a same-sex relationship, or a Catholic prostitute, or any other case) might receive communion temporarily if her situation was so toxic or controlling that it could not be easily escaped. So did the related argument-from-ignorance—that a divorced and remarried Catholic who had been misled by the ambient culture, who did not understand that remarriage was adultery, could provisionally receive communion while being educated in the full truth of the faith. But in both cases, the provisional nature of receiving communion was crucial to the logic of the argument, since it required that eventually, with sufficient spiritual and moral growth, the Catholic in question would either have to leave the adulterous/sinful relationship or cease to take communion once again.

The original Kasper proposal was roughly the opposite. It envisioned a temporary abstention from communion, while a given divorced-and-remarried person reckoned with the failings of the past, followed by a permanent reintegration even as the second marriage advanced in stability and happiness. It proposed communion for the remarried not as a temporary gift for people in chaos and great difficulty, but as a permanent grace for divorced Catholics who had rebuilt their lives, entered in a new and happier relationship, and achieved the proper psychological posture toward their past. It wanted to make a distinction, as the Australian Archbishop Coleridge put it during the synod, between "a second marriage that is enduring and stable and loving" and "a couple skulking off to a hotel room for a wicked weekend," and provide for people in the first category while still potentially withholding communion from people in the second.[13] The official view of the church, that separation or civil divorce was sometimes acceptable (and that merely divorced people were welcome to the Eucharist) but remarriage always wrong, was implicitly reversed: The past divorce became the key sin in need of atonement to make the new marriage morally acceptable.

Which meant that the Catholic prostitute, under the liberal vision's logic, might be a poor candidate for communion because her personal situation was so unstable, her relationship to her sins so obviously fraught . . . whereas the happily remarried Catholic divorcée would be in a much more appropriate situation to receive the Eucharist. And the language of *Amoris* seemed at times closer to this view—portraying reintegration (again, never specifically defined) as a reward for the "responsible and tactful" Catholic, as a response to a "a second union consolidated over time, with new children, proven fidelity, generous self giving"—than to the narrow reading that its more conservative, continuity-focused defenders tried to offer.[14]

But multiple readings were possible and reasonable, and because the pope had declined to choose explicitly between them, all of them were embraced, by theologians and Catholic scribblers and bishops all around the Catholic world, as the true interpretation of *Amoris*. The synod had rejected the German vision of a devolution of doctrinal authority, of a local-option Catholicism in which each bishops conference or bishop adapted the church's teaching to cultural conditions. But by issuing such an ambiguous document Pope Francis had pushed Catholicism toward exactly that kind of devolution, toward a geographical and cultural variation in what his church would teach.

Thus in the months following the release of *Amoris* some bishops declared that the rule of prior centuries was still fully in effect, and that the pope's message of reintegration was limited and that "accompaniment" for the remarried could only lead to communion if they obtained an annulment or lived as brother and sister with their new spouse. These conservatives included the Polish bishops and a number of bishops across North America— led by Charles Chaput in Philadelphia, and eventually joined by bishops in Phoenix, Portland, Lincoln, Portsmouth in England, Western Canada, the unlikely traditionalist bastion of Kazakhstan, and more.

Then at the same time there were bishops who quickly announced their intention to welcome the remarried back to communion. In some cases they did so sweepingly: Bishop Robert McElroy in San Diego, a Francis appointee, essentially operationalized the full liberal endgame, treating the decision to receive communion as an individual decision, to be assisted but not challenged by priest-confessors, and thus for most people a matter of when, not if. In other cases the movement was more cautious: in Rome and Brazil and Pope Francis's native Argentina, guidelines emerged that allowed for exceptions, but seemed (in different ways in each locale) to emphasize their rarity, the key role of the priest-confessor in discerning when such an exception might be made. The German bishops' guidelines were likewise a little more circumspect when they inevitably opened communion to some of the remarried. Meanwhile, the two bishops of tiny, very Catholic Malta put out guidelines that seemed expansive, welcoming to communion any remarried Catholics who felt "at peace with God." [15]

A few bishops seemed intent on having it both ways. In Florence, the cardinal archbishop, Giuseppe Betori, instituted a "diocesan course of formation" to instruct priests and laypeople on *Amoris* and its implications. The first lecture was given by his predecessor, Cardinal Ennio Antonelli, a conservative who told listeners that the ban on communion for the remarried was still very much in force. But then when the lecture series came around to the contentious eighth chapter, Cardinal Betori's invited speaker was a supporter of the most liberal interpretation, Monsignor Basilio Petra, who had argued that for the "enlightened faithful" contemplating whether to take communion after a divorce and second marriage, there might be no need for confession at all.

These varying responses made it clear that there was no consensus about what *Amoris* meant even among Catholic leaders who read it as an opening to communion. Instead, like functionaries in a somewhat capricious dictatorship, they all were effectively "working toward the pope," trying to offer guidelines that differed with one another but also tried to fit what they thought his ambiguities intended. And when challenged or critiqued they appealed to the papal will—even acknowledging, in the process, that their papal positivism required ignoring what prior popes had rather clearly said. "Whoever wishes to discover what the true will of Christ is for him," the Maltese archbishop declared in a sermon given amid the swirl of controversy, "he must ask the Pope and the bishops who are in communion with the Pope. . . . Whoever wishes to discover what Jesus wants from him, he must ask the Pope, this Pope, not the one who came before him, or the one who came before that. This present Pope." [16]

Yet most of those "bishops who are in communion with the Pope" seemed less confident. While a few conservatives and traditionalists went one way and a few liberals and papal loyalists another, the vast majority of the world's five-thousand-odd bishops, regardless of their theological position, declined to take any firm stance. They talked about other sections of *Amoris*, they praised Pope Francis in generic terms—and then they waited, like good ecclesial politicians, to see what might happen next.

In effect, then, the immediate result of *Amoris Laetitia* was to move the church from a situation in which Catholic teaching on marriage and the sacraments was defined universally but implemented variously to a situation in which that teaching was defined variously as well—one way in Krakow and Philadelphia and Winnipeg, another way in Buenos Aires and Rome and San Diego, but in most places ambiguously, left up to whichever reading of *Amoris*'s relationship to the prior magisterium the individual pastor or individual Catholic found most convincing.

A waspish English priest, Father John Hunwicke, borrowed a phrase from the famous nineteenth-century English convert John Henry Newman and dubbed this "a suspense of the magisterium"—meaning a situation in which the pope was deliberately declining to exercise his teaching role.[17] Alternatively, you could say that Francis was offering Catholics a choice of multiple magisteria. There was the formal teaching of the church, which had not been explicitly altered, and then there was the informal teaching of the pope, delivered by implication and through semiofficial interviews and in the footnotes.

Perhaps the plan was to allow conservatives to keep the first magisterium, the formal teaching, since then they would have no grounds for fearing that the pope had fallen into error or that the church had broken faith with Christ . . . while liberals from Chicago to Cologne could have the more liberalized teaching as a permission slip for pastoral experiments. The theory being, presumably, that so long as this doubled approach continued, there would be no crisis point, no danger of the church imitating the Anglican communion and skidding into schism. Denied the support he sought and the cover he needed for explicit change, Francis had taken the unofficial route—and perhaps found a new, politically brilliant way to keep the church together, to preserve its stability, even as he liberalized its rules.

Archbishop Forte, the synod secretary, suggested as much when he discussed *Amoris* shortly after its release. In a pithy way he confirmed everything that conservatives had sensed about the synodal process and the pope's intentions. "If we talk explicitly about communion for the divorced and remarried," Forte paraphrased the pontiff telling him, "you have no idea what a mess these guys will make for us. So let's not talk about it directly, you get the premises in place and then I will draw the conclusions." [18]

Which now the pope was doing—but in a way that remained ambiguous, leaving his critics baffled as to how they should respond.

But was it really so brilliant, and would it really bring stability after the storms of the synods? There were reasons to be doubtful. The first problem was that the Catholic Church was not designed for major decentralization of controverted questions (its selling point had always been the reverse), and Francis had not actually done much in the way of the formal restructuring that might make such decentralizing plausible. If anything, his personal style and tendency to ignore the bureaucracy had concentrated more effective power in his hands. A rhetoric of "synodality" did not obscure the fact that Rome was still the final arbiter, and if *Amoris Laetitia* was magisterially ambiguous most of Francis's powers continued to be exercised in ways that made it very clear which side of the controversy he was actually on.

His appointments became more liberal after the synods. In choosing cardinals in early 2016 he passed over not only Chaput of Philadelphia but also José Gomez of Los Angeles, the leader of America's largest and most Hispanic archdiocese and a crusader for liberal immigration policies. In a different moment Gomez would have been a natural appointment for a church moving to the peripheries and championing social justice causes . . . but he was seen as too theologically conservative, not enough of a Francis loyalist, and perhaps a dangerously *papabile* figure for conservatives to champion at the next synod. Instead the cardinals' hats in the United States went to Blase Cupich and the more obscure Joseph Tobin of Indianapolis, who was installed in Newark as a kind of Francis-friendly counterweight to Timothy Dolan (one of the signatories to the thirteen cardinals' letter during the synod) in New York across the river, and who wasted little time in aligning himself with the liberal interpretation of *Amoris* and critiquing fellow bishops (Chaput, notably) who differed.

Meanwhile, Francis also moved to undermine and isolate the conservatives who remained in prominent Vatican positions. Letter-of-thirteen signatory Robert Sarah, the head of the Congregation for Divine Worship, had his wings clipped after he gave a speech urging priests to celebrate mass *ad orientem*—toward the altar, toward the east, the traditional manner abandoned after Vatican II. He was summoned to a meeting with Francis, the Vatican spokesman slapped him down publicly, and then in a remarkable purge most of his subordinates were removed, and a more liberal roster of cardinals and bishops put in place—effectively leaving Sarah as a conservative figurehead with no effective power. Other purges followed: Several priests were fired from Müller's CDF for no apparent reason (the real reason seemed to be that Francis had heard through back channels that they had criticized *Amoris*), and lesser entities like the Pontifical Academy for Life found their membership rolls emptied and replaced with a new roster of papal favorites.

The sharpness of these moves was distinctive. Both John Paul II and Benedict had prodded the Vatican and the episcopate in a more conservative direction by degrees, promoting their own men while also respecting the normal processes that turned auxiliary bishops into archbishops, archbishops into cardinals. In general but especially after the synods, Francis seemed to be on a more hurried timetable, more determined to put his stamp on the church while there was time to do it, lest a successor be elected who might reverse the informal changes he had made. It was a high-reward but polarizing strategy. "I am happy that he is increasing the odds that the next pope will be like him," noted Father Thomas Reese, the dean of liberal Jesuits in the United States, "and all my progressive friends are certainly pleased with these appointments . . . but then I had to be honest with myself by asking the question, 'How would I have reacted if Pope John Paul or Pope Benedict had done the same thing?' Frankly, I would have been outraged."[19] And the precedent being set, Reese acknowledged, created a risk of counter-purges under a more conservative pope, thus raising rather than lowering the stakes of ecclesial appointments and debates.

Nor did the pope's own words make the post-*Amoris* truce or devolution look like something built to last. He might be allowing conservative bishops to stick with the old magisterial line rather than his ambiguous update, but he wasn't just denying them red hats; he continued to let them have it verbally, in the same style as his concluding synodal remarks, in sermon after sermon. The balancing act, the attempt to plant himself in a middle ground between liberal and conservatives, was a thing of the past. The synthesis of theological conservatism and social justice seemed to evaporate. What had been one theme among many in his early days as pope—the dangers of pharisaism and legalism, the evils of rigidity, the closed hearts of the doctors of the law—became a constant one, repeated weekly in varying contexts, whether the pope was addressing the state of seminaries and priestly formation (where Francis deplored the return of a "black and white" mentality among younger priests and told apocryphal stories about young priests standing on the sidewalk yelling at people, "You'll go to hell!"[20]) or talking about the state of priestly dress (where Francis mocked the cassocks and hats favored by some tradition-minded clerics—"and it is said that the Church does not allow women priests," he jibed[21]) or sermonizing on the Decalogue (do not "hide in the rigidity of the closed Commandments," he warned[22]) or speaking, at Christmastime, about the journey of the Magi (which became an opportunity to denounce "prophets of doom" who cling to the "usual fare" instead of embracing the radical and new[23]).

At the same time, Francis escalated his unofficial interventions on behalf of a more liberal interpretation of *Amoris*. When the Buenos Aires bishops produced their guidelines allowing priests to admit some remarried divor-cées to communion, it was arranged that the pope would write them a "pri-vate" letter praising the guidelines and saying that "no other interpretations" were possible.[24] The letter then leaked to the press from the pope's inner circle, to be cited repeatedly as evidence that the debate over what *Amoris* meant was settled. This claim was not theologically accurate, as private let-ters have no magisterial weight. But as a signal to the church the leak strongly suggested that the devolution on remarriage and communion was intended to be temporary, a means to buy time so that the consensus Francis had failed to win at the synod could gradually emerge ... at which point the Polish-German and Philadelphian–San Diegan differences would vanish, and all the Catholic world would be united in Francis's understanding of what mercy for the remarried should require.

Meanwhile, there was the further problem that the logic of communion for the remarried really *did* point beyond itself to further change, just as conservatives had argued. And not only on issues related to sexuality, as the German bishops quickly made clear: Once communion for the remarried was established, what they envisioned next was intercommunion with Prot-estants, or at least with their Lutheran fellow countrymen, beginning with the Lutheran spouses in mixed-faith marriages.

This was an idea as theologically fraught in its own way as communion for the remarried. Intercommunion, in limited forms, was allowed with the Orthodox churches because they shared the Catholic understanding of tran-substantiation and the priesthood. But the Lutheran churches did not, and to admit Lutherans to regular communion was an effective statement that one could take the Eucharist not only without going to confession but without even believing what Catholicism believed about it. Still, the *Amoris*-style argument of pastoral necessity was invoked on its behalf. In late 2016, with the five hun-dredth anniversary of the Reformation looming, Walter Kasper declared his hope that the "the next declaration [from the pope] will open the Eucharistic sharing in particular situations, especially in mixed marriages and families and in countries like Germany and the United States where this pastoral problem is extremely pressing."[25] And indeed, Pope Francis had hinted at sympathy for this idea, in a stream-of-consciousness answer to a Lutheran questioner after the second synod, which ended with him telling her to "talk to the Lord and then go forward. I don't dare to say anything more."[26]

Then there was the case of physician-assisted euthanasia, legal in an increasing number of Western nations, and offered to (or, in some cases, effectively imposed upon) the non–terminally ill in several European countries. When Canada passed a law legalizing suicide across the dominion, the bishops of Western Canada issued a pastoral letter reminding Catholics that it wasn't possible for priests to give last rites to people preparing to kill themselves, since you can't absolve someone of mortal sin when they're consciously planning their own quietus for the next day or even hour. But the bishops of the Maritime Provinces had a different take: Citing Pope Francis's pastoral innovations as a model, they wrote that in some cases pastoral accompaniment *could* include giving last rites to people about to receive what they (following the government) euphemistically described as "medical assistance in dying," because it was more important to be there for people, to accompany them, than to impose any kind of one-size-fits-all rule.[27] And just like that, the same kind of quasi-schism that separated Polish and German Catholics on remarriage and the sacraments separated Albertans from Nova Scotians on the sacraments and suicide.

So there was no reason, in Rome and elsewhere, to think that the ambiguities of *Amoris* would leave conservatives with anything but a provisional stability, or that the ripples from its quasi-innovations would not spread. For many conservative bishops and cardinals, including most of the letter-of-thirteen signatories, this realization didn't suggest an obvious course of action, beyond a mix of caution, prayer, and hope that Francis's bench-stacking would fall short and the next conclave would allow for a major course correction. But those with less to lose saw a case for open confrontation, which produced the peculiar drama of the *dubia*.

●　●　●

A *dubium*, in Vatican parlance, is a question raised about a particular issue of church teaching or canon law: "Does document X allow for practice Y?," etc. In the autumn of 2016 four cardinals—Burke, naturally, joined by Walter Brandmüller, Carlo Caffarra, and Joachim Meisner, all theological heavyweights but also all retirees—posed four *dubia* in a private letter to Pope Francis and to the Congregation for the Doctrine of the Faith, requesting clarity on *Amoris*. The first *dubium* asked the pope to clarify whether the church's ban on communion for divorced Catholics in new marriages remained in place. The remaining three asked whether the church's traditional opposition to situation ethics still held, whether *Veritatis Splendor*'s declaration that "circumstances or intentions can never transform an act intrinsically evil . . . into an act 'subjectively' good" had been superseded, and whether the church now taught, as it had not before, that individual consciences could discern "legitimate exceptions to absolute moral norms." [28]

These were all reasonable questions, to which the various readings of *Amoris* suggested various responses—some clearly orthodox, some tipping toward heresy or rupture, some ambiguously in between. But Francis chose not to answer, and declined to authorize a response from the CDF as well. After an interval had passed, Burke and his coauthors took the unusual step of making the *dubia* public; this was just before another consistory in Rome, when the pope was to present red hats to the newest cardinals. The pope continued to ignore the questions, but took the equally unusual step of canceling a general meeting with the cardinals (the same meeting at which Kasper had delivered his address three years before). Perhaps he was "boiling with rage," as some sources claimed,[29] or perhaps he was entirely calm and focused on more important matters, as Father Spadaro suggested in one of his many tweets against the pontiff's critics. But either way it seemed that he wanted to avoid any opportunity for the larger number of prelates who tacitly endorsed the four cardinals' line of questioning to make their voices heard.

So the *dubia*, no less than *Amoris* itself, hung there, unanswered and unresolved. And as with *Amoris* itself, there was a small rush to take sides and a larger hanging back. The pope's inner circle and leading allies, including

Spadaro, Kasper, and Cupich, dismissed the questions as a pointless stunt and insisted that the meaning of *Amoris* was clear; somewhat more intemperately, the head of Greece's bishops conference accused the *dubia* authors of heresy and possibly apostasy for questioning the pope. At the same time a smattering of bishops spoke up on behalf of the questioners, and a few of the key cardinals—including Pell and Sarah—offered ambiguous support. But when the conservative journalist Sandro Magister tallied up the numbers a month after the controversy began, he found fewer than twenty-five comments from bishops and cardinals—about ten in support of the pope, about fifteen giving some kind of encouragement to the *dubia*. From everyone else, again—silence. Watchful waiting. A refusal either to defend the pope or to question him openly, until they knew what moves he intended to make next.

What happened was a response, but of a different sort. The Knights of Malta, the charitable order to which Cardinal Burke was posted, had their own version of the larger church's ongoing battles, which came to a head shortly after the *dubia* were publicized when a German knight, Grand Master Albrecht von Boeselager, was sacked by his English superior, Prince and Grand Master Fra' Matthew Festing. The proximate issue was a condom distribution program; the deeper issue was a split over the order's overall trajectory, how much it should insist on Catholic identity, and all the other inevitable questions of the age. Boeselager protested and appealed to allies in the Vatican, and Pope Francis intervened—which would not have been surprising except that the Knights were, in fact, their own sovereign country, owing religious fidelity to the pope but with an ancient constitution that made them self-governing and not subject to Rome in choosing their leaders or their rules. So Francis's move, which led to Festing's resignation and Boeselager's reinstatement, was a kind of soft annexation with no clear grounds in international law—a move, a few observers pointed out, that offered a kind of precedent for Italian or European Union intervention in some future papal conclave.

These legal niceties aside, the Knights business wasn't so very different from John Paul II's intervention in Jesuit elections in the 1980s, when the pontiff tried (without obvious success) to change the order's liberal drift. But it had a more personal edge, given that it was Burke who had been advising the Order of Malta, Burke who had possibly encouraged Festing to fire Boeselager, and Burke's authority that the papal intervention superseded. That the traditionalist cardinal was soon thereafter dispatched to far-flung Guam to supervise a sex abuse tribunal did not feel particularly coincidental.

Around this time the inhabitants of Rome awoke to find the city plastered with posters bearing the visage of a dyspeptic-looking pope. "Ah Francis," they read in colloquial Italian, "you've taken over congregations, removed priests, decapitated the Order of Malta . . . ignored Cardinals . . . but where's your mercy?"[30] Such a public Roman protest was an unusual thing, indeed without precedent since the nineteenth century. The authorities pulled them down; Father Spadaro, ever ready on Twitter, called them "a sign that he's doing well and causing A LOT of annoyance."[31] Shortly thereafter Francis's handpicked kitchen cabinet of nine cardinals met in Rome and issued a statement of support, also unusual, for the pontiff: "In relation to recent events," the statement said, "the Council of Cardinals expresses its full support for the work of the Pope, assuring at the same time its full adhesion and backing for His person and His Magisterium."[32]

The recent events were not specified, nor were the details of "His Magisterium." And from Francis himself, and from most of the world's uneasy, watchful bishops, there was still only silence.

Nine

ATHANASIANS
AND ARIANS

T he bishops were watching, but were ordinary Catholics? The two synods and *Amoris* had polarized the hierarchy, the theologate, and the
commentariat, but their impact on the pope's image and popularity among
the faithful seemed modest, even negligible. In most surveys of public opinion Francis remained popular with most Catholics, generally slightly more
so than Benedict and slightly less than the beloved John Paul II. If you
peered closely at the polling, in the United States and worldwide, you could
sometimes discern the existence of conservative discontent—but you had to
peer very closely indeed, making distinctions between "very favorable" and
"somewhat favorable" responses, to find anything that looked like disillu-
sionment.

Here and there a parish controversy flared up: a priest in Italy clashing
with his congregation after he criticized the pope, priests in Latin America
and Malta clashing with their bishops over the interpretation of *Amoris*.

But these were minor, sporadic, exceptional. There were many anecdotes about how the synods were received, with liberals talking eagerly about ex-Catholics returning to the fold and conservatives talking grimly about confusion and discouragement. But the data didn't suggest anything all that big was happening—neither a sudden renewal nor major, post–Vatican II–style turmoil. At most you could say that just as nations and dioceses were polarizing in response to Francis's decentralization of doctrine, so were parishes to some extent—that Francis was giving more liberal parishes and priests a license to experiment, and traditional and conservative congregations a reason to act a little more militant and embattled. But such modest polarization was not an active crisis. The *Amoris* wars raged fiercely on the Internet, but in everyday parish life they came up as just one controversy among many, if at all.

In the summer of 2017 the American bishops organized a big event in Orlando, Florida—a "convocation of Catholic leaders" in which about thirty-five hundred priests and nuns and laypeople from around the country crowded into a convention center to hold panels and talks and networking events, all organized around "The Joy of the Gospel," Pope Francis's blueprint for evangelization from the distant-seeming first year of his pontificate. John Allen, the Vatican reporter, was at the event, and he remarked on the gap between the polarizing elite debate over Francis and the way that most convocationgoers talked about him—mostly with enthusiasm, sometimes with a "but" included on the *Amoris* debate or the pope's incautious interview style or some other specific point, but without the fear or rancor evident in Rome or among some cardinals and theologians or on Twitter. There is "a mismatch between the public debate about Francis and the reality on the ground," Allen argued: Vatican conflicts grab headlines in the press and inspire furious online argument, but "if you want to know what most Catholics are actually thinking about Francis, get off Twitter and into the trenches."[1]

This gulf was ofted cited by the pope's partisans: Because there was no crisis in the pews in the strange months after *Amoris*, they argued that there was no crisis whatsoever. Just as they had suggested during the synods that any conflict was a creation of the media, in the wake of *Amoris* and the *dubia* many of Francis's admirers argued that the division over the pope's teaching wasn't very serious, that Burke was a melodramatist and other critics attention seekers and the journalists giving them aid and comfort were desperate for a headline, that the document itself was quite clear and not remotely controversial to most Catholics, that anyone who murmured about schism or fretted about heresy was a hysteric . . . and that conservative discontent under Francis was just the mirror image of liberal discontent under John Paul II and no more threatening to church unity.

In the end, wrote Austen Ivereigh, the papal biographer and his subject's most indefatigable English-language advocate, the agita about changes to church teaching was confined to a narrow claque. They were "lay, educated and from the wealthy world or the wealthy parts of the developing world . . . mostly intellectuals and lawyers and teachers and writers who put great store in their reason." But the mass of Catholics didn't share their insistent textual criticism and scrupulosity. "Even as they insist that there is a debate to be had, a case to answer, a matter to be settled, the train is leaving the station, and they are left on the platform, waving their arms."[2]

Ivereigh was echoing what Archbishop Fernández, the papal ghost-writer, had said a year earlier, between the two synods, when he was asked if he saw a risk of "two churches" developing under Francis—one loyal to the official magisterium as conservatives understood it, and one to the pope's potential innovations. The archbishop was dismissive: "There's a schism when a group of important people share the same sensibilities that reflect those of a vast section of society," he said. "Luther and Protestantism came about this way. But now the overwhelming majority of the people are with Francis and they love him. His opponents are weaker than what you think. Not pleasing everyone does not mean provoking a schism."[3]

There was some truth to these points. As yet, nothing Francis had done had transformed the day-to-day life of the church in the way that Vatican II had reshaped things for ordinary Catholics. The specific debates of the synods and *Amoris* and the *dubia* turned on questions that could seem abstract and technical, and the groups most excited by them were what you might call professional Catholics—clerics and theologians and the church watchers in the press. There was no massive grassroots rebellion brewing, no vast army of restive Catholics ready to march out of their parishes in protest if their bishops or pastors interpreted the pope's reforms in one particular fashion or another. The unsettled and unhappy constituted a minority of churchgoers, and they didn't exactly have somewhere else to walk out *to*. When observers wrote about the possibility of schism, it was far easier to envision in theory than in practice.

So the crisis, for the time being, was clearly an elite battle, not parish-by-parish trench warfare. But even with that important concession made, the situation was still rather extraordinary. The wrestling matches between conservative bishops and the pope's allies at the synods, the thirteen cardinals' intervention, the tension between the pope and his own Congregation for the Doctrine of the Faith, the *dubia* and the idea of a "correction" of the pope— all of these had no obvious precedent in the modern history of the Catholic Church. The dissent after *Humanae Vitae* and John Paul II's conflicts with liberal factions had been serious, but they hadn't produced these kinds of fractures in the very heart of the hierarchy, this level of rhetorical escalation on both sides. No liberal cardinal had gone as far as Burke in challenging a reigning pope, and neither John Paul nor Benedict had been so personal, persistent, and direct in attacking the motives and indeed the morals of their critics. To the extent that there were precedents for this level of open controversy, they belonged more to the early-modern and medieval periods, and to late antiquity—and they were precisely the cases that scholars and theologians long remembered as major theological crises for the church.

That those past crises had often been accompanied by massive turbulence and this one, as yet, has not, suggested that it might yet be defused. But the turbulence of the past, when arguments over Jesus's divinity or the nature of the sacraments were tangled up with major popular upheavals, also reflected the church's greater temporal power and cultural importance in those eras. The *political* and *populist* intensity of the Lutheran-Catholic struggle or the Christological battles of the late Roman era were always unlikely to be replicated in an age with a secularized mass culture and a church that no longer wields much temporal power. What was happening in the Francis era—a war of words between Catholic elites, with the mass of churchgoers watching uncertainly or indifferently—was how you would expect a major theological controversy to begin in a more disenchanted and less zealous era, in which theology matters less than in the medieval or Reformation-era past because the church itself is less politically powerful and culturally dominant.

And Francis's defenders, when it suited them, seemed to understand that. They only downplayed the stakes when the pope faced some sort of setback or opposition; the rest of the time, they tended to play up the significance of what he was attempting to accomplish. Ivereigh's biography was subtitled "The Making of a Radical Pope"—and he was one of the more moderate, continuity-focused of the pope's defenders. In the Archbishop Fernández interview in which he dismissed the risk of schism, the archbishop also promised that Francis aimed at "irreversible" changes in the life of the church, with a "deep impact" that would endure and prevent any "turning back."[4] The rhetoric of papal admirers generally was replete with talk of a great renewal, a move of the Holy Spirit, a train rushing down the track, a "Francis revolution," a struggle for Catholicism's very soul.

Their sense of the high stakes involved was also clear enough from the way their own arguments slipped, very easily, from defending the Kasper proposal as the most modest of changes in one breath to cheering sweeping changes in the next. The Kasper proposal is just a change of discipline, not doctrine . . . *but* by the way, the church should also establish intercommunion with Protestants as soon as possible. Conservatives are wildly overreacting when they interpret *Amoris* as a kind of surrender to the sexual revolution . . . *but* by the way, the church should offer recognition to gay couples and grant last rites to suicides and revisit *Humanae Vitae* and for heaven's sake stop obsessing about abortion. It is ludicrous to suggest that Francis was changing doctrine on marriage . . . *but* by the way, his casual comments on the death penalty and just war meant that he was developing church teaching on those issues too, and soon any Catholic who favored capital punishment would be out of step with the modern magisterium. It is absurd to suggest that any core Catholic teaching was at stake in the synodal debates . . . *but* by the way, Jesus's strict teachings on marriage probably reflected his mistaken view that the world was about to end, or maybe we just don't know what Jesus really said, because after all the gospel writers didn't have tape recorders. It is ludicrous to draw analogies between the *Amoris* controversies and the great debates over Arianism or Gnosticism or Lutheranism . . . *but* in fact, now that you mention it, some semi-Arian understandings of Jesus, some semi-Gnostic concepts of the human person, some semi-Lutheran understandings of sin or the sacraments, might actually deserve a home in the Catholic Church. It was ridiculous to say that Catholicism's intellectual integrity and theological consistency were at stake in the remarriage debate . . . *but* in fact it's time for the church to acknowledge that "theology is not Mathematics," and if necessary "2+2 in theology can make 5."[5]

I am plucking from a variety of pro-Francis Catholic sources for these examples—bishops, theologians, and journalists—and one could easily add more. (The tape recorder comment belongs to the new Jesuit superior-general, Arturo Sosa, delivered to a slightly stunned Italian interviewer early in 2017; the 2+2=5 to the indefatigable Father Spadaro, answering his critics on Twitter.) The ease and frequency with which this slippage happened—from support for "modest" reform to support for every reform proposed since 1962; from support for Walter Kasper to questioning the Nicene Creed—suggested that certain Francis's apologists knew very well that they weren't just defending simple pastoral flexibility against the rigor of conservatives. Flexibility they surely wanted, but there was also clearly a more revolutionary vision implied and waiting underneath.

The heart of this vision, appropriately for an idea with such strong support in Germany, was Hegelian—the idea that God's revelation was perpetually unfolding in history, and that therefore it was a mistake to consider Catholicism a closed system in which questions were settled permanently. The liberal Protestant line, "Never put a period where God has put a comma," was the basic presupposition for this liberal Catholicism as well. Nothing, save Christ's divinity and not necessarily even that, could be closed to debate, and the message that the church was called to preach in one era might be very different in the next.

Of course this idea was not new to the Francis era. It was woven into liberal Catholicism in the 1960s and 1970s and into modernist Catholicism before that. And the slippage from modesty toward revolution, from a subtle change to a more sweeping follow-up, was likewise characteristic of the long battle over Vatican II's implications.

So it was fair to say that in the hindsight of, say, twenty-fifth-century Catholic scholarship, the crisis of the Francis era would not be studied in isolation, as a theological storm breaking unlooked-for on the church. Rather it was a particularly dramatic moment in the longer-lasting conflict over how much the church should accommodate to liberal modernity, how much revelation could be revised in the light of new historical contingencies, and how closely Catholicism could imitate Episcopalianism while doing so.

But in the context of that long conflict, the debate that Francis ushered in was not only dramatic but possibly decisive—opening possibilities for reform that had been heretofore only theoretical, opening scenarios for division that had been heretofore seen as dangers only for Protestant churches, and distilling, in the question of communion for the remarried, all the ways that liberals believed that the church must change and all the reasons why conservatives insisted that it could not change and still remain the church.

Which still left open the question of how it would end. And if it were analogous to past theological controversies, perhaps one of them could provide a template.

For conservatives scrambling to find examples in the Catholic past where a pope had imperiled orthodoxy and then been corrected, two instances— both mentioned in the first chapter of this book as cautionary tales for pontiffs—came up repeatedly. One was John XXII, pope from 1316 to 1334, while the papacy was based in Avignon but before the Great Schism that eventually followed from this relocation. Born Jacques Dueze to a shoemaker in Cahors, educated in medicine and canon law, and elevated to the papacy with the support of France's Philip V, his relatively long reign (which forms the backdrop to Umberto Eco's intellectual potboiler *The Name of the Rose*) featured a number of controversies, but one that was particularly memorable, because the pope ultimately lost.

Late in his reign, John XXII began preaching on the question of whether Christians experienced the beatific vision—in layman's terms, "heaven"—immediately after death (or immediately after being purified in purgatory). He argued that they did not, that until the end of the world and general resurrection of the dead they were kept in a kind of semi-heaven, "under the altar," in a state of happiness at one remove from the divine. (To reconcile his position with Jesus's words to the good thief on the cross that "today you will be with me in paradise," John argued that Jesus's human nature somehow would be present to console and bless the blessed dead, even as his divine nature remained hidden with the Father.)

Debates about the next life were as potent in medieval Christendom as debates about sexual ethics are in late modernity, and John had placed himself on the wrong side of both popular piety and much of the church's tradition. (Thomas Aquinas had pre-butted his argument in the century previous.) "The whole Christian world was troubled" by his sermons, a contemporary wrote, and various theologians wrote to rebuke him; when he attempted to impose his views on the university of the Sorbonne, they were joined in the rebuke by the king of France himself. So severe was the controversy that the pope, on his deathbed, agreed to a kind of retraction. He stated that he had delivered the sermons strictly as a private theologian, without the binding authority of papal teaching. Then his successor, Benedict XII, swiftly moved to correct his predecessor and clarify Catholic teaching, formally defining as a dogma of the church that "the souls of all the saints . . . before they take up their bodies again and before the general judgment, have been, are and will be with Christ in heaven," where they see God "face to face, without the mediation of any creature."[6]

The implications of this case for conservative critics of the Francis papacy were obvious. Here was an instance where a pope's own preaching had expressed a heretical position, less ambiguously by far than anything in *Amoris Laetitia*, and where resistance from the wider church had forced him to essentially back down.

Similar implications could be drawn from an earlier case, involving Pope Honorius I, pontiff from 625 to 638, who presided over the theological controversy on whether Christ had a single, divine will; or two wills, human and divine, working in harmony with one another. Honorius, in his correspondence and in negotiation with the emperor and the churches of the East, favored the one-will view, known as Monothelitism. The church as a whole did not, and both Monothelitism and Honorius himself were condemned and anathematized by an ecumenical council forty years later, and by one of Honorius's papal successors, Leo II, who judged him guilty of "profane treachery" against the truths of Catholic faith.

When the debate over papal infallibility was joined more than a millennium later, however, the official view was that Honorius had never formally defined Monothelitism as a doctrine. He had strayed only in correspondence, not in public teaching, and therefore his error, even his treachery, was compatible with the limited view of papal infallibility that the First Vatican Council ultimately defined in 1870. Nonetheless there was no question that he had tacitly supported a heresy—and so again, for Catholics who feared Francis's moves on marriage, he offered precedent for pushing back against the pope.

But the analogy that had the most appeal to Francis-resisting conservatives was a much more famous one: the grand controversy of Arianism, which consumed the church for much of the fourth century and flared periodically thereafter.

The Arian heresy was named for an Alexandrian theologian, Arius, who rejected Jesus's full divinity in favor of a kind of halfway position that made the Nazarene a kind of demi-god—adopted and divinized by God the Father, not preexisting and eternal with him. The Council of Nicaea, which helped produce the creed that Catholics (and many other Christians) still proclaim, was summoned by the Emperor Constantine in 325 to address the rise of Arianism, and its attendees voted overwhelmingly for what we know now as the orthodox position on Christology—that Jesus was "consubstantial," *of one being*, with the eternal God.

But its settlement was steadily undermined for the next few decades. Despite what Nicaea had ruled, Constantine's successors favored the Arian position, and so did the imperial elite and many bishops. Under their influence, a succession of church synods adopted various semi-Arian and Arian formulations (until the Christian world "awoke with a groan to find itself Arian," Saint Jerome wrote) and the defenders of the orthodox position were pressured, silenced, and exiled. Only in the late fourth century, after the Emperor Julian's pagan interregnum and another round of pro-Arian efforts by one of his successors, Valens, did the orthodox emperor Theodosius ratify and enforce the Nicene position once again. Meanwhile, Arianism had been exported to the newly Christianized Germanic tribes, so the controversy simmered for centuries as Vandals and Visigoths and Franks adapted to orthodoxy.

This summary skims over a controversy in which theological distinctions were parsed exceedingly finely, and as one pagan writer sniped, "the highways were covered with galloping bishops." But for the purposes of contemporary analogies a few points stand out. First, while the details of the theological arguments could get esoteric quickly, at bottom the appeal of Arianism was the appeal of a more rationalized Christianity, in which the mystery and paradoxes of the Trinity would give way to a more straightforward doctrine that posed fewer problems for philosophical assumptions about the unity of God. This appeal explains why Arian ideas have returned, under various guises, in many eras: There are Arian influences in the Islamic view of Jesus, in various Enlightenment revisions of Christianity, Unitarianism especially, and in certain tendencies in liberal Christianity and Catholicism in the present day.

Second, the Arian controversy featured numerous attempts to revive the heresy through deliberately ambiguous formulations, designed to allow what remained a minority viewpoint among the church's bishops to appear as a consensus view. To quote John Henry Newman's theological history of the period, Arianism presented itself as "a sceptical rather than a dogmatic teaching . . . proposing to inquire into and reform the received creed, rather than to hazard one of its own."[7] As the church historian Claudio Pierantoni notes, even during the high tide of Arian power, the councils of 357–60, "the pro-Arian minority does not venture to put forward a position too clearly in opposition with the traditional view . . . it does not expressly state that the Son is inferior to the Father . . . although holding the reins of power, it seeks to conceal itself."[8] Instead, in synod after synod, debate after debate, there was an attempt to find (to quote Newman again) some formula "so faintly precise and so decently ambiguous, as to embrace the greatest number of opinions possible"[9]—a formula that did not express Arianism clearly but undermined the orthodox position nonetheless.

Third, in part because they had the refuge of ambiguity, many of the era's bishops found reasons to go along with the Arianizing drift, sometimes under pressure and sometimes of their own accord. This was the original "suspense of the magisterium," the period to which Newman's line was actually applied: It was a period in which, as he wrote, "the body of Bishops failed in their confession of the faith. They spoke variously, one against another; there was nothing, after Nicaea, of firm, unvarying, consistent testimony, for nearly sixty years."[10]

Whether this failure included the pope himself remains a matter of some debate. The pontiff in the crucial years, Liberius, was a staunch-enough defender of the Nicene Creed that the Arian emperor Constantius exiled him to Thrace in 355 and installed an antipope, Felix, in his place. While in exile, Liberius supposedly agreed to sign on to Arian formulas in a trio of letters; the letters that have come down to us, however, are likely forgeries, and historians are uncertain whether Liberius actually succumbed to imperial pressure. In either case, no one considers letters written under duress to constitute infallible teaching: "If he really consorted with heretics," the editors of the 1912 *Catholic Encyclopedia* wrote, "it was a momentary human weakness which no more compromises the papacy than does that of St. Peter." [11]

But nonetheless, if Liberius did not fully succumb to Arianism, the papacy was certainly not orthodoxy's greatest champion either. That honor belongs to Athanasius of Alexandria, bishop of that city for forty-five years, and memorialized with the phrase *Athanasius contra mundum*—Athanasius against the world—for the seventeen years he spent in varying periods of exile ordered by four separate emperors, and the multiple condemnations he endured from various Arian-dominated church councils. Turbulent and disputatious, Athanasius and his allies—among them Saint Hilary of Poitiers, the "Athanasius of the West"—are the reason what we know as orthodoxy survived imperial edicts and episcopal compromises, and why Catholics today still say "begotten, not made, consubstantial with the Father" every Sunday between the sermon and the Eucharist. The papacy did not turn back Arianism: Stubborn bishops and laypeople played that role, at a time when authorities both secular and sacred were on the other side.

From the conservative perspective, all these elements of the Arian controversy are also present in today's confusion. In liberal Catholicism as in Arianism you have an interpretation of the faith that seems tailored to the reasonable person, the moderate and balanced mind, and that the leading authorities of the age tend to favor over more traditional ideas. In liberal Catholicism as in Arianism you have a set of positions and aspirations that keep being proposed despite clear and authoritative condemnations—from the Council of Nicaea in the Arian case, from John Paul II and Benedict in the case of the reforms favored by progressive churchmen today. In the present controversies as in Arianism you have an attempt to use ambiguous formulations to do an end-around, to shift teaching without a frontal confrontation with the dogmatic roadblocks, to be "faintly precise" and "decently ambiguous" to coax the orthodox along.

Finally, with Pope Francis's interventions on behalf of the liberal side, the division of the bishops and the simple silence of so many, you have a case not unlike the situation facing figures like Athanasius—where for orthodoxy to win out, it must do so against long odds, in defiance of seemingly authoritative proclamations, without (at certain moments) the clear support of the pope himself. The various synods summoned to push Arianism offer a precedent for the two synods on the family. Athanasius and his fellow troublemakers offer a precedent for Burke's resistance, for the letter from the thirteen cardinals, for the *dubia*, for all the objections raised by conservative bishops and theologians to *Amoris* and its interpretations. And the Athanasians' eventual success, the victory of orthodoxy and the defeat of Arianism, is the template for the victory that today's conservatives hope for and expect.

How might this victory transpire? In one scenario, the simplest, Francis might be succeeded by a vigorous conservative—Cardinal Robert Sarah, as Pope Pius XIII—who issues a clarifying teaching on the disputed points, and who uses Francis's own tactics as a model for stacking the ranks of bishops and bringing doctrinal order to the church. But as this vision is basically a stronger version of what John Paul II already (and unsuccessfully, it seems) attempted, and as a College of Cardinals increasingly filled with Francis appointees seems unlikely to elect a Sarah as his successor, such a scenario seems a little fanciful, leaving aside the escalation of the civil war it would entail. Maybe a revolutionary pope could have a counterrevolutionary successor, but only if the Holy Spirit *really* wills it, and sees to it that some truly martial figure is elected without most of the assembled cardinals realizing what they're doing.

The more plausible scenario for conservatives involves a much longer period of theological crisis, in which a succession of weak popes try and fail to contain the fissiparous process Francis has set in motion. The church's divisions widen rather than close, experiments both doctrinal and liturgical proliferate, and at first it seems that the church will become a liberalized institution with conservative dissenters and traditionalist holdouts. But nothing definitive prevents the two factions from coexisting, conservatives and traditionalists persist in leadership roles because the faithful in many areas demand it, over many decades the conservatives gain ground as their rivals dwindle (or dwindle further, in the case of the Northern Europeans), and reach a level of influence sufficient enough to take over a future ecumenical council—call it the Council of Nairobi, say, circa 2088—as decisively as the reformers took over Vatican II, and use it to rule as firmly for restoration as Trent ruled against Protestantism.

At which point there might come a mess, a parting of the ways, a larger version of the "Old Catholic" breakaway that followed Vatican I, in which some group of liberal clergy and believers depart and form some new World Catholic Church. But in the Roman Catholicism they've left behind both continuity and clarity would be restored, the bishops and priests and theologians and laypeople who resisted near-heresy from the hierarchy would be remembered as heroic figures (*Saint Raymond Burke, lion of orthodoxy, pray for us,* murmur Catholics in the Martian colonies in 2234 AD), and Francis himself, in the memory of the church, would join Honorius and John XXII in the ranks of popes who proved themselves fallible indeed.

This is no more necessarily a fantasy than a similar scenario would have been in 357, when Athanasius was in his third exile, Arian-leaning councils were being organized, and Pope Liberius had been packed off to Thrace. But there is this one key difference: The church of today has spent sixteen hundred years becoming more centralized than the church of the fourth century, and in that centralized church it matters a great deal if the pope is firmly on the side of innovation.

So the conservative hope assumes that the age of ambiguity, the suspense of the magisterium, will last long enough for conservatives to gain a great deal of institutional ground even with the pope and much of the hierarchy against them. It assumes that a Franciscanized Vatican will allow figures like Burke and Sarah to continue to hold major offices in the church. And it assumes that the popes of this Franciscan age will continue to be constrained—by fear of conservatives and their residual power, fear of the Holy Spirit, or both—from simply changing the magisterium directly, and teaching explicitly what for now is only implicit in *Amoris Laetitia*'s pastoral yearnings and suggestive footnotes. It assumes, that is, that the full theological crisis, the pope-as-heretic, won't come for conservative Catholics, that it can't come, and that there will never be a moment where they find themselves forced to contemplate either simple surrender or a schism.

But how might all of this be settled if this assumption proves wrong?

Ten

JANSENISTS
AND JESUITS

Because the liberal side has incentives to downplay the seriousness of the Francis controversies, and because the liberal position involves the assumption that the pre–Vatican II past need not bind the church, fewer cases from Catholic antiquity get invoked as models for how a liberalizing vision might simply triumph and Francis's conservative critics simply lose. Liberals are more likely to either cite Vatican II itself as a precedent, or else to emphasize issues where the church has evolved more gradually—like slavery, which the church once critiqued but tolerated (with popes and priests alike owning slaves) and now more sweepingly condemns, or usury, where the medieval church once forbade all lending of money at interest while the modern church only criticizes predatory interest rates.

Of these examples the more obscure one, usury, is the stronger one for liberal purposes. The church's full-throated modern condemnation of slavery builds on clear biblical themes, a long-standing Christian recognition of the institution's evils, and frequent papal condemnations of the slave trade. Slavery was nearly regulated out of existence in medieval Europe, and the religious arguments in its defense from the fifteenth century onward look like adaptations to the new economic incentives for slaveholding created by the Age of Discovery and early modern capitalism—making pro-slavery arguments more analogous, in certain ways, to progressive arguments for why the church must adapt to the sexual revolution than to conservative arguments for maintaining traditional teachings. At the very least, as the Anglican theologian Ian Paul has written, rather than representing a "revolution in the Christian understanding of the scriptures and the moral law, as though everyone up till that point thought that slavery was just fine," the modern Christian and modern Catholic condemnations of the institution represent a "ceasing of tolerance for exceptions to the natural law which had hitherto been thought intractable."[1] The change is real enough, but it looks much more like development than reversal.

Usury is a somewhat different matter. When the medieval church taught that interest-based moneylending was a grave evil, it used language not so different from that applied to sexual sins throughout the church's history. (In his *Inferno*, Dante placed usurers and sodomites in the same circle of hell.) The subsequent evolution was plainly an adaptation to pressures created by modern capitalism, it began with exceptions that look a bit like the expansive use of annulments in today's marriage controversies, and it proceeded to a point where the exceptions essentially emptied out the rule. The conservative claim to discern a continuous and consistent teaching here is weaker than on other issues, and when conservative Catholics defend the shift by arguing that the medieval church did not fully understand the science of economics, they sound a bit like contemporary liberals who argue that the church of the past did not understand the science of human sexuality.

The more consistent view is held by traditionalists who argue that the church's shift on usury is a cautionary tale, and that properly much of modern finance capitalism should be condemned as firmly as adultery. But presuming that this is unlikely to happen, usury looks like the strongest example for the liberal case that what the church once condemned firmly as an evil, it can find a way to ultimately accept.

However, in the case of usury the change was contained, sealed off from issues more central to the faith, and came in without much real resistance in the end. The shift was confirmed under otherwise conservative nineteenth-century popes, there was no major theological struggle within the church, no immediate or obvious ripple effect for other teachings, and no widespread contention among conservatives that condemning every interest-bearing loan was essential to fidelity to Christ. So while the usury debate offers ammunition for the liberalizing cause, it doesn't tell us much about what might happen when a larger constellation of teachings are all at stake and the theological battle lines are clearly drawn.

If you're looking for a case where a sustained battle *was* joined between a self-consciously conservative faction and a group of modernizers and the modernizers won, the most interesting example is suggested by the very occasional liberal swipe at Pope Francis's critics as "Jansenists." This is a reference to a theological school that flourished in seventeenth-century France, warred with that era's Jesuits, and ended up having its key institutions dissolved and some of its key theological premises officially rejected by the church. Indeed, the Jansenist-Jesuit clashes look enough like present-day debates within Catholicism that it's somewhat surprising that Pope Francis's defenders don't invoke their memory more often.

Jansenism takes its name from Cornelius Jansen (or in his native Dutch, Corneille Janssens), the bishop of Ypres in the early seventeenth century and the author of a posthumously published treatise on the thought of Saint Augustine, the *Augustinus*. His French disciples, including the tormented genius Blaise Pascal, took from him (and, they argued, from Augustine himself) a view of predestination and free will that emphasized the utter insufficiency of human effort, the deep corruption of the human soul, and the need to depend absolutely on God's unmerited and irresistible grace for both virtue and salvation. (Their perspective was effectively summarized in the title of the Polish philosopher Leszek Kolakowski's book on the controversy: *God Owes Us Nothing.*) Jansenism's critics accused these ideas of imitating Calvinism, with which the school did share some common ground. The Jansenists answered that it was simply Augustinianism, the view of the church's most ancient and greatest father, and accused the Jesuits of being Pelagians, the heresy (opposed by Augustine in his time) that claimed that human beings could achieve salvation through their own efforts alone.

This was the theological bedrock of the Jesuit-Jansenist dispute, but the conflict was much broader, having to do with the entire Catholic response to early modernity. The Jansenists were moral rigorists, foes of corruption both clerical and political, willing—like some conservative Catholics today—to accept a smaller, purer church rather than make various accommodations to humanism, commerce, and (in the Parisian context) upper-class libertinism. Like certain Calvinists they regarded a great deal of human activity as dangerous frivolity, leading souls ever more astray. Amusements, honors, luxuries, the secular arts (Jansenists penned stern condemnations of the theater), sexual pleasure—these were all dangerous snares, distractions for human beings who ought to be focused at every waking moment on the only Reality that mattered. Jansenists urged the sternest penances for sinners, the infrequent reception of communion (perfect contrition, the pure love of God rather than merely the fear of hell and its punishment, was required in their lights for a good confession), an ascetic spirit for every Christian worthy of the name. They saw themselves both returning to the spirit of the early church and building a Christianity strong enough to remain Christian amid the secularizing tendencies of the emerging modern world.

Meanwhile, the French Jesuits were, then as now, more adaptationist, preaching a Christianity that was flexible enough, merciful enough, and sufficiently aware of human weakness to shape and influence the ordinary people who liked the theater and poetry and other secular arts, who spent their days making money and their evenings spending it, who sometimes fought duels or slept with people not their spouse. They wanted to Christianize the new humanism, to baptize the emerging commercial society, not reject all of it outright. In practical terms, they wanted the church to still *matter* in a society where it no longer enjoyed medieval prerogatives and intellectual monopolies. In theological terms, they wanted to slip as many modern souls as possible into heaven even if most of them required a long, long stint in purgatory beforehand.

The Jansenists' rigor could make them rigid to the point of cruelty, whether they were consigning unbaptized infants to hell or consigning baptized children to their own ruthlessly ascetic schools. But Jesuit adaptationism could lead to a ludicrous laxism, an excuse making for sinfulness that Pascal ridiculed in his *Lettres Provinciales*. He has priests telling well-to-do adulteresses that it's licit to accept money from their paramours because their favors are certainly worth more than a prostitute's; priests telling men that they may frequent brothels so long as they have some vague intention of converting the fallen women therein; priests telling trigger-happy aristocrats that it's not murder if the man they killed had slapped them in the face; priests excusing all manner of miserliness on the grounds that we are only obligated to give to the poor from our excess, and even kings don't really have excess; and so on down an extraordinary list, which made sport of extreme cases (most Jesuits were not so lax) but did reflect at least some Jesuit advice accurately.

So the Jansenists were sometimes brutal and the Jesuits sometimes ridiculous—but they represented the poles of a crucial debate, which resembles the debate that roils the church today. Here is how Kolakowski distills it:

> [Both Jesuits and Jansenists] knew that they lived at a time when the norms of their world were being relentlessly and mercilessly undermined by the new civilization—in science, in customs, in philosophy and in art. Naturally enough, in view of the danger, each side within the Church perceived the other as enemies intra muros: the Jesuits, in the eyes of their foes, had entered into friendly negotiations with the devil and thus, whatever their true intentions, let him take his place triumphantly in the temple; the very identity of the Christian Church was thereby jeopardized and open to question. The Jansenists, in the eyes of the opposite

side, were trying to make the Church into a besieged fortress, closing their eyes to reality, losing contact with the world, depriving the church of any efficient tools to convert the pagan environment, and ultimately leading Christianity to disaster. Both were faced with an eternally recurring dilemma that never has a satisfactory solution: all concessions to the enemy are risky, but so is an intransigent attitude that allows no concessions. In this sense both were right.[2]

The debate recurs, but in institutional terms the Jesuits won its seventeenth-century round. The Holy Office, the predecessor of today's Congregation for the Doctrine of the Faith, condemned Jansen's *Augustinus* as early as 1642. Then came various truces and half-measures and political complexities that kept the controversy open and bubbling for more than half a century. Over this period the Jansenists used various ingenious arguments to explain why what seemed like formal papal rulings were actually nonbinding or incomplete or misinformed, or why propositions condemned by the papacy weren't actually in the Jansenist texts, so the condemnation wasn't binding. (The possible resemblance to contemporary conservatives explaining why *Amoris* isn't really a binding papal teaching is worth noting.) But the core of Jansenist theology, their view of the relationship between grace and the human will, was condemned consistently as tantamount to Calvinism, while what Jansenists derided as a "semi-Pelagian" idea—the view that grace is offered to all, and that we choose whether or not to cooperate with it—was defined as Catholic teaching.

By the latter decades of the controversy, the Jansenists were dealt with harshly by the church—their schools were closed, their great convent at Port-Royal was forbidden to accept new novices. In the last great moment of tension, the papal bull *Unigenitus Dei Filius* in 1713 that condemned the works of Jansenist author Pasquier Quesnel, several thousand French priests appealed for a general council that might overrule the pope—but they were a remnant, even their appeal was condemned, and Jansenism passed into church history as a heresy. (Meanwhile, the Jansenist critique of Jesuit laxity was repurposed, in one of history's many twists, as a rhetorical weapon for anticlerical revolutionaries later in that century.)

So to the extent that today's late-modern argument between Burke and Kasper, or between conservative "John Paul II Catholics" and liberal "Pope Francis Catholics"—or between the Pascals of Twitter and Father Antonio Spadaro, even—seems to echo the Jansenist-Jesuit dispute over how the church should respond to early modernity, that the Jesuits won back then might offer a precedent for how they might win today. Not because they necessarily have the more theologically decisive argument; the Jansenist exegesis of scripture was brilliant in its way and the Jansenist interpretation of Augustine's thought plausible. But because, as Kolakowski suggests, Catholicism could not have survived as a global faith along the lines the Jansenists imagined: "In the new world, full of novelty and excitement . . . Christianity had to make itself, if not 'easy,' at least much easier, in order to survive. One could not resurrect as a universal norm the ethos of the apostolic time when the faithful really lived in the shadow of imminent apocalypse. But that is precisely what the [Jansenists] tried to do—to their doom."[3]

Perhaps a similar judgment will be rendered on the rigorists of today, on Pope Francis's various conservative critics. Perhaps they will find a way to accept his changes, bending the knee as many of the Jansenists eventually did, or enduring as a beleaguered faction within the church, waiting a restoration that will never come. Perhaps there will be a small pseudo-schism, in which Catholics who reject *Amoris* and its implications end up in a position much like the Society of Saint Pius X, declaring themselves officially loyal to Rome but governing themselves and ignoring the novelties of Francis and his successors. Or else, more radically but also on a small scale, perhaps the highly unusual circumstances of Benedict's resignation and Francis's election will eventually lead to a mainstreaming of "sedevacantism" (the belief, currently held by a scattering of traditionalists, that the chair of Peter is actually vacant), producing an opportunity for a new papal election in some Avignon of Cardinal Burke's successors' choosing. Or perhaps, like Jansenism in the era of the French Revolution, today's conservative Catholicism will mutate into something new—a religious right-wing nationalism, for an age of mass migration and cultural anxiety, that folds its grievances against the Vatican into a general Euro-populism, and calls itself "Catholic" without necessarily showing up for church.

In all of these scenarios, history's likely verdict on this era in the church would be that Pope Francis had understood, as his critics do not, what the Catholic faith must accept to move forward and continue preaching Christ. Like the Jansenists before them, with their desperate quest for purity in a changing world, the "more orthodox" church of today's conservatives could only be a sect, not a universal faith, so great is the gap between our own new world and their kind of rigorism. So the faith must change, and in changing, the conservatives must diminish, and like the Jansenists before them, lose.

There are conservative Catholics whose faith is strong enough, whose theological confidence is perfect enough, to simply assume that this cannot be their future. But for those critics of Pope Francis who harbor more uncertainty about God's purposes, Kolakowski's final verdict on the Jansenists— that a form of Catholic Christianity has survived and thrived in modernity, but "it is not the Christianity that the Jansenists carried in their hearts"—is an epitaph that they might reasonably fear could someday be applied to them.[4]

But should this scenario come to pass, should the conservatives lose in today's controversy and pass into Catholic history with Cornelius Jansen and Port-Royal, it would involve a more profound shift in the self-understanding of the church than did rigorism's seventeenth-century defeat. The analogy between the two eras is fascinating but imperfect, and should today's liberal Catholicism carry the day, the differences would lead to a far greater transformation.

Consider first that the Jansenists, unlike today's conservatives, were moral rigorists but also theological rebels. As much as they protested otherwise, they were at least somewhat at odds with an existing body of church teaching, at least somewhat close to the Calvinism their foes accused them of embracing. Unlike today's conservatives, who are arguing on behalf of papal pronouncements less than half a century old and defending a larger tradition whose consistency is reasonably clear, the Jansenists were effectively going over the head of medieval Catholic tradition and the papacy to claim Augustine and the early fathers as their model. Which means that in condemning Jansen and his heirs, the popes of the seventeenth and early eighteenth centuries were in no real danger of falling into glaring self-contradiction, or undercutting their own theological authority.

It also means that when Jansenism was condemned, it did not threaten to take a much larger body of church teaching and tradition with it. That could have happened, arguably, if the church of that era had embraced the most accommodating theories of Jesuit confessors at the time. But Rome did not do that. In condemning Jansenism, the popes never came close to endorsing any of the egregious moral relativism attacked by Pascal's *Provinciales*; indeed, they specifically condemned it.

Moreover it is a slur on the Jesuits to suggest the most egregious relativism was the order's official stance or norm, especially since the seventeenth century was also the high tide of Jesuit missionary zeal, of heroism and martyrdom around the world. As much as there were Jesuits who fit Pascal's stereotype, the order as a whole sought a middle way between laxism and rigorism—and so too did the seventeenth-century papacy. If it refused the Jansenist insistence on near-perfection as the price of full communion, Rome accepted the Jansenist argument that modernity did not require suspending moral absolutes. (Which is why certain liberal Catholics have suggested that the church remained functionally Jansenist until Vatican II—or, perhaps, until Francis.) The theater and poetry, yes; adultery and prostitution and fornication, no. Running a business, yes; exploiting your workers, no. Going to confession with imperfect contrition, yes; not bothering to confess an ongoing serious sin, no.

The church after the Jansenist-Jesuit battles was sometimes seen as too easy on individual sinners; it was a frequent claim of Protestant polemic that the confessional on Sunday was an excuse for Saturday-night debauchery.

But nobody doubted the church's official clarity on moral matters, its enduring willingness to call a mortal sin a sin. And in the long arguments about papal infallibility, about whether the popes have been consistent on faith and morals across the centuries and millennia, almost nobody cites the Jansenist-Jesuit era as a period of possible papal discontinuity.

So what is happening in our own era, then, is not precisely a replay of those battles. Once again you have rigorists and laxists, conservatives and adaptationists, Jesuits on the church's left flank and their critics on the right. But each side occupies very different territory, in part because so much adaptation has taken place since then. The center of theological and cultural gravity has shifted sufficiently that what was once the "left" is now the "right"—all but the most "lax" seventeenth-century Jesuits would be strict conservatives by today's standards. And what is now the "left" is offering a vision of Catholic doctrine and pastoral practice that the papacy of the seventeenth century would almost certainly condemn as vigorously as it did the Jansenists.

After all, Cardinal Burke is not defending a Jansenist theology of grace, nor is Cardinal Sarah or Cardinal Müller arguing that most people should receive communion once a year or never, nor are most of the theologians criticizing *Amoris Laetitia* suggesting that going to the movies or reading a novel is a betrayal of the Christian life. Nor, indeed, are most of the pope's critics—some traditionalists excepted—rejecting the adaptations to modernity that the church has made *since* the days of Pascal, including all the aspects of Vatican II that the recent conservative popes, John Paul and Benedict, embraced and celebrated and maintained. They are not defending the proposition that modernity corrupts, and absolutely; they are not demanding a return to the perfectionist church of the first century; they are not even demanding a return to the rigorism of the church circa 1940. Though regularly called intransigent they have accepted a great host of reforms, a revolution in the liturgy and politics and public language of the church, and a wide array of accommodations (including, in the case of marriage and divorce, much easier annulments) to the new world that the 1960s made.

We are almost all adaptationists, in other words, in contemporary Catholic debates, and we all fall far short of the standard that was demanded by the Jansenists. Which from the liberal perspective is a crucial part of the argument for adapting further: We have come this far, and at each stage, from Pascal in the 1600s to Cardinal Ottaviani in the time of Vatican II, voices have warned that accommodation leads to ruin . . . yet Catholicism still endures.

But while there is power to this logic, it is also true that Catholicism cannot both be a ship of Theseus in which every single part can be replaced and also be the church founded by Jesus Christ, the embodiment of a perfect and eternal Godhead. And if it is the latter, if it has a changeless core, there must come a time when a given set of proposed reforms would mean not adaptation but rupture, not reading the signs of the times but surrendering to the spirit of the age. There must come a point at which the rigorists are right about what cannot be surrendered and the accommodationists are wrong. There must come a point at which the Jansenists of the right, too scrupulous and too ascetic, find their mirror image in an anti-Jansenism of the left, too worldly and self-satisfied and no less destructive in its effects upon the faith.

And there is a sense in which the worldview of Cardinal Walter Kasper does mirror the worldview of the Jansenists. The late-modern German laxist, like the early-modern French rigorists, believes that New Testament living and modern conditions are, in a deep sense, incompatible. For the Jansenists this conclusion led to a harshly antimodern perspective, a rejection of the new civilization as all frills and fripperies dressing up damnation. For the Kasperites, and the pope whom they have influenced, it leads to an acceptance of modern conditions joined to a shrugging, "what they meant was . . ." attitude toward some of the clearer words of Jesus and Saint Paul. The Christian standard is too hard to reach in the modern world, the Jansenists suggested, therefore reject the modern world. The Christian standard is too hard to reach in the modern world, Kasper has suggested, therefore we must accept that most Christians cannot reach it. The conclusion in each case is very different—but the implicit premise, that the fullness of the Christian life becomes impossible in certain contexts and amid certain particularly power-ful temptations, is basically the same.

So for all of their manifold differences, a church that once rejected Jansenism could also reject Kasperite and Bergoglian liberalism on similar grounds: for being too pessimistic about whether Christian virtue is actually within the ordinary modern person's reach.

Unless, of course, what present liberal theology proposes is not a lowering of Christian standards but the grasping, under the guidance of the Holy Spirit, of a higher Christianity than the one the church has previously taught. If we are to give the present liberal perspective its due, this possibility must be given consideration—especially since it was providentially elevated, in the midst of the Francis controversies, by one of Hollywood's greatest Catholicism-haunted filmmakers.

This was Martin Scorsese, whose adaptation of the novel *Silence*, Shu-sako Endo's story about Jesuit missionaries in seventeenth-century Japan, reached theaters around the time that the pope was conducting his bloodless cross-border aggression against the Knights of Malta. The project's connec-tion to the Francis era was intimate rather than coincidental: Scorsese had as his theological adviser Father James Martin, the popular Jesuit author and a frequent champion of papal policy; the movie was screened for Jesuits in Rome and its director welcomed in a papal audience; and the varying inter-pretations of its story soon became a synecdoche for the larger controversies of the pontificate.

That story takes place in a period of maximal Catholic suffering and cour-age: the massive persecutions visited upon the nascent Japanese church, in which thousands upon thousands of Christians, natives and missionaries alike, were put to death with the most elaborate tortures by a shogunate in-tent on ridding its islands of any Western influence. Against this backdrop the movie depicts the particular agonies of a young Portuguese Jesuit, Father Rodrigues, who travels to Japan along with a companion in search of his mentor, Father Ferreira, who had been a leading missionary but who is rumored to have apostatized under torture.

Rodrigues finds an underground church in Japan's rural villages, where he hears confessions and says mass and is concealed from the local samurai. But eventually he is betrayed into the hands of a much feared inquisitor, Inoue. He expects martyrdom, but Inoue has a much more subtle strategy in mind. He tortures and kills the fervent Christian peasants, tying them to crosses in a rising tide, dropping them from boats and burning them alive and hanging them upside down above a pit with a single cut to let their life flow out by inches. Throughout all of these barbarisms, he bids the priest watch, telling him that he can end their suffering and save their lives at any time. He need only apostatize—plant his foot upon a fumie, a sacred image of Christ, and in so doing abjure Jesus and the Catholic faith.

For a time Rodrigues holds out. But then Inoue has the missing Father Ferreira brought to him, and reveals that the older Jesuit faced the same test and decided to step on the fumie and apostatize. Ferreira tells his former student that their mission is hopeless, that the Japanese mind cannot comprehend Christianity, that the Japanese lack a distinction between the natural and the supernatural and so don't understand the concept of Jesus's divinity. He tells him that he is studying Buddhism, and that the ethical component of the two religions is basically the same—so it is a good thing to have Christianity for Europeans, and Buddhism for the Japanese. He tells him that a higher charity requires him to apostatize, that relieving suffering is more important than witnessing for the faith. "It will be the greatest act of mercy," he promises him. And then, at the last, when Rodrigues is near the breaking point, the image of Jesus on the fumie seems to speak, to tell the young priest to go ahead and plant his foot—because "it was to be trampled on by men that I was born into this world." And Rodrigues, undone, takes that step.

Is it really Jesus speaking? The film, like the book, leaves multiple possibilities open. (In both, a cock crows just after Rodrigues steps on the fumie, linking his act to Saint Peter's betrayal—but what that implies too is ambiguous.) But the answer supplied by Scorsese's official Catholic adviser, Father

Martin, was straightforward: Yes, it was Jesus, telling his priest-follower to commit what would ordinarily be the gravest of sins in order to relieve the suffering of others.

Does this seem strange, illogical, contrary to the Catholic teaching that one cannot do evil for the sake of some good end? Well, yes, Father Martin concedes. But then again he notes that many of Jesus's own acts seemed strange and illogical and even immoral at the time, including to his own disciples. Being willing to commit what is objectively a grave sin because Christ asks you to do it is not so different, he suggests, from Jesus's own willingness to submit to the crucifixion because his Father in heaven asked it of him. And this has implications for contemporary Catholic controversies, Father Martin argues:

> Some of the discussion surrounding this movie may even reflect the debates going on inside the church today about Pope Francis' emphasis on "discernment" for people facing complicated situations, where a black-and-white approach seems inadequate. A Jesuit friend felt the essential question the movie poses is: Can we trust that God works through a person's conscience, and that God helps us discern the right path in complex situations, where the normal rules seem inadequate to the reality of the situation?[5]

The implication here is that there are effectively two levels in Christian morality—one for ordinary circumstances and one for more complex cases, cases in which the moral law seems cruel or the consequences of persisting in the ordinary sort of virtue particularly impossible to live with. Under those circumstances, the higher law of mercy kicks in: What would be wrong under the normal, everyday sort of rules becomes for those who are working on a higher level not just understandable but *what Jesus wants*. It might be something as extreme as an act of apostasy, or as commonplace as receiving communion after a second marriage. But in either case, where the moral law seems to impose too much, Jesus does not want you to suffer indefinitely. He wants to take the weight of the impossible choice, for his yoke is easy and his burden light.

This idea is thrown into particular relief by the stakes in *Silence*, but in a not much subtler form it recurs throughout the papal rhetoric of the Francis era. There is the law, the pope and his allies and champions constantly suggest, and the law matters—but to insist on it too forcefully is to be as the Pharisees were, rather than to imitate Jesus Christ. Those "doctors of the law," to borrow from a representative papal sermon, did not "consider people's lives but only their own rules of laws and words," whereas Jesus was constantly willing to "go beyond the law, the letter," in the service of human needs.[6] Whenever the religious law of his time seemed to impose needless suffering, he acted to lift the burden and relieve the suffering—healing on the Sabbath, embracing the unclean, sweeping away dietary regulations and other rituals that made people believe themselves defiled. And when confronted with people suffering under its own laws, the church that Jesus founded should do the same. Just as Jesus transcended Jewish legalism, Catholicism under Pope Francis must transcend its own legalities for the sake of a higher Christianity.

When it is his admirers rather than the pope himself making this argument, there is often a strong direct identification between Francis and Jesus himself. Like Christ in the gospels the pope is now the one calling the faithful to "conversion," in the words of a 2017 editorial in *L'Osservatore Romano*, the Vatican newspaper, which accused "many" priests and bishops of imitating "the Sanhedrin" instead of being Francis's/Christ's disciples, of clinging to their "devotion to the past" but ignoring the revelation in their midst.[7]

Perhaps this close identification between the pope and the Son of God is just natural enthusiasm carried a little bit too far. But at the very least Francis's admirers clearly believe that his efforts to change the church, no less than his vivid public gestures, are an *imitatio Christi* for our times—demonstrating that just as Jesus set mercy and forgiveness and the relief of suffering above the law, so must his contemporary disciples, and accept that what we think of as "Christian morality" is sometimes not the Christian thing to do.

This idea is powerful. But it is not an idea to be found anywhere in the traditional teachings of the church; it is an idea, indeed, that the church has confronted in various forms across the centuries and rejected—whether in the form of Roman-era Gnosticism or in medieval visions of a "church of the spirit" finally set free from law and hierarchy or in the 1960s-era death-of-God theology. And not just rejected out of fidelity to its own prized moral system, its natural law theories and complicated philosophical architecture. It has been rejected out of fidelity to the New Testament, the gospels, the words of Jesus.

To read the gospels, to reenter their world, is to find a Jesus whose anger at legalism is directed against the *ritual* law of first-century Judaism—the rules related to purity, diet, Sabbath observance, and so on, all of which he insists can and must give way in the name of mercy, healing, encounter, love. But the moral law, the Ten Commandments and their corollaries, Jesus never qualifies or relativizes. He never suggests that there exists some shades-of-gray world in which apostasy or adultery (or fraud or murder or theft or gluttony or any other sin) are actually part of God's complicated plan. Instead he heightens moral demands—urging purity of heart as well as purity of action, proposing a more sweeping rule of charity toward the poor, a more sweeping warning against the temptations of great wealth, and a more exalted view of sex and marriage.

Meanwhile, he often condemns the Jewish traditionalists and legalists of his time not because they are simplistic or harsh in their moral demands, but because their ritualism obscures the clarity of the moral law, or turns the law into a too clever means for people to avoid their clear moral obligations. Consider, for instance, this passage from Matthew's gospel—the first half famous, the second more obscure:

> And the Pharisees and the scribes asked him, "Why do your disciples not walk according to the tradition of the elders, but eat with defiled hands?"
> And he said to them, "Well did Isaiah prophesy of you hypocrites, as it is written,

'This people honors me with their lips,

but their heart is far from me;

in vain do they worship me,

teaching as doctrines the commandments of men.'

You leave the commandment of God and hold to the tradition of men."

And he said to them, "You have a fine way of rejecting the commandment of God in order to establish your tradition! For Moses said, 'Honor your father and your mother'; and, 'Whoever reviles father or mother must surely die.' But you say, 'If a man tells his father or his mother, "Whatever you would have gained from me is Corban"' (that is, given to God)—then you no longer permit him to do anything for his father or mother, thus making void the word of God by your tradition that you have handed down.[8]

The passage begins with Jesus rejecting a dead conservatism, in a very Francis-like style. But then he swiftly pivots to chastising the Pharisees on moralistic grounds, warning them that an absolute moral obligation—to support one's parents in their old age—cannot be undone through some sophisticated legalism, some clever scheme in which the duty to honor your father and mother gets fulfilled through religious donations instead.

It's a discourse that parallels his more famous discourse on marriage and adultery. There too it is precisely the allowance for divorce that he attacks as a legalism and a human tradition, which is superseded by the intent of God's creation and the clarity of God's law. In both cases, legalism is rejected because it relativizes morality, not because it makes the moral law too stringent. And while there are many moments, just as Father Martin says, where Jesus does something or asks something that leaves his disciples confused, there is never a moment where he asks them to do something that violates the Ten Commandments for the sake of a higher or more complicated or nuanced moral vision.

This doesn't mean that Jesus's mercy isn't absolute. It is more absolute, indeed, than Jewish law: The repentant sinner must be forgiven not seven times but seventy times seven, which is to say perpetually. But this absolute mercy is always linked to repentance; it is never deployed to supersede the Commandments, never used to suggest that they are too simplistic for dealing with the complexities of human situations, or that there is a landscape beyond or above them where the law does not apply.

Jesus doesn't urge Peter to "go ahead, betray me, I understand." Jesus doesn't tell the woman taken in adultery, "go back to your lover, because your situation is complex." Jesus doesn't tell Zacchaeus the tax collector, "actually, keep the money you may have unjustly taken, because you need it to support your family." Jesus dines with sinners, he hangs out with prostitutes and publicans, he evangelizes the much married Samaritan woman, he welcomes thieves into eternity. But he never confirms them in their sins, or makes nuanced allowances for their state of life; that sort of rhetoric is alien to the gospels. The ritual law—yes, that can and must be superseded. But the moral law—no, that is bedrock.

This is not some complicated esoteric reading of the New Testament; it is the boringly literal and obvious one, which is why it takes a professional theologian to dispute it. And this is why, in the end, it is justifiable to call the Francis moment a potentially revolutionary one in the life and history of the church. The reforms of Vatican II were dramatic, but what they changed was mostly aspects of church life and Catholic teaching that stand at one remove, one extrapolation if not more, from the words of Jesus of Nazareth. There is nothing in the gospels about whether the mass should be in Latin and exactly which prayers it should include, nothing about whether the church should necessarily prefer one sort of government to another. Some Vatican II shifts and reforms and changes might have been mistaken, they might have tended to weaken Catholic belief in more essential things. But nobody who defended them was required to argue that they proceeded from a higher understanding of Christian morality than the one supplied by Matthew, Mark, Luke, and John. Nobody had to go all the way to where the death of God theology ended up, around the same era as Vatican II—to the idea that in some sense Christianity "must will its own death" to fulfill its mission, that the destiny of the true Christian is to abandon all authority, all certainty, even about the commandments of Jesus Christ himself.

Yet this is where Francis-era liberal Catholicism has so often ended up— in arguments that imply that the church must use Jesus to go beyond Jesus, as it were, using his approach to the ritual law as a means to evade or qualify the moral law, which means essentially evading or qualifying his own ex- plicit commandments, and declaring them a pharisaism that the late-modern church should traffic in no more. To fulfill Jesus's mission, to follow the Jesus of faith, even the Jesus of Scripture must be left behind.

While this is pitched as mercy, as a more perfect fulfillment of God's love, its effective Hegelianism—its vision of a church evolving toward a higher morality over time—implies something very strange about Jesus and, indeed, about God himself. Because if there is a higher morality than the stark commandments of the Decalogue, if there is a more sophisticated form of mercy than the literal words of Jesus seem to offer, then one wonders why could it not have been offered two thousand years ago rather than being left to discovery by the adepts of the twenty-first century anno Domini? It is not as if first-century Jews and Greeks were unfamiliar with the understandable and very human reasons why a man or woman might want to marry twice (or enter a same-sex relationship or practice polygamy), any more than the early Christians were unfamiliar with all the understandable reasons why a perse- cuted believer might apostatize. Why couldn't Jesus, so confident in over- turning traditions and scandalizing audiences, give us some scriptural hint that sometimes committing what seems objectively like a sin is fine, or even necessary for the higher good? Why leave us to labor for two thousand years with the idea that taking up the cross requires accepting suffering, sometimes extraordinary suffering, if the truth is that there is no need to even abstain from communion when you break the moral law?

If God wills the suspension of his own law when things get particularly difficult or complicated, whenever too much emotional or physical suffering would be imposed, from the point of view of every Christian who ever suffered or even died for the sake of their hardest passages, the gospels look less like a revelation than a somewhat cruel trick. And just as it is difficult to maintain an ideological regime once you decide that the ideology has been misleading people on various essential points, the idea that Catholicism can thrive by embracing a theory that makes the gospels' moral vision at best incomplete, at worst actively cruel, and the church's historical interpretation a further cruelty needlessly imposed . . . well, let us call that theory unduly optimistic.

One of the striking aspects of Catholic life is the thread that runs backward through time and culture—through novels, poetry, essays, devotional literature, and the wider arts—linking the experiences of believers across two thousand years. Of course ideas change, cultures change, and the experience of Catholic culture today is necessarily different from the experience of believers a century or a millennium before. But not entirely so: Read John Henry Newman and Thomas Aquinas and Augustine back to back to back, or read Evelyn Waugh and Dante together, or read Teresa of Ávila and then Thérèse of Lisieux. In each case the gulf of years and difference in cultural expression does not obscure the fact that they belong to the same tradition, the same story, and that there are ways in which Catholic Christianity really is a time machine: You can step into those worlds, the worlds of the Catholic past, find your footing and realize that you are not somewhere altogether alien; that the past is another country but also somehow yours; you can in some sense think *with* the letter writers of the New Testament and the church father scribbling in late antiquity and the medieval monk in the north of England and the Florentine poet and the philosopher-nun dealing with hapless popes and the mystic in Spain and the philosopher-martyr in Henry VIII's court and thence back around to the saints and novelists and polemicists of the modern world.

But this is not the case with the church that seems to be imagined by the reformers of the Francis era. The Jesuits from the era in which Scorsese's *Silence* is set, the men who either died for the faith or apostatized only under the most horrible of torture, would not recognize the moral theory under which some of today's Catholics justify apostasy. The popes who condemned Jansenism would, under the theories now current in the Vatican, look like Jansenists themselves. In the Walter Kasper vision, Saint Thomas More becomes a Pharisee, the Council of Trent an exercise in misguided zealotry, the church's ancient elevation of celibacy a needless imposition on the ordinary Christian. The implicit logic of *Amoris Laetitia* would make much of Catholic literature incomprehensibly strange: Whether in the pages of Waugh or Graham Greene or Sigrid Undset, all the characters struggling with the tension between their personal lives and their Catholicism become neurotics in need of reassurance, not sinners wrestling with grace. And if the Diocese of San Diego's rhetoric on marriage eventually becomes the Catholic standard, then every papal document on marriage, family, and morality written prior to 1965, or 1981, or 2013 would become a dispatch from an alien religion, with a cruel demiurge masquerading as its god.

What I'm suggesting here sounds extreme, and perhaps it is. Perhaps this fear of auto-demolition is like the fears of Jansenists four hundred years ago, and eventually it will be clear that Catholic Christianity *can* synthesize the vision of Walter Kasper with two thousand years of Catholic history, that the liberal vision and the core of New Testament morality are far more compatible than my journalist's analysis implies. I am sure that most of Pope Francis's admirers sincerely believe this to be true. I am aware that they may be proven right.

But their confidence still seems misplaced, the tension between their higher Christianity and historical Catholicism much more overt and devastating than they concede—and thus the likelihood of crisis, breakage, schism far too high to justify their blithe assumptions about inevitable continuity. The church has broken in the past, not once but many times, over tensions and issues that did not cut as deeply as the questions that undergird today's Catholic debates. Other communions have divided very recently over precisely the issues that the pope has pressed to the front of Catholic debates.

And for good reason: Because these issues, while superficially "just" about sexuality or church discipline, actually cut very deep—to the very bones of Christianity, the very words of Jesus Christ.

Eleven

THE FRANCIS LEGACY

At the beginning of 2017, after the *dubia* and the pope's annexation of the Knights of Malta, HBO premiered a new hour-long Sunday drama entitled *The Young Pope*. During the John Paul II and Benedict eras it would have been easy enough to predict what a pop cultural treatment of a youthful American pope would look like. From 1979's *The Vicar of Christ*, Walter F. Murphy's bestseller about an American-born "Pope Francesco" who is assassinated when he launches a crusade for pacifism, to the priest-novelist Andrew M. Greeley's 1996 novel *White Smoke*, in which two wily Irish American prelates ensure the election of a modernizing Spanish cardinal, the idea of a liberal pope who sets out to bring sweeping change to Catholicism has long been tinder for artistic imaginations. It nearly was again in 2012, when Showtime shot a pilot for a series called *The Vatican*, in which Kyle Chandler (most famous for embodying Coach Taylor from *Friday Night Lights*) played a rising-star New York cardinal with progressive views—only to have the network spike the show, perhaps feeling overtaken by events, ten months after Pope Benedict resigned.

But *The Young Pope* was something else. The work of the Italian film-maker Paolo Sorrentino, a gifted visual stylist and not a practicing Catholic, it was inspired by a comment someone in the Vatican reportedly made to its creator, to the effect that Francis's successor could well be a reactionary. From that idea Sorrentino invented Lenny Belardo, a New York kid abandoned by hippie parents and raised by the tough nun Sister Mary (played by Diane Keaton) who grows up to look like Jude Law (who plays him), become a priest and then a bishop and a cardinal, and get elected—somehow, no one seems sure how—as the youngest pope of modern times.

As pontiff he turns out to be some strange combination of cynic, saint, and supervillain. But whatever he is, he is not a liberal: He takes the name Pius XIII, dons sumptuous vestments and red shoes, buys back and wears the papal tiara, celebrates mass *ad orientem* ("the liturgy will no longer be a social engagement," he decrees), rejects the papal cult and refuses to make public appearances, and declares that henceforward the church will not accommodate to the world, but will instead retreat back into a glorious mysteriousness—while demanding not lukewarm affection, not mere loyalty, but fanaticism from its faithful.

He also drinks Cherry Cokes and chain-smokes, terrorizes liberal cardinals and evades their counterplots, winks at the camera and alternates between outrageous hubris and paralyzing self-doubt. Which is to say that the show does not have a clear theological program: It traffics in various blasphemies along with the inevitable-for-HBO nudity, occasionally displays a gross ignorance of Catholicism, and offers a studiously ambiguous verdict on its protagonist. But it does have an insinuating implication—that the old-time form of Catholic faith is more fascinating, more transfixing, and more charged with divinity than the various attempts to update Catholicism for a more disenchanted age.

The Young Pope was a hit in Sorrentino's Italy, and it did well on HBO. Its most ardent partisans, though, often seemed to be young, conservative-leaning

Catholics with social media accounts. For them it seemed to be at once a form of escapism and a resonant acknowledgment of one of the Francis era's strange unstated truths: that the struggle for the future of Catholicism might be generational, but not in the way we are conditioned to expect, with the young as a liberal vanguard and the older generation hunkered in resistance. Instead Pope Francis and his progressive allies belong to an older generation of Catholics that in its youth was revolutionary, and now in its twilight has been given a chance to carry the revolution forward.

The question facing the church is whether the next generation, Francis's inheritors, will actually want to carry the same revolution forward in their turn—or whether, like Lenny Belardo's Pius XIII, they might tire of a church that assumes liberal modernity is as permanent as Catholicism itself, and might yearn for the tiara once again.

The immediate prospects for such a restoration, admittedly, do seem somewhat dim. Soon after *The Young Pope* wound up its first season, several of the real pope's more conservative opponents were abruptly ushered off the Roman stage. The first to go was Cardinal George Pell, who was summoned to his native Australia to face charges of sexual abuse. Often a lightning rod during his years as Sydney's archbishop, Pell had been accused of abuse years before and cleared, and his defenders were vehement that the new case was a put-up job, involving dubious accusations plus prosecutorial overreach in a society increasingly secular and hostile to Pell's version of the faith. But such certainty had been proven wrong too often in the past to instill confidence. The most one could say was Pell's trial would be a dramatic culmination either way—a last Vatican scandal to pile atop the mountain of clerical sins, or proof that the abuse scandal had left the church hopelessly vulnerable to anti-Catholic attacks.

The next to depart was Gerhard Müller from the Congregation for the Doctrine of the Faith. The German cardinal had walked a tightrope on *Amoris Laetitia*, insisting in interviews and writings that it did not change church teaching on remarriage and the sacraments, critiquing those bishops who moved to sweepingly welcome the remarried to communion, refusing to acknowledge evidence that the pope agreed with them and not with him—while also looking for ways to reconcile the competing positions, to find exceptional cases where a remarried person might be able to return while also insisting that such exceptions were self-limiting. (He would later write an introduction for a book by Rocco Buttiglione, the John Paul II confidant who argued for continuity between Francis and his predecessor.)

Müller's hope seemed to be that by simply remaining in his office he could mitigate or suppress the theological crisis. But then his five-year term expired, and though such terms are generally renewed at least once (and Müller was not old) he was ushered into retirement, and in such a brusque manner that the highly circumspect German cardinal aired his grievances in the press. Francis "did not give a reason," he complained. "As a bishop, one cannot treat people in this way." [1]

The real reason, or one of them, seemed to be that Francis blamed him for the *dubia* even though he hadn't been a signatory—and indeed, one of the phone calls Müller made after his firing was to one of the four *dubia* cardinals, Joachim Meisner, the retired archbishop of Cologne and a longtime friend of both the cashiered CDF head and Benedict XVI. Meisner, Müller said later, "was particularly upset at the news" [2] that the pope had fired him—and the cardinal died that very night at eighty-three, passing away after falling asleep over his breviary, reducing the *dubia* signatories' numbers to just three. Two months later he was followed to the grave by Cardinal Carlo Caffarra, another signatory, leaving only Burke and Walter Brandmüller among the living.

Pope Emeritus Benedict, still very much alive, sent a personal eulogy to be read aloud at Meisner's funeral. It included this striking passage:

What particularly impressed me from my last conversations with the now passed Cardinal was the relaxed cheerfulness, the inner joy and the confidence at which he had arrived. We know that this passionate shepherd and pastor found it difficult to leave his post, especially at a time in which the Church stands in particularly pressing need of convincing shepherds who can resist the dictatorship of the spirit of the age and who live and think the faith with determination. However, what moved me all the more was that, in this last period of his life, he learned to let go and to live out of a deep conviction that the Lord does not abandon His Church, even if the boat has taken on so much water as to be on the verge of capsizing.[3]

That last line was quickly interpreted by both allies and critics of Pope Francis as a swipe at Francis's papacy. The pope's allies speculated on who had really written it (presuming that Benedict was senile and malleable); the critics cited it as Benedict's implicit endorsement of the *dubia*. Both theories were dismissed as a "fantasy" and the work of "stupid people"[4] by the pope emeritus's personal secretary, and indeed, it was true that the image of the church as a beleaguered boat was a recurring one in Benedict's writings. At the same time, reaching for such an image at this particular moment, at a funeral for a man who had come close to accusing Benedict's successor of heresy—well, it did not feel like the most ringing endorsement of the pontificate of Francis.

But neither did it call for rebellion or resistance, or hint at any regret for Benedict's own fateful choice. Instead its major chord was a kind of faithful resignation, tinged with self-justification. *In this last period of his life, he learned to let go and to live out of a deep conviction that the Lord does not abandon His Church . . .* this was a description of Joachim Meisner, but also surely of Joseph Ratzinger, who had retired in confidence and then watched his successor set about dismantling his legacy. And if it implied a message to Francis's open critics, it was one of patience, trust, and prayer. If the conservatives were ultimately right about the controversies of the Francis era, then by their own premises their vindication was already somehow prepared—in God's time, not man's. In the meantime, their own powers were obviously insufficient—because Francis was pope, and they were not.

After Pell's clouded departure and Müller's firing and the two *dubia* cardinals' deaths, this insufficiency seemed like the hard truth for the opposition.

Conservative resistance had won the battles of the synods, but the pope's other powers were not subject to vote, and he could still use them to effectively boil the frog with conservative opponents, taking small step after small step to instantiate a liberal reading of *Amoris*, none of them decisive enough to provoke a crisis but each one bringing the church closer to officially teaching what he had desired from the synod and been denied. A move he made shortly after Meisner and Caffarra passed away was an example: In a kind of backhanded answer to the *dubia*, the pontiff ordered his "private" letter endorsing the Argentine bishops' cautious opening to the communion for the remarried published in the *Acta Apostolicae Sedis*, the official "Acts of the Holy See." The publication gave the letter some magisterial weight, and his critics and defenders immediately fell to squabbling over how much—but meanwhile the modesty of the step meant that few in the conservative wing of the hierarchy were prepared to publicly oppose it. Thus the pope's agenda advanced by degrees, and the conservative position weakened—all without an obvious crisis point where a great mass of conservative cardinals and bishops would be obliged to join hands with Raymond Burke and issue some kind of formal, schism-threatening rebuke. (A group of traditionalist theologians and clergy did issue a "filial correction" of Francis in early autumn of 2017, but its small media splash did not provoke any follow-up from within the hierarchy.)

Then, too, there was the pope's power to make appointments and shape his own succession. Francis was an old man but not obviously declining, and were he to reign for five more years, still more of his remaining critics in the College of Cardinals could be effectively retired, many troublesome bishops replaced or "promoted" out of influence, and more conservative-leaning Catholic institutions neutered or remade. And then should he be succeeded by a similarly inclined successor—perhaps a liberal "young pope," elected to confirm the Francis revolution—the space for further alteration could widen even more. Francis's pontificate would be interpreted as proof that the limits on papal action that seemed to make prisoners of his predecessors were not nearly as binding as they seemed. With those limits weakened, the papal office would carry with it a more sweeping power, and it would be in the hands of the current pope's disciples, with many obstacles that he had faced cleared away.

Not that such a successor would lack for opposition if he sought to push the liberal project further. But for all the words that can be written (and this book has written many) about the theological problems facing innovators, it is harder to tell a straightforward institutional story about how the conservative side of the Catholic argument could successfully block reforms imposed by a papacy increasingly in tune with liberal Catholicism's hopes and plans. The past precedents, ancient and medieval, show how orthodoxy can win out when a pope is indecisive or flirts with heresy. But in none of them did a faction that the church now considers heretical take full control of the highest reaches of the church, and in several of them a secular power—a Roman emperor, a French king—actively helped settle the debate in what we now call orthodoxy's favor. What power could conceivably play that role, if a Pope Francis II or a John XXIV announces new developments of doctrine, further steps toward an Episcopalian future for the church?

There is a historical irony here. It was conservative Catholics who backed the strongest possible understanding of papal authority—first in the controversies of the late nineteenth century and again following Vatican II— as an essential bulwark against liberal currents in religion. There were doubters, among them John Henry Newman, who wondered if placing too much of a stress on the papacy's importance as a guarantor of orthodoxy threatened to obscure the higher importance of, well, orthodoxy itself. The doubters did not anticipate, or not exactly, a moment such as this, but some of their caution does seem vindicated by the Francis era—by the ease with which a rhetoric of "being in unity with Peter" and obeying "the Pope, this Pope, this present Pope" can be used to justify reversal of prior teaching, by the speed with which liberals who once complained about the papal authoritarianism of John Paul II have switched to complaining about the un-Catholic disloyalty of conservative "dissenters" from the papal line, and by the difficulties that Francis's critics have faced in persuading the average Catholic that the pope might somehow be a danger to the church.

If more average Catholics can't be so persuaded, can the Francis revolution really be resisted? To imagine a future in which it succeeds, one need only extrapolate some of the institutional patterns of his pontificate forward: His appointees continue to fill in the highest ranks within the church and his critics age and retire and die; his approach to remarriage and communion is accepted as a legitimate development of doctrine because after a time there are no Burkes or Sarahs to contest it; there is no rebellion in the pews because enough Catholics are either liberal or indifferent or conditioned to accept whatever the pope has handed down . . . and finally conservative resisters, like similarly situated believers in certain Protestant denominations, either depart for some schismatic alternative or remain as an unhappy church-within-the-church, noisy and grumbling but sidelined and irrelevant.

So by staying alive and forging ahead, in this analysis, the man who was Jorge Bergoglio can ensure that the future of Catholicism will be progressive, liberal, *new*—whatever that may ultimately mean.

But history is never so straightforward as this. The Francis era has made conservative overconfidence of the John Paul II era look foolish in hindsight. But it hasn't made liberal confidence look justified, or at least not yet. Francis is powerful and popular, but in reviving the spirit of 1970s Catholicism he has solved none of the problems that have bedeviled liberal strains in Christianity for the last two generations.

The main challenge for the present pope's legacy is that five years into his pontificate the much discussed "Francis effect" seems to be largely a media phenomenon, a shift in how the papacy is perceived by outsiders rather than an actual revival of enthusiasm within the church. There is no evidence beyond the anecdotal that a liberalizing pontificate is actually bringing the lapsed back to faith, increasing mass going, inspiring new vocations, or otherwise ushering in the great progressive renewal that John Paul allegedly choked off.

Instead, the only (spotty) evidence points the other way. Mass attendance in the United States is flat since Francis's election; among younger Catholics religious observances have modestly dropped off.[5] Record numbers of Italian Catholics took steps to disaffiliate from the church in 2015.[6] In Brazil the decline of Catholic numbers steepened in the Francis era, with 9 million fewer Brazilians identifying as Catholics in 2016 than just two years before.[7] Likewise Australia: What had been a gentle decline in Catholic identification under John Paul and Benedict has accelerated in the 2010s.[8] Worldwide, seminary enrollment went down in each of the first few years of Francis's pontificate, after seeing (small) annual increases up until 2011 under Benedict.[9] In Rome itself, the numbers for pilgrimages and papal audiences are down from the Benedict years, notwithstanding the boost from Francis's Jubilee Year of Mercy.[10]

These are short-term trends, and most of them cannot be plausibly blamed on the pope. It will be decades before we can look at any "Francis effect" in full and assess its consequences for Catholic practice and belief, and even then placing too much emphasis on the papacy would be unreasonable, given the limits on its power and the swamping influence of cultural and demographic effects.

But they are evidence against the frequent suggestion from Francis's admirers that his attempted renewal will rescue and revive the faith. Indeed, given the disappointing experience of 1970s Catholicism, and the strong historical correlation between progressive theology and institutional decline, the burden of proof is on the liberalizers to show that *this time things are different.* So far they cannot: Under Francis there is no break with the patterns that made liberal Catholicism seem moribund before his surprise election, no sign that this time, under this pope, liberalization will be a path to expansion rather than decline.

Meanwhile, it remains the case that the younger generation of Catholic priests is more conservative than its elders, which in an institution built around sacramental life and run by clerics creates obvious long-term difficulties for progressives. These are problems of which Francis seems well aware, since his sermons against rigidity and clericalism and ritualism so often cast younger priests in an unflattering light—as merciless hellfire preachers one day, as swishy liturgy snobs the next. His Vatican has been very eager to investigate and scrutinize growing traditionalist orders, and in an audience in early 2017 he remarked that "when they tell me that there is a congregation that draws so many vocations, I must confess that I worry"[11]—a reference, presumably, to the unhappy history of the Legionaries of Christ and its sociopathic founder, but also a very strange way for a pope to phrase things. HBO's saturno-sporting Pius XIII sometimes seems like the specter that haunts the present pope, as though he senses that his liberalization project is in a race against time, that young conservatives in the clergy could come along and undo all his work.

That fear is understandable, because if it is difficult to see exactly how conservative Catholics could resist a progressive pope and hierarchy, it is equally difficult to see how the progressive faction can sustain its vision of Catholicism in the long term if it is not reproducing itself within the priesthood and religious life in greater numbers than today. Liberal Catholicism's difficulty, now as forty years ago, is that it has the most appeal to Catholics with the loosest connections to the church, and its appeal weakens as the intensity of commitment increases. This means it can do well in opinion polls of all Catholics, well enough in polls of churchgoers . . . and still fail to generate the level of commitment that induces men and women to give their lives in service to the faith.

Consider, as a particularly striking case, the situation in France, where the aging of the Catholic clergy is proceeding at a particularly brisk clip. But not all the clergy: When you include both the Society of Saint Pius X and the traditionalist orders in full communion with the church, the number of French priests associated with the Latin Mass is growing steadily, fast enough that if current trends continue there will be more traditionalist (not merely John Paul II–esque conservative) French clergy in 2040 than priests in the diocesan clergy and other religious orders.[12] Meanwhile, the clergy shortage is also leading the French church to import priests from Africa—hundreds and hundreds every year—who likewise lean theologically conservative (though not liturgically so, or not yet). So in one of the key countries in liberal Catholicism's heartland, Western Europe, the future of the Catholic clergy looks more Burkean or Sarahesque than Kasperite . . . which does not necessarily seem to promise a near-future landscape in which a liberal Vatican can simply impose a progressive vision on the church.

Next, consider Africa itself, whose Christians have resisted liberalizing tendencies within Protestant bodies (global Anglicanism, the United Methodists) and whose Catholic bishops provided the firmest resistance to the German party at the last two synods. In the post-*Amoris* landscape, African churchmen, with the partial exception of Cardinal Sarah, have mostly been silent rather than active, avoiding direct conflict with the pope, and leaving it to Western bishops to stake out specific interpretations of the papal teaching. But the consensus African position is clearly conservative. When various African theologians and bishops showed up in Rome in early 2017 for a conference on the continent's theology, the main organizer, Father Paulinus Odozor of Nigeria and the University of Notre Dame, preempted questions about the *dubia* with a two-step move. He first suggested that the West was too obsessed with the divorce-communion question and was ignoring the "incredible richness" in the other portions of *Amoris*. Second, on the question of the remarried receiving communion, he kept it short: "We settled that long ago. They can't." [13]

Right now Africa's conservatism still belongs to the church's peripheries. The Catholic population of Africa is still smaller than the (nominally) Catholic population of Europe—220 million versus 280 million[14]—and Africans are even more underrepresented in the hierarchy than that difference would imply. But if present demographic trends continue, in 2040 there will be *460 million* African Catholics, while the Catholic population of Europe will have shrunk, leaving it barely over half the size of the African church.[15] Meanwhile, African mass attendance is presently close to 70 percent; mass attendance in Europe in 20 percent, and lower still in Western European countries.[16]

So no matter how liberal the next pope, how practical will it be for theologians and liberal prelates from Germany and Italy and Belgium to set the agenda for the church a generation hence, if the African church is larger and its members considerably more active and devout? Suppose that the Francis-stacked College of Cardinals elects a like-minded successor, and another after that: Can the institutional power of the papacy really be sufficient to override such a stark shift in numbers, such a wide gap in religious intensity, if the Africa of 2040 still prefers the Catholicism of Cardinal Sarah to the Catholicism of Cardinal Kasper?

Now of course not every African Catholic leader agrees with Sarah or Father Odozor, and with time African Catholicism might change, might follow the same path as Germany and the Low Countries, if growth and modernization and shifting sexual mores lead to secularization. The liberal Cardinal Danneels of Belgium, in a 2015 interview, imagined exactly that— acknowledging that "European churches have been overrun by the effects of secularization that have also led to rising individualism," but suggesting that "this very individualism could reach Africa sooner or later. . . . It is possible that the crisis we have had will spread there too, with all that this entails. Africans may also experience a situation similar to ours. Then they might call us up to see how we dealt with it. To get some useful tips." [17]

But it is also easy, in an age of resurgent nationalism and civilizational tensions, to imagine African Christianity continuing to define itself against European styles of theological liberalism for the same reasons that African nations and thinkers might define themselves against the liberal West's political and economic power. In the past conservative forms of Catholicism often flourished for centuries in societies that felt themselves exploited and oppressed (Ireland, Quebec, Poland, and others). If a more liberal Catholicism is understood as the faith of moneyed Westerners and European church bureaucrats, it is difficult to see it taking root south of the Mediterranean absent massive political and economic transformations—which may come, but not on any predictable timetable.

The same might be true within Europe itself, where the more conservative Catholic churches are in Eastern European nations—Poland and

Hungary, especially—that are wary of a German-dominated European Union and its secular-cosmopolitan ruling class. Will Polish Catholics be easily won to a liberal Catholicism that seems identified with the same cosmopolitan project, with German ideas and influence and money? And if not, the question recurs—how easily could a progressive-run Vatican impose its vision on their churches?

Framed this way, the real Francis legacy might be less a swiftly unfolding progressive revolution than a new impasse. He could leave liberal Catholicism with control of the most important levers of power within the church—but without having solved its long-standing manpower-and-enthusiasm problem. There might be fewer cardinals equipped to stop his would-be heirs—but also too few priests enthusiastic about following them. There might be a clear institutional path to a continuing liberal revolution, but at the same time good reasons for liberals in the hierarchy to tread carefully, to avoid chasing innovations to their logical (and desired) conclusions, to simply maintain a studious ambiguity as a default style for liberal pontificates.

This is, sometimes, what Francis himself has seemed to be aiming at with his footnotes and fraught silences—a legacy of theological liberalism in effective power, but with enough room left for theological conservatives (including all those "rigid" priests he dislikes but whom the church obviously needs) to feel like their understanding of Catholicism still has life. But as we have seen just in the two years since *Amoris* was published, this kind of truce is difficult to sustain. The old truce worked, sort of, because both sides thought of themselves as playing a long game: Conservatives had a (complacent) confidence that papal authority would gradually overcome dissent, and liberals accepted that they would not enjoy power for the foreseeable future, which meant that it almost didn't matter what happened in Rome day to day, because when the necessary changes came, all of the mistakes of the John Paul era would be swept away together.

Under the new truce, though, the day-to-day stakes for conservatives are much higher—with more popes like Francis, Catholic truth will stand on a knife's edge—and the promise for liberals much more immediate and tempting and hard to resist pursuing further. That seems to be the attitude of many people around Francis, his intellectual intimates and kitchen cabinet and tweeting Jesuit apologists, who often seem much more eager than the pope himself to forge ahead on multiple fronts. This is hubristic in one sense but completely understandable in another: If you believe that the church's traditional teachings are cruel and unmerciful and pharisaical, then there is a strong moral case against delaying changing them. Especially since the kind of twilit terrain created by *Amoris Laetitia* risks leaving reformers in a kind of late-Soviet position—maintaining an official pretense that the old dogmas are still in force while sending constant signals to anyone with eyes and ears that they don't believe in them. This model didn't work for Gorbachev for very long, and Francis's successors may decide that his example makes a case for hastening the revolution forward, cries of "heresy" be damned.

Such has been the pattern in most Protestant communions where liberal theology has gained a permanent institutional advantage. The Lutheran-turned-Catholic priest-intellectual Richard John Neuhaus's quip that "where orthodoxy is optional, orthodoxy will sooner or later be proscribed" isn't always accurate, but overall liberal Christianity has not been notably more tolerant in power than the conservatism that it overthrew—even in the Anglican communion, where ambiguity on doctrine is practically written into the church's DNA. Even under Francis, for that matter, despite all the talk of dialogue and mercy: Across 2017, criticism of *Amoris Laetitia* got the eminent Catholic philosopher Josef Seifert dismissed from his specially created chair at the International Academy of Philosophy in Granada, Spain; an open letter critical of the pope got the eminent American theologian Father Thomas Weinandy dismissed from a position with the United States Conference of Catholic Bishops; and around the world conservative academics and priests complained of what one described, in England's conservative-leaning *Catholic Herald*, as "a toxic atmosphere of intimidation"[18] around the remarriage-and-communion debates.

Again, there are understandable reasons why liberals once in power would move to limit conservative dissent. Once you have persuaded yourself that a given reform is *what the Holy Spirit wants*, the toleration of conservatives who want to fence or cage the Spirit is no virtue, and rolling over their resistance is no vice. In theory the twilight may seem clever, but how long can you tell people that their intimate choices are to be tolerated but not blessed, accepted but not celebrated—or accepted by one parish but not by another, by this bishop but not by that one? Jesus's admonition to be hot or cold but not lukewarm applies here: If a second marriage or a same-sex partnership (or, for that matter, a physician-assisted death or a biotechnology-assisted reproduction) isn't really sinful but just sort-of not-ideal, the desire for a blessing will be pressing, powerful, and ultimately inexorable.

Moreover, even if an empowered progressive Catholicism could resist forging ahead with its program, some of the trends noted above may force its hand. That is, if liberal Catholicism isn't generating the vocations required to run parishes or keeping the numbers of believers in the pews required to maintain the larger Western Catholic apparatus, if the youthful priesthood is not only smaller but conservative and traditionalist, the future of a liberal church will depend on radical revisions in liturgy and practice. Abandoning a priest-centered sacramental life, embracing lay-led worship as a norm rather than an exception, finding ways to unite with liberal Lutherans and Anglicans not just in prayer but in actual ecclesial communion—these are all steps that might seem not only desirable but necessary to a Catholic hierarchy whose theological liberalism places it at odds with a large part of its own clergy. (Lay-led, priestless parishes are already on the German bishops' agenda.) If the choice is either taking radical steps toward unity with Protestantism or ceding the future to a younger cadre of conservative priests, the pressure for the first option may seem irresistible.

And it may be stronger still if that younger cadre swings further to the theological right, abandoning the terrain of John Paul II Catholicism—with its acceptance of the new mass, its embrace of the ecumenical spirit, its assumption that liberal democracy and the church are basically compatible—for a more reactionary or antiliberal stance. For this too may be part of the Francis legacy: If his attempts at a revolution have encouraged liberal Catholicism to become more ambitious, more aggressive, more optimistic about how far the church can change, they have encouraged many conservative Catholics (again, younger ones especially) to take a darker view of the post–Vatican II era, and to reassess whether there might have always been more wisdom in the traditionalist critique than they wanted to believe. If the conservatism of John Paul and Benedict led only to Francis, perhaps it didn't conserve enough; if those popes' attempted synthesis was so easily challenged and unraveled, perhaps it wasn't a successful synthesis at all; if their project of restoration still left fertile soil for a new revolution, perhaps the entire project needed to be reassessed.

Such a reassessment could be intellectually and spiritually healthy, since even before Francis's ascension it should have been clear that John Paul II–era conservative Catholicism was neither as robust nor as theologically persuasive in all respects as its adherents wanted to believe. In an ideal world conservatives might take the Francis era as an opportunity to think harder about what development of doctrine allows and what it doesn't, which teachings are inviolate and which ones might evolve, which rulings from Rome have to be accepted and which might inspire a faithful, Catholic critique. This project might conclude that traditionalists are correct about certain errors that crept in with Vatican II, certain blind alleys that the council and subsequent papacies led Catholics down, but also accept that liberals are right about certain innovations that are possible even as they are provisionally rejected. It might enable conservatives to internalize part of the present pope's critique of pharisaism and legalism without abandoning their commitment to doctrine, and might point beyond current controversies to an eventual transcending of the church's civil war.

But that seems too optimistic. If this reassessment is happening against the backdrop of constant progressive pressure, a constant sense that a liberal revolution backed in Rome is advancing on all fronts, it's more likely to inspire a purely reactive sensibility, and with it the abandonment of any hope of a new center for the late-modern church. Naturally this is what traditionalists themselves believe is necessary—a simple rejection of modernism and all its pomps and works and empty promises, which would eventually carve away much of the post–Vatican II church as you would cleave a rotten branch, and only then see growth begin anew. They could be right, but the history of counterrevolutions makes this counsel seem doubtful; the genuine rigidity and cruelty that afflicted the pre–Vatican II church make it seem less than desirable. But the more that Francis's heirs press for a Church of the Future, the more conservatives are likely to be radicalized in their turn.

In this widening gyre, what holds the church together for the time being might not be a sincere center but a cynical one, led by the curial operators and timeservers whom Francis was elected to clear out—but most of whom remain securely in their place. Life in Rome is more uncomfortable and unsettled than under Benedict, the threat of firings or purges ever present, the power of certain offices reduced, the likelihood of a papal tongue-lashing increased. But the blueprints for dramatic reforms, produced at some expense by various consultants, have been argued over endlessly and then abandoned until the next kitchen cabinet meeting. The church's finances have been clarified somewhat but large budgets have been left in the same not exactly trustworthy hands; financial reform was Pell's project, and as his conservatism cost him papal favor the Vatican's old guard pecked away at his agenda and steadily reduced its scope. The push for further protocols on sex abuse has stalled amid conflicts between the pope's commission and the Congregation for the Doctrine of the Faith. And some of the ecclesial princes who helped make Benedict's years a misgoverned mess have found, if anything, more power under Francis.

Which is not to say that they've all been happy with him. It was these men—the bureaucrats and operators, not the conservatives and traditionalists—who were reported in the *Times* of London in early 2017 to be talking about some sort of "coup" against the pope (this was shortly after his kitchen cabinet's loud vote of confidence), with the idea being that Francis could be induced to resign so as to be replaced by Cardinal Pietro Parolin, the present Vatican secretary of state and a man with substantial bureaucratic skill and no obvious commitment to any theological party.

The "coup" part of the idea was a mix of rumor and rubbish; there is nothing in Francis's personality that suggests a man who might be induced to step aside. But the report rested on the real truth that the pope's ambiguous revolution worries even some of his allies and appointees. Not because they necessarily feel strongly about the issues at stake, but because it threatens to disturb the normal running of the church and their own sinecures within it. Heresy might be tolerable, but schism is bad for business.

Meanwhile, the church's controversies are not happening in a vacuum. While Francis was seeking to change the church, the world around him was changing as well. Indeed, it was almost as if Benedict's resignation had super-naturally shifted something in secular politics as well—as though the gears of history, rusted since the Cold War's end, were grinding back to life.

This sudden return of history has undercut some of the basic common ground shared by John Paul II–era conservative Catholicism and its progressive-Catholic critics—a baseline acceptance of liberal democracy, the mixed economy, and the broad features of the post–Cold War Western order. Instead ideas at once older and newer are shouldering their way into the West's debates—illiberalism or post-liberalism in various forms, reaction and radicalism both, secessionist nationalisms in Western Europe and more aggressive nationalisms on Europe's eastern fringes, plus the complicated influence of Islam. The 1930s may not have returned in full, but old ideas are current once again: The younger left is reading Marx; the new right is dabbling in fascist and nationalist thinkers; and from Jeremy Corbyn and Bernie Sanders to Marine Le Pen and Viktor Orbán to, yes, President Donald Trump, the neoliberal consensus is being hacked away at by a multitude of populists.

In certain ways as the "people's pope" Francis was a harbinger of this trend. His highly personalized style, his willingness to "make a mess" in the service of internal revolution, his insult-rich rhetoric, his impatience with circumspection, tradition, and taboo . . . in all this and more he resembles many of the Western populists who have risen toward power, or in the case of Trump attained it.

The comparison to Trump is a fraught one, of course. Many of Francis's admirers have cast him as the anti-Donald and in certain ideological ways he clearly is—a populist of the left rather than the right, a defender of the rights of migrants who dismisses talk of a confrontation with Islam, a universalist and near-pacifist rather than a nationalist, and so on. But mirror images resemble one another even when the features are reversed, and as a ruler of the church, in the context of existing Catholic doctrine and discipline and norms, the pope has turned out to be far more Trumpian than most of the cardinals who elected him ever anticipated. Rome under Francis is much like Washington under Trump—a paranoid and jumpy place, full of ferment and uncertainty. Francis's opponents, like Trump's, feel that they're resisting an abnormal leader, a man who does not respect the rules that are supposed to bind his office. Meanwhile to his supporters, as to many of Trump's, all these discontents are vindication, evidence that he's bringing about the changes required to Make Catholicism Great Again.

But in reality what may be happening is that the populist pope is Missing Catholicism's Opportunity. Under the last two pontiffs the church's engagement with Western politics was often polarized between a conservative Catholicism that upheld church teaching on marriage and family while sometimes compromising the church's message of economic solidarity, and a more liberal Catholicism that basically did the reverse. Both John Paul II and Benedict tried to fight this polarization, pressing a moral critique of capitalism's contradictions that they linked to individualistic policies on abortion, sexuality, suicide. But their synthesis found only limited political constituencies, because the lines of political battle in the West did not allow the space for a larger one to form. There were neoconservatives and neoliberals and not much on offer further to their right or left, let alone in the kind of radical center where Catholic teaching seemed to properly belong.

Now, though, everything is more fluid. Technocracy is cracking up, the right is turning from libertarianism to populism, there is more impatience with existing ideologies and more doubts about the utopia that secular elites have long imagined themselves building. Which makes it an ideal moment to raise the church's banner, to offer a distinctively Catholic sort of synthesis—one that would speak to the right's fear that the West's civilizational roots are crumbling *and* to the left's disappointment with the rule of neoliberalism; one that would offer a Christian alternative to the aridity of secularism, the theocratic zeal of Islamism, and the identity politics of right and left.

Such was the great promise of Francis's pontificate, five long years ago—that by stressing anew the church's themes of economic and social solidarity without compromising its metaphysical and moral commitments, he could offer a vision of Catholicism that unified its warring factions and made it more attractive and influential in the wider world. Such a vigorous, recentered Catholicism's influence could make right-wing politics less bigoted and left-wing politics less materialistic, social democracy less sterile and capitalism less ruthless, devout Muslims less frightening and political Islam less like secular liberalism's only comprehensive challenge. From its own rediscovered center, the church could offer a different center—religious solidarity, rather than secular technocracy—to an aging, fragmenting, increasingly fearful developed world, while building a religious bridge between the still Christian elements in Western civilization and the increasingly Christian global South.

At times this pope has reached for such a goal—the early attempts to correct the errors of liberals and conservatives alike, the critique of modernity offered in *Laudato Si'*, the insistence that the church must be more than a comfortable NGO, the attacks on the colonial mentality of secular liberalism. One of his favorite images, the idea of a "throwaway culture," offers a vivid link between the everything-is-disposable ethos of hypercapitalism and the way that liberal societies treat the unborn and the aged, the human embryo and the natural family.

But much more often, as the debate over communion for the remarried has proceeded, the papal message has lost any distinctively conservative element, instead offering simply liberalism in theology and left-wing politics—German theological premises, Argentine economics, and liberal-Eurocrat assumptions on borders, nations, and migration. The stress on what liberalism gets wrong has faded, and meanwhile, less charity is extended rightward: As theological conservatives have turned on him, he has turned on conservatism generally, so that instead of correcting its errors he is ignoring its insights, its warnings, its understandable appeal. The Vatican under Francis always seems to have time for secular and liberal and non-Catholic opinion, whether it's organizing conferences that feature population control advocates or searching for common ground with pro-abortion politicians or sending the pope off to celebrate the Reformation's anniversary in Sweden while sticking Martin Luther on its stamps. But the theological concerns of conservative Catholics are waved off as pharisaism, and the cultural-political fears driving large parts of Francis's flock into the arms of Trump and other right-wing nationalists are left unacknowledged or dismissed.

Which sometimes they deserve to be, partaking as they do of racism and chauvinism and xenophobia. But the taproot of these anxieties is not always race. Sometimes it is religion, the pope's own faith. People in France and Britain and the United States fear Western Christianity's eclipse, they fear the collapse of community outside the posh mega-cities and the disappearance of the natural family everywhere, they fear what global capitalism, elite secularism, and Islamic self-assertion will mean for what remains of Christian civilization in Europe. These fears are not irrational, and recent trends have sharpened them, which is part of why Western politics has moved in a more populist and nationalist direction. But under Francis Rome has moved the other way, so that instead of a fully Catholic alternative to right-wing nationalism the Vatican seems to be offering conservative Catholics only judgment on their shortcomings, their chauvinism, their anxieties and lack of charity toward all.

Judgment is a father's right. But Francis has judged his church's conservatives harshly while confirming the fears that pushed many of them toward conservative politics in the first place—the fear that a left-wing Catholic politics is inextricably linked to revolution in theology as well. Part of the promise of his pontificate was that there could be once again in the developed world an *orthodox* Catholic liberal-left, as in the time of Dorothy Day and Catholic New Dealers and the Christian Democrats of Western Europe. The hope in

Francis's early days was that he would revive a form of Catholic engagement with modern political economy that was populist or anti-plutocratic . . . but also orthodox in its theology, countercultural in its attitude toward the sexual revolution, zealous in its commitment to the essentials of the faith.

Instead he has thrown away the opportunity, by wedding his economic populism instead to Kasperism and the moral theology of the 1970s, making enemies of conservatives (African, American, and more) who might have been open to his social gospel, treating economic moralism not as a complement to personal moralism but as a substitute . . . and driving the church not toward synthesis but toward crisis.

Francis must know that it did not have to be this way. At every point between Walter Kasper's address and *Amoris*'s release he could have stepped back to safer ground, achieved the practical goal of mercy by easing the path to annulments while reaffirming what his predecessors taught, and seen much of the conservative resistance to his efforts melt away. Strip away the marriage controversy, and he had already found many ways to please progressives without having conservatives murmur about heresy and schism. Strip away the marriage controversy and all his other large projects—the reform of the curia, the pursuit of a "poor church, for the poor," the various diplomatic and ecumenical endeavors—would have become far easier to pursue.

Why did he choose as he did? There are two possibilities. One is that he always intended a kind of revolution, and the appearance of conservative-leaning moderation that enabled his election was either something he had left behind in the 1970s, something that fell away with his elevation to the papacy, or else a kind of mask that he had worn in order to advance under John Paul II. This theory implies that the St. Gallen faction, the European liberals, knew exactly what they were doing when they championed his candidacy, that the pope himself explicitly understood the Kasper proposal as the entering wedge for broader changes, and that he chose to risk the church's unity because he believed, in effect, that he was a man of destiny—and that a full liberalization, a permanent openness to change, was the path that God required of the church in this particular age.

The other possibility is that Francis never had a programmatic vision in mind for church reform, never thought of himself as a sweeping liberalizer, and instead consciously intended the balancing act, the synthesis of conservative and liberal tendencies, that he seemed to be seeking in his first years. But because of his impatience with theological niceties, his irritation with legalisms, he did not understand the consequences of making the issue of remarriage and communion the place where he pushed for change, and did not expect the kind of resistance that it met. He imagined that it would be a small thing, an easy thing—after all, it didn't touch the hottest buttons, like homosexuality or abortion. And then when conservatives fought him to a standstill their intransigence effectively turned him against *them*, pushing him toward the more radical vision of some of his intimates, letting an ideological inner circle—the liberal cardinals, advisers like Spadaro and Fernández—close around him and seek a more sweeping transformation than he intended to pursue.

Probably the psychological reality is more complicated than either of these alternatives suggests. But the important thing is that Francis chose as he did, and the fact of the choice has consequences. For the pope himself it means that his legacy cannot ultimately be ambiguous or modest; for good or ill he will go down as one of the most significant popes of modern times. By pressing papal authority to a possible breaking point in pursuit of crucial liberal goals, he could be remembered as a heroic revolutionary, a more courageous progressive than the behind-the-scenes popes of Vatican II, and the man who broke free of the prison in which his office seemed contained. If, that is, his successors sustain his revolution. If they do not, if it collapses from self-contradiction and the halfway house of *Amoris* gets demolished, he will be remembered with Boniface VIII in the ranks of ambitious popes who overreached, and with Honorius and John XXII in the ranks of popes who failed to teach and keep the Catholic faith.

Either way, he will probably not be remembered for achieving the goal that he set in the conclave speech that made him pope—the goal of a less "self-referential" church, a church less consumed with its own internal controversies, a church no longer stuck "within itself" but ready to go outward to evangelize and save the world. Instead the theological crisis that he set in motion has made Catholicism more self-referential, more inward-facing, more defined by its abstruse internal controversies and theological civil wars. The early images of the Francis era were missionary images, an iconography of faith-infused outreach. The later images have been images of division—warring clerics, a balked and angry pope, a church divided by regions and nationalities, a Catholic Christianity that cannot preach confidently because it cannot decide what it believes.

If one wished to look for a providential element in all this conflict, it might be that given the depth of the divisions within Catholicism, something like the Francis crisis—and whatever comes next—simply had to happen before the faith could regain its footing and become a missionary force again. In this sense Francis might ultimately serve his declared purposes by forcing divisions back up onto the surface, by allowing liberal Catholicism to be honest about its goals and premises and forcing conservative Catholics to defend church teachings in their own terms, even to the point of criticizing a reigning pope. Long is the road and hard the path that out of disunity leads to a new evangelization—and by exposing the weakness of the Catholic center, the width of the gulf separating cardinals from cardinals and theologians from theologians, perhaps Francis's willingness to risk a crisis has set the church on that hard but necessary path.

This would be the view of some of his supporters, eager to complete the revolution that they think will help make Catholicism vital once again. It might also be the view of some of his traditionalist critics, eager for conservative Catholics to accept that the church since the 1960s has been deep in crisis notwithstanding the efforts of John Paul II and Benedict. And the Francis era has revealed certain truths that make the case for open conflict: It's clearer than ever that the John Paul settlement was unstable, that the level of dissent extended far beyond just birth control and political priorities to touch the deepest questions of the faith, and that many arguments conservative Catholics believed were settled were always destined to be litigated anew. Today it seems possible, indeed reasonable, that the church will need to gradually feud its way toward another and more decisive ecumenical council, in which many post-1960s questions will be explicitly resolved—a Chalcedon to Vatican II's Nicaea, if you want to flatter Vatican II; if not, a Trent to its Fifth Lateran.

But to borrow from the Gospel of Matthew and Abraham Lincoln—*it must needs be that offences come, but woe to that man by whom the offence cometh.* For Francis has not just exposed conflicts; he has stoked them, encouraging sweeping ambitions among his allies and apocalyptic fears among his critics. He has not just fostered debate; he has taken sides and hurled invective in a way that has pushed friendly critics into opposition, and undercut the quest for the common ground. Like Boniface after Celestine, Francis has pressed papal authority to its limits—theological this time, not temporal, but more dangerous for that.

Yes, truces are unsatisfying and instability is exciting and wars can be worth waging. But sustaining a for-the-time-being Catholicism, even amid tensions and contradictions and divisions, is not an achievement to be lightly dismissed. And risking a war or launching one, when your office is charged with maintaining unity and continuity above all, is a very serious business—and especially when an eventual endgame, a unifying resolution, is so bafflingly difficult to envision or predict.

So yes, the story could end with Francis as its hero. But to choose a path that might have only two destinations—hero or heretic—is an act of great and dangerous presumption, even for a pope. *Especially* for a pope.

Earlier in this book I quoted a line from a Latin American Jesuit, cited in Paul Vallely's sympathetic papal biography, on the state in which Jorge Bergoglio's Argentine Jesuits were left after his years as their superior. To end this account of a not yet ended papacy, it's worth quoting the Jesuit's comments in full:

As provincial he generated divided loyalties: some groups almost worshipped him, while others would have nothing to do with him, and he would hardly speak to them. It was an absurd situation. He is well-trained and very capable, but is surrounded by this personality cult which is extremely divisive. He has an aura of spirituality which he uses to obtain power. It will be a catastrophe for the Church to have someone like him in the Apostolic See. He left the Society of Jesus in Argentina destroyed with Jesuits divided and institutions destroyed and financially broken. We have spent two decades trying to fix the chaos that the man left us.[19]

Hagan lío! Francis likes to say. "Make a mess!"

In that much he has succeeded.

Acknowledgments

This book was written in America, not in Rome, so before anything else I am grateful to all the journalists who have covered the daily life of this always interesting papacy, and without whose reporting a book like this could not exist. In particular, John Allen and his team at *Crux*, Edward Pentin at the *National Catholic Register*, and Sandro Magister at *L'Espresso* supplied a lot of the meat of this story; I also relied upon publications as old as the *National Catholic Reporter*, *Commonweal*, and *America* and as young as the revamped *Catholic Herald*, *OnePeterFive*, and *LifeSiteNews*—as well as my colleagues Laurie Goodstein and Jason Horowitz among others at the *New York Times*, Francis X. Rocca at the *Wall Street Journal*, and many more. I am also grateful to the legions of voices arguing (often with me) about the pope and the church on Catholic Twitter—a world which displays many vices of the online realm but in the end, I think, has the stakes of the current pontificate about right.

My wonderful editor, Ben Loehnen, made this book better at every stage, and my agent, Rafe Sagalyn, has been a reliable source of wisdom and support as always. I am grateful to my editors at the *Times* for allowing me to use my space on their page to indulge in theological arcana over the last few years, and to Scott Stossel and Ann Hulbert at the *Atlantic* and R.R. Reno and Matthew Schmitz at *First Things* for commissioning essays that laid the foundation for this book. April Lawson, Evelyn Behling, and Rishabh Bhandari supplied essential editorial help and saved me from a number of egregious errors. Michael Brendan Dougherty was a source of private help while his public writings allowed me to look moderate and circumspect by comparison. Debbie Whitney was a source of immense practical support when my household needed it most.

Without Father Carleton Jones of the Dominican Order, I would not have become this particular kind of Catholic; hopefully this book does not make him regret his influence. Various other members of his order and some prayerful monks have been helpful more recently; the same hope applies to them.

My mother and father, in different ways, played more direct roles in making this book possible than any previous book I've written—through intellectual and religious formation, but also through recent consolation and support. I love you both. My children are not precisely supportive at this age, but their love is also a reason this book exists; hopefully some of these controversies will have passed by the time they are old enough to decide what to make of their strange Catholic inheritance.

And finally, Abby, my love, thank you for everything—*in sickness and in health*, but God willing in the latter soon enough.

Notes

CHAPTER 1: THE PRISONER OF THE VATICAN

1. The Holy See, Central Office of Church Statistics, "The Pontifical Yearbook 2017 and the 'Annuarium Statisticum Ecclesiae' 2015," news release, June 4, 2017, https://press.vatican.va/content/salastampa/en/bollettino/pubblico/2017/04/06/170406e.html.
2. "Earthly Concerns; the Catholic Church in America," *The Economist (U.S.)*, August 18, 2012.

CHAPTER 2: THREE STORIES ABOUT VATICAN II

1. Pope John XXIII, "Gaudet Mater Ecclesia" (speech), October 11, 1962, trans. Fr. Joseph Komonchak, https://jakomonchak.files.wordpress.com/2012/10/john-xxiii-opening-speech.pdf.
2. Roger Finke and Rodney Stark, *The Churching of America, 1776–2005: Winners and Losers in Our Religious Economy* (New Brunswick, NJ: Rutgers University Press, 2011), 269.
3. John Zmirak, "The Shame of the Catholic Subculture," "The Catholic Thing," February 1, 2014, https://www.thecatholicthing.org/2014/02/01/the-shame-of-the-catholic-subculture/.

4. Ibid.

5. Paul Elie, "The Year of Two Popes," *The Atlantic*, January/February 2006, https://www.theatlantic.com/magazine/archive/2006/01/the-year-of -two-popes/304498.

CHAPTER 3: A POPE ABDICATES

1. Boniface VIII, *Unam Sanctum*, http://www.newadvent.org/library/docs _bo08us.htm.

2. Dante Alighieri, *Inferno*, Cantos 59–60, trans. Allen Mandelbaum, https:// digitaldante.columbia.edu/dante/divine-comedy/inferno/inferno-3/.

3. Joseph Ratzinger, "Homily to the College of Cardinals," April 18, 2005, http://www.vatican.va/gpII/documents/homily-pro-eligendo-pontifice _20050418_en.html.

4. Benedict XVI, "Homily of His Holiness Benedict XVI," April 24, 2005, https://w2.vatican.va/content/benedict-xvi/en/homilies/2005/docu ments/hf_ben-xvi_hom_20050424_inizio-pontificato.html.

5. Joseph Ratzinger and Peter Seewald, *Salt of the Earth* (San Francisco: Ignatius Press, 1996), 16.

6. Pope Benedict XVI and Peter Seewald, *Last Testament* (London: Bloomsbury, 2016), 24.

7. Ibid., 20–21.

8. Ibid., 17.

CHAPTER 4: THE BERGOGLIO SURPRISE

1. John Hooper, "Italy Mourns Cardinal Who Said Catholic Church Was 200 Years Out of Date," *The Guardian*, September 3, 2012.

2. Paul Vallely, *Pope Francis: The Struggle for the Soul of Catholicism* (New York: Bloomsbury, 2015), 29.

3. Austen Ivereigh, *The Great Reformer: Francis and the Making of a Radical Pope* (New York: Henry Holt, 2014), 193.

4. Sergio Rubin and Francesca Ambrogetti, *Pope Francis: Conversations with Jorge Bergoglio* (Hodder & Stoughton, 2015), quoted in Vallely, *Pope Francis*, 131.

5. Joseph Ratzinger, "Theology and the Church" (lecture), March 22, 1986, trans. Francesca Romana, Rorate Caeli, https://rorate-caeli.blogspot.com/2014/07/ratzinger-hierarchy-theologians-cannot.html.

6. Jorge Bergoglio, "Bergoglio's Intervention: A Diagnosis of the Problems in the Church," Vatican Radio, http://en.radiovaticana.va/storico/2013/03/27/bergoglios_intervention_a_diagnosis_of_the_problems_in_the_church/en1-677269.

7. Ivereigh, *The Great Reformer*, 363.

CHAPTER 5: THE FRANCIS AGENDA

1. "Pope Calls Argentine Kiosk Owner to Cancel Paper Delivery," Catholic News Agency, March 21, 2013.

2. "Press Conference of Pope Francis," Holy See Press Office, July 28, 2013, http://w2.vatican.va/content/francesco/en/speeches/2013/july/documents/papa-francesco_20130728_gmg-conferenza-stampa.html.

3. Pope Francis, Interview by Father Antonio Spadaro, August 19, 2013, https://w2.vatican.va/content/francesco/en/speeches/2013/september/documents/papa-francesco_20130921_intervista-spadaro.html.

4. Benedict XVI, "Europe and Its Discontents," *First Things*, January 2006.

5. Hannah Roberts, "Bishop Calls for Church to Listen to Calls for Communion for Divorcees," *The Tablet*, May 13, 2014.

6. Pope Francis, "Homily of the Holy Father Pope Francis," March 14, 2013, http://w2.vatican.va/content/francesco/en/homilies/2013/documents/papa-francesco_20130314_omelia-cardinali.html.

7. John L. Allen, *The Francis Miracle: Inside the Transformation of the Pope and the Church* (Des Moines, IA: Time Books, 2015), 36.

8. Ibid.

9. Ibid.

10. Pope Francis, "*Evangelii Gaudium*: Apostolic Exhortation on the Proclamation of the Gospel in Today's World," November 24, 2013, http://w2.vatican.va/content/francesco/en/apost_exhortations/docu ments/papa-francesco_esortazione-ap_20131124_evangelii-gaud ium.html.

CHAPTER 6: THE MARRIAGE PROBLEM

1. Pope John Paul II, *Familiaris Consortio*, November 22, 1981, http:// w2.vatican.va/content/john-paul-ii/en/apost_exhortations/documents /hf_jp-ii_exh_19811122_familiaris-consortio.html.

2. "Maradiaga Says Müller Needs to 'Be a Bit More Flexible,' " *La Stampa*, January 21, 2014, accessed December 16, 2014, http://www.lastampa .it/2014/01/21/vaticaninsider/eng/news/maradiaga-says-mller-needs -to-be-a-bit-more-flexible-vZdAXTfW8PCqOqYloLM4oM/pagina .html.

3. "Cardinal Kasper's Speech on Divorce, Remarriage, and Communion," Catholic News Agency, March 4, 2014, https://www.catholicnews agency.com/news/cardinal-kaspers-speech-on-divorce-remarriage-and -communion.

4. Ibid.

5. Mark 10:2–4.

6. Mark 10:4–12.

7. "Shepherd of Hermas," trans. F. Crombie, from Alexander Roberts et al., *Ante-Nicene Fathers*, Vol. 2 (Buffalo, NY: Christian Literature Publishing Co., 1885), http://www.newadvent.org/cathen/05054c .htm.

8. J. Ziegler, "Annulment Nation," *Catholic World Report*, April 28, 2011, http://www.catholicworldreport.com/2011/04/28/annulment-na tion/.

9. "Divorce (Still) Less Likely Among Catholics," Center for Applied Research on the Apostolate, September 26, 2013, http://nineteensixty-four.blogspot.ca/2013/09/divorce-still-less-likely-among.html.

10. Pamela Engel, "Divorce Rates Around the World," *Business Insider*, May 25, 2014, http://www.businessinsider.com/map-divorce-rates-around-the-world-2014-5.

11. Anian Christoph Wimmer, "In Germany, Mass-Goers, Priests and Sacraments All in Decline," Catholic News Agency, July 18, 2016, https://cruxnow.com/global-church/2016/07/18/germany-mass-goers-priests-sacraments-decline/.

12. Walter Kasper, "Merciful God, Merciful Church: An Interview with Cardinal Kasper," interview by Matthew Boudway and Grant Gallicho, *Commonweal*, May 17, 2014, https://www.commonwealmagazine.org/interview-cardinal-walter-kasper.

CHAPTER 7: TO CHANGE THE CHURCH

1. "Vatican Statement on Pope's Phone Call to Divorced/Remarried Woman," *National Catholic Register*, April 24, 2014, http://www.ncregister.com/blog/edward-pentin/vatican-statement-on-popes-phone-call-to-divorced-remarried-woman.

2. Homily of Pope Francis, October 5, 2014, https://w2.vatican.va/content/francesco/en/homilies/2014/documents/papa-francesco_20141005_omelia-apertura-sinodo-vescovi.html.

3. John Thavis, "A Pastoral Earthquake at the Synod," JohnThavis.com, October 13, 2014, http://www.johnthavis.com/a-pastoral-earthquake-at-the-synod#.WiR5q0qnE2xty.

4. https://twitter.com/joshjmac/status/521573906030030848.

5. *Relatio post disceptationem* for 2014 Synod of Bishops, published by *National Catholic Reporter*, October 15, 2014, https://www.ncronline.org/news/vatican/relatio-post-disceptationem-2014-synod-bishops-family.

6. John Allen, " 'Lifestyle Ecumenism' May Be the Real Breakthrough at 2014 Synod," *Crux*, October 13, 2014, https://cruxnow.com /church/2014/10/13/lifestyle-ecumenism-may-be-the-real-break through-at-2014-synod/.

7. Edward Pentin, *The Rigging of a Vatican Synod* (San Francisco: Ignatius Press, 2015), chapter 5, Kindle.

8. Ibid.

9. John Allen, "Africans Are no Longer Junior Partners in Catholicism Inc.," *Crux*, October 17, 2014, https://cruxnow.com/church/2014/10/17/afri cans-are-no-longer-junior-partners-in-catholicism-inc/.

10. Edward Pentin, "Statement on Cardinal Kasper Interview," Edward-Pentin.co.uk, accessed December 16, 2017, http://edwardpentin.co.uk /statement-on-cardinal-kasper-interview/.

11. "The Pastoral Challenges of the Family in the Context of Evangelization," Synod of Bishops, October 2014, http://www.vatican.va/roman_curia /synod/documents/rc_synod_doc_20141018_relatio-synodi-familia _en.html.

12. "Address of His Holiness Pope Francis for the Conclusion of the Third Extraordinary General Assembly of the Synod of Bishops," October 18, 2014, http://w2.vatican.va/content/francesco/en/speeches/2014/octo ber/documents/papa-francesco_20141018_conclusione-sinodo-dei -vescovi.html.

13. Ibid.

14. Ibid.

15. Sandro Magister, "The Closed Door of Pope Francis," *L'Espresso*, May 11, 2015, http://chiesa.espresso.repubblica.it/articolo/1351045 bdc4.html?eng=y.

16. Edward Pentin, "German Bishops: 'We Are Not Just a Subsidiary of Rome,' " *National Catholic Register*, February 7, 2015, http://www .ncregister.com/daily-news/german-bishops-we-are-not-just-a-subsid iary-of-rome.

17. Pope Francis, *Laudato Si'*, June 18, 2015, paragraph 21.

18. John Allen, "Pope's Annulment Reform Will Recalibrate the Synod of Bishops, and More," *Crux*, September 8, 2015, https://cruxnow.com/church/2015/09/08/popes-annulment-reform-will-recalibrate-the-synod-of-bishops-and-more/.

19. Sandro Magister, "Thirteen Cardinals Have Written to the Pope. Here's the Letter," *L'Espresso*, October 12, 2015, http://chiesa.espresso.repub blica.it/articolo/1351154bdc4.html?eng=y.

20. Fr. Raymond de Souza, "How 13 Cardinals Changed the Course of History," *Catholic Herald*, October 13, 2016, http://www.catholicher ald.co.uk/issues/october-14th-2016/how-13-cardinals-changed-the-course-of-history/.

21. Andrea Tornielli, "Pope Urges Bishops Not to Give in to Conspiracy Theories," *La Stampa*, October 8, 2015.

22. "Conspiracy Theory," *America Magazine*, October 14, 2015, https://www.americamagazine.org/issue/conspiracy-theory.

23. Archbishop Mark Coleridge, "On the Road Together—Invective, Fear, Surprise," "Synod on the Family" blog, October 20, 2015, https://bris banecatholic.org.au/articles/on-the-road-together-invective-fear-sur prise/.

24. "Address of His Holiness Pope Francis," Ceremony Commemorating the 50th Anniversary of the Institution of the Synod of Bishops, October 17, 2015, http://w2.vatican.va/content/francesco/en/speeches/2015/october/documents/papa-francesco_20151017_50-anniversario-sinodo.html.

25. "The Final Report of the Synod of Bishops to the Holy Father, Pope Francis," October 24, 2015, paragraph 86, http://www.vatican.va/roman_curia/synod/documents/rc_synod_doc_20151026_relazione-finale-xiv-assemblea_en.html.

26. Francis X. Rocca, "Bishops Hand Pope Defeat on His Outreach to Divorced Catholics," *Wall Street Journal*, October 24, 2015, https://www.wsj.com/articles/bishops-hand-pope-a-defeat-on-outreach-to-divorced-catholics-1445715350.

27. Laurie Goodstein and Elisabetta Povoledo, "Amid Splits, Catholic Bishops Crack Open Door on Divorce," *New York Times*, October 24, 2015, https://www.nytimes.com/2015/10/25/world/europe/synod-makes -overture-to-the-divorced-but-rejects-gay-marriage.html.

28. "Address of His Holiness Pope Francis," Conclusion of the Synod of Bishops, October 24, 2015, http://w2.vatican.va/content/francesco /en/speeches/2015/october/documents/papa-francesco_20151024 _sinodo-conclusione-lavori.html.

29. Alexander Stille, "Pope Francis's First Crisis," *The New Yorker*, October 16, 2015, https://www.newyorker.com/news/daily-comment/con flict-at-the-vatican.

CHAPTER 8: HIS HOLINESS DECLINES TO COMMENT

1. Eugenio Scalfari, "The Pope: How the Church Will Change," *La Repubblica*, October 1, 2013, http://www.repubblica.it/cultura/2013/10/01 /news/pope_s_conversation_with_scalfari_english-67643118/.

2. "Vatican Confirms Scalfari Interview Was "an After-the-Fact Reconstruction," *Catholic World Report*, October 5, 2013, http://www .catholicworldreport.com/2013/10/05/vatican-confirms-scalfari-inter view-was-an-after-the-fact-reconstruction/.

3. "Pope Francis Reportedly Promises 'Solutions' to Priests' Celibacy," CBS News, July 13, 2014, https://www.cbsnews.com/news/pope-fran cis-reportedly-promises-solutions-to-priests-celibacy/.

4. Francis X. Rocca, "Fr Lombardi: Words in Scalfari Interview 'Cannot Be Attributed to the Pope,'" *Catholic Herald*, July 14, 2014, http://www .catholicherald.co.uk/news/2014/07/14/fr-lombardi-words-in-scalfari -interview-cannot-be-attributed-to-the-pope/.

5. John-Henry Westen, "About That Pope Francis 'Interview' Where He Denied the Existence of Hell," *LifeSiteNews*, March 24, 2015, https:// www.lifesitenews.com/blogs/about-that-pope-francis-interview-where -he-denied-the-existence-of-hell.

6. Ibid.

7. Edward Pentin, "Fr. Lombardi: Latest Scalfari Article on Pope 'In No Way Reliable,'" *National Catholic Register*, November 2, 2015, http://www.ncregister.com/blog/edward-pentin/fr.-lombardi-latest-scalfari-article-on-pope-in-no-way-reliable.

8. Sandro Magister, "Francis Is Silent. But Another Jesuit Is Speaking for Him," *L'Espresso*, November 7, 2015, http://chiesa.espresso.repubblica.it/articolo/1351172bdc4.html?eng=y.

9. Raymond de Souza, "What Will the Pope Say? His Friends Tell Us," *Catholic Herald*, November 12, 2015, http://www.catholicherald.co.ukwww.catholicherald.co.uk/issues/november-13th-2015-2/what-will-the-pope-say-his-friends-tell-us/.

10. Pope Francis, *Amoris Laetitia*, March 19, 2016, 232, https://w2.vatican.va/content/dam/francesco/pdf/apost_exhortations/documents/papa-francesco_esortazione-ap_20160319_amoris-laetitia_en.pdf.

11. Ibid., 228.

12. Ibid., 237.

13. Junno Arocho Esteves, "New Pastoral Approach Does Not Change Doctrine, Australian Archbishop Says," Catholic News Service, October 19, 2015, http://www.catholicnews.com/services/englishnews/2015/new-pastoral-approach-does-not-change-doctrine-australian-archbishop-says.cfm.

14. *Amoris Laetitia*, 227.

15. Dan Hitchens, "Malta's Bishops Tell the Remarried: Take Communion if You Feel at Peace with God," *Catholic Herald*, January 13, 2017, http://www.catholicherald.co.uk/news/2017/01/13/maltas-bishops-tell-the-remarried-take-communion-if-you-feel-at-peace-with-god/.

16. Edward Pentin, "Archbishop Scicluna: We Are Following the Pope's Directives," *National Catholic Register*, January 30, 2017, http://www.ncregister.com/blog/edward-pentin/archbishop-scicluna-we-are-following-the-popes-directives.

17. John Hunwicke, "Suspense of the Magisterium?," Fr Hunwicke's

Mutual Enrichment, November 25, 2016, http://liturgicalnotes
.blogspot.com/2016/11/suspense-of-magisterium.html.

18. Sandro Magister, "Yes, No, I Don't Know, You Figure It Out. The Fluid
Magisterium of Pope Francis," *L'Espresso*, May 13, 2016, http://chiesa
.espresso.repubblica.it/articolo/1351297bdc4.html?eng=y.

19. Thomas Reese, "Pope Francis Gets a C+ on Reforming Vatican Curia,"
National Catholic Reporter, December 29, 2016, https://www.ncron
line.org/blogs/faith-and-justice/pope-francis-gets-c-reforming-vatican
-curia.

20. "In-Flight Press Conference of His Holiness Pope Francis from Azerbai-
jan to Rome," October 2, 2016, https://w2.vatican.va/content/francesco
/en/speeches/2016/october/documents/papa-francesco_20161002
_georgia-azerbaijan-conferenza-stampa.pdf.

21. "Pope Francis: Rigidity, Worldliness a Disaster for Priests," Vatican Radio, September 12, 2016, http://en.radiovaticana.va/news/2016/12/09
/pope_francis_rigidity,_worldliness_a_disaster_for_priests/1277926.

22. "Pope Francis at Mass: Be Open, Receptive to God's Gifts," Vatican
Radio, June 2, 2017, http://en.radiovaticana.va/news/2017/02/06
/pope_francis_at_mass_be_open,_receptive_to_gods_gifts/1290724.

23. John Allen, "Pope Decries 'Prophets of Doom' Wanting Only 'the
Usual Fare,'" *Crux*, January 6, 2017, https://cruxnow.com/vatican
/2017/01/06/pope-decries-prophets-doom-wanting-usual-fare/.

24. Ines San Martin, "Pope Okays Argentine Doc on Communion for Divorced and Remarried," *Crux*, September 12, 2016, https://cruxnow
.com/global-church/2016/09/12/pope-okays-argentine-doc-commu
nion-divorced-remarried/.

25. Jan Bentz, "Cardinal Kasper: Pope's 'Next Declaration' Should Allow
'Shared Eucharistic Communion' with Protestants," *LifeSiteNews*, December 14, 2016, https://www.lifesitenews.com/news/cardinal-kasper
-continues-to-push-for-intercommunion.

26. Edward Pentin, "Pope Tells Lutheran to 'Talk to the Lord' About Receiving the Eucharist," *National Catholic Register*, November 16, 2015,

http://www.ncregister.com/blog/edward-pentin/pope-tells-lutheran-to
-talk-to-the-lord-about-receiving-eucharist.

27. "Canadian Bishops Take Different Stands on Sacraments for Catholics Planning Assisted Suicide," *Catholic Culture*, December 14, 2016,
https://www.catholicculture.org/news/headlines/index.cfm?storyid
=30191.

28. "Full Text and Explanatory Notes of Cardinals' Questions on 'Amoris
Laetitia,'" *National Catholic Register*, November 14, 2016, http://www
.ncregister.com/daily-news/four-cardinals-formally-ask-pope-for-clar
ity-on-amoris-laetitia.

29. Claire Chretien, "Vatican Expert: Sources Say Pope Francis 'Boiling
with Rage' over Amoris Criticism," *LifeSiteNews*, November 18, 2016,
https://www.lifesitenews.com/news/vaticanist-pope-francis-boiling
-with-rage-over-amoris-criticism.

30. Delia Gallagher, "Posters Critical of Pope Francis Appear Around
Rome," CNN, February 5, 2017, http://www.cnn.com/2017/02/05/eu
rope/pope-francis-posters-rome/index.html.

31. https://twitter.com/antoniospadaro/status/827874222047379457.

32. John Allen, "Could C9 Cardinals Backing the Pope Have Unintended
Fallout?," *Crux*, February 15, 2017, https://cruxnow.com/analy
sis/2017/02/15/c9-cardinals-backing-pope-unintended-fallout/.

CHAPTER 9: ATHANASIANS AND ARIANS

1. John Allen, "Interested in Catholic Reaction to Francis? Get off Twitter and into the Trenches," *Crux*, July 3, 2017, https://cruxnow.com
/interviews/2017/07/03/dinardo-popes-joy-gospel-key-american-cath
olic-future/.

2. Austen Ivereigh, "As Anti-Amoris Critics Cross into Dissent, the Church
Must Move On," *Crux*, December 11, 2016, https://cruxnow.com/anal
ysis/2016/12/11/anti-amoris-critics-cross-dissent-church-must-move/.

3. John-Henry Westen and Maike Hickson, "One of Pope's Closest

Advisors: How Pope Francis Is Changing the Church," *LifeSiteNews*, June 4, 2015, https://www.lifesitenews.com/news/one-of-popes-closest -advisors-how-pope-francis-is-changing-the-church.

4. Ibid.

5. https://twitter.com/antoniospadaro/status/817144723093733377.

6. Benedict XII, *Benedictus Deus*, http://www.ewtn.com/library/papaldoc /b12bdeus.htm.

7. John Henry Newman, *The Arians of the Fourth Century* (New York: Longmans, Green and Co., 1908), chapter 2, available at: http://www .newmanreader.org/works/arians/.

8. Claudio Pierantoni, "The Arian Crisis and the Current Contro- versy About *Amoris Laetitia*: A Parallel," *Catholic Culture*, Novem- ber 2, 2016, https://www.catholicculture.org/culture/library/view.cfm ?recnum=11457.

9. Newman, *The Arians of the Fourth Century*, chapter 4.

10. John Henry Newman, "On Consulting the Faithful in Matters of Doc- trine," *The Rambler*, July 1859, http://www.newmanreader.org/works /rambler/consulting.html.

11. John Chapman, "Pope Liberius," *The Catholic Encyclopedia,* Vol. 9 (New York: Robert Appleton Company, 1910), http://www.newadvent .org/cathen/09217a.htm.

CHAPTER 10: JANSENISTS AND JESUITS

1. Ian Paul, "The Church Changed Its Mind on Slavery. Why Not on Sex?," *Psephizo*, July 24, 2017, https://www.psephizo.com/biblical -studies/the-church-changed-its-mind-on-slavery-why-not-on-sex/.

2. Leszek Kolakowski, *God Owes Us Nothing: A Brief Remark on Pascal's Religion and on the Spirit of Jansenism* (Chicago: University of Chicago Press, 1998), 98.

3. Ibid., 105.

4. Ibid., 110.

5. James Martin, "Fr. James Martin Answers 5 Common Questions About 'Silence,' " *America Magazine*, January 18, 2017, https://www.america magazine.org/arts-culture/2017/01/18/fr-james-martin-answers-5-com mon-questions-about-silence.

6. "Pope: The Doctors of the Law 'Have Hearts Closed to Life,' " *Asia News*, April 11, 2016, http://www.asianews.it/news-en/Pope:-The-doc tors-of-the-law-have-hearts-closed-to-life-37192.html.

7. "Vatican Article Says 'Main Obstacle' for Pope Francis Is Bishops, Priests," *Crux*, July 23, 2017, https://cruxnow.com/vatican/2017/07/23 /vatican-article-says-main-obstacle-pope-francis-bishops-priests/.

8. Mark 7: 5–13.

CHAPTER 11: THE FRANCIS LEGACY

1. "Cardinal Müller Criticises the Way Pope Francis Dismissed Him," *Catholic Herald*, July 8, 2017, http://www.catholicherald.co.uk/news /2017/07/08/cardinal-muller-criticises-the-way-pope-francis-dismis sed-him/.

2. Maike Hickson, "Just Before Death, Cardinal Meisner Spoke to Cardinal Müller of Distress Over His Dismissal," *OnePeterFive*, July 5, 2017, https://onepeterfive.com/just-before-death-cardinal-meisner-spoke-to -cardinal-muller-of-distress-over-his-dismissal/.

3. Steve Skojec, "Pope Benedict's Message at Funeral of Cardinal Meisner: 'The Lord Does Not Abandon His Church,' " *OnePeterFive*, July 15, 2017, https://onepeterfive.com/pope-benedicts-message-funeral-cardi nal-meisner-lord-not-abandon-church/.

4. Inés San Martín, "Benedict Aide: It's a 'Fantasy' and 'Stupid' to Use Him Against Francis," *Crux*, July 19, 2017, https://cruxnow.com/vati can/2017/07/19/benedict-aide-fantasy-stupid-use-francis/.

5. Matthew Schmitz, "Has Pope Francis Failed?," *New York Times*, September 28, 2016, https://www.nytimes.com/2016/09/28/opinion/has -pope-francis-failed.html.

6. Patrick Browne, "Losing Faith: Why Italians Are Spurning the Church," *The Local*, January 8, 2016, https://www.thelocal.it/20160108/losing -faith-why-italians-are-spurning-the-church.

7. Kenneth Rapoza, "Catholic Shrinkage: Has Brazil Given Up on Jesus?," *Forbes*, December 17, 2016, https://www.forbes.com/sites /kenrapoza/2016/12/27/brazil-jesus-catholic-datafolha-survey /#641ce3bb1760.

8. Gary Bouma, "Census 2016 Shows Australia's Changing Religious Profile, with More 'Nones' Than Catholics," *The Conversation*, June 27, 2017, http://theconversation.com/census-2016-shows-australias-chang ing-religious-profile-with-more-nones-than-catholics-79837.

9. "Latest Statistics: Seminarians Down in the USA and the World, Priests Worldwide in Decline, Catastrophic Decline in Women Religious," *Rorate Caeli*, May 17, 2017, https://rorate-caeli.blogspot.com/2017/05 /latest-statistics-seminary-entries-down.html.

10. Alessandra Nucci, "Large Decrease in Visitors to Papal Events in 2015; Jubilee Numbers Low So Far," *Catholic World Report*, January 2, 2016, http://www.catholicworldreport.com/2016/01/02/large-decrease-in -visitors-to-papal-events-in-2015-jubilee-numbers-low-so-far/.

11. "Pope Francis Challenges Religious Communities," *Aleteia*, August 10, 2017, https://aleteia.org/2017/08/10/pope-francis-challenges-religious -communities/.

12. "Traditional Priests in France Until 2050," *Centurio*, July 6, 2014, http://centurioweblog.blogspot.com/2014/07/traditional-priests-in -france-until-2050.html.

13. John Allen and Ines San Martin, "Theologian Says 'Amoris' Communion Debate Is Settled in Africa," *Crux*, March 21, 2017, https:// cruxnow.com/africaund/2017/03/21/theologian-says-amoris-commu nion-debate-settled-africa/.

14. Iacopo Scaramuzzi, "Catholics Rise in Africa and Asia, Decline in Europe," *La Stampa*, April 7, 2017, http://www.lastam pa.it/2017/04/07/vaticaninsider/eng/world-news/catholics-rise

-in-africa-and-asia-and-decline-in-europe-1WppBzSKyNQo
qC05R9qASL/pagina.html.

15. Philip Jenkins, "Catholicism's Incredible Growth Story," *Catholic Herald*, September 9, 2016, http://www.catholicherald.co.uk/issues/september-9th-2016/catholicisms-incredible-growth-story/.

16. "Global Catholicism: Trends & Forecasts," Center for Applied Research on the Apostolate, June 4, 2015, 8–10, http://cara.georgetown.edu/staff/webpages/global%20catholicism%20release.pdf.

17. Jeanne Smits, "Cardinal Danneels Warns African Bishops to Avoid 'Triumphalism,' " *LifeSiteNews*, November 13, 2015, http://www.lastampa.it/2015/11/12/vaticaninsider/eng/inquiries-and-interviews/church-reform-and-francis-apostolic-sufferings-76STX5VXXIVbH0W GNXyyAK/pagina.html.

18. Dan Hitchens, "Climate of Fear: The New Crackdown on Catholic Theologians," *Catholic Herald*, October 13, 2017, http://catholicherald.co.uk/issues/october-13th-2017/climate-of-fear-the-new-crackdown-on-catholic-theologians/.

19. Vallely, *Pope Francis*, 129.

Index

About the Author

ROSS DOUTHAT is an op-ed columnist for the *New York Times*. He is the author of *Bad Religion: How We Became a Nation of Heretics, Privilege: Harvard and the Education of the Ruling Class*, and the coauthor, with Reihan Salam, of *Grand New Party: How Republicans Can Win the Working Class and Save the American Dream*. He is the film critic for *National Review*. He lives in Connecticut with his wife and three children.